IMAGES
of America

LAURELTON

On the Cover: Excited Laurelton children await their chance to select a book from the library bus in 1934. Please see page 23 for additional information. (Courtesy of Queens Borough Public Library.)

IMAGES *of America*

LAURELTON

Roberta Kossoff and
Annette Henkin Landau

ARCADIA
PUBLISHING

ISBN 978-0-7385-7401-1

Published by Arcadia Publishing
Charleston, South Carolina

Printed in the United States of America

Library of Congress Control Number: 2010931330

For all general information, please contact Arcadia Publishing:
Telephone 843-853-2070
Fax 843-853-0044
E-mail sales@arcadiapublishing.com
For customer service and orders:
Toll-Free 1-888-313-2665

Visit us on the Internet at www.arcadiapublishing.com

For Philip Landau, who made Laurelton shine for me —AHL

Thank you to my Annie Sullivan —RDK

Contents

Acknowledgments

There are a few people without which this book would simply not have been possible. Tom Smith, hot air balloonist, stilt maker, and a "Mentone," became an integral part of the project, and we are grateful beyond words for the staggering amount of effort he exerted for this book. We are also immensely indebted to those individuals who opened up their photo albums and memories and let us peek into their own private Laurelton: Ernest Engerer and Frederick Engerer, son and nephew respectively of Capt. Ernest Engerer; Jean Schmitt Garvey, daughter of Anthony Schmitt, the last farmer on Merrick Boulevard; and Larry and Bill Lederer, grandsons of one of Laurelton's first residents, Peter Gannon. A tremendous thank you is owed to Bernard Kavaler, grandson of one of Laurelton's first dentists, Dr. David Kavaler; Ron Miller; Reba Harris Solomon; Joel Karpay; Paul Frommer; Dr. Michael Rauch; Emil Schaffer; and Charles Stein Sr. A special thanks to Skip Weinstock for posting my urgent pleas for help on his Laurelton website.

Eric Huber of the Long Island Division of the Queens Borough Public Library was extremely helpful to us, as was Richard Hourhan of the Queens Borough Historical Association. Jasmine Harrison of the Laurelton branch of the Queens Borough Public Library was very generous with her time when we visited. Roger Madiou, Laurelton historian, provided assistance with community research. Erin Vosgien, our publisher, has our deepest gratitude and respect for being so patient and encouraging.

Roberta Kossoff would like to say a special "zank" you to son Ben Weinstock and daughter Hannah. A special thanks also goes to Dasha Weinstock for taking wonderful photographs of modern-day Laurelton. And finally, we offer a deep and gracious bow to Cynthia Lee for her spectacular assistance throughout.

INTRODUCTION

Laurelton is a place in time
And a state of mind,
A love and warmth
That will always be,
And can never be again.

—Charles Stein Sr., 1998

By 1900, parts of Queens were becoming bedroom communities for other parts of New York City. The Long Island Rail Road electrified its line, opened tunnels under the East River, put an end to ferry service, and positioned Queens within commuting distance. The Queensboro Bridge did the rest.

In 1906, a former New York state senator, William H. Reynolds, advertised the sale of lots on which only expensive one-family houses could be built. Laurelton was advertised as the "Garden Suburb in New York City," 25 miles from Manhattan and "highly restricted," a code term meaning "no Jewish people." Only a few lots were sold and a few houses constructed. The senator soon abandoned Laurelton.

Laurelton languished underdeveloped for most of the prosperous 1920s, but in the summer of 1928, an advertisement appeared that another "group of 204 Spanish type houses has been started on the old Laurelton golf course, bringing the total . . . to more than 900 homes."

The stock market crashed famously in October 1929, but it did not seem to deter the builders. Eighty new homes were opened for inspection on 226th Street, bringing the total to 2,000. The developers announced plans for 500 more. Soon, they announced that $1.3 million worth of dwellings had been sold, bringing the four-year level to $35 million. "There is never a shortage of potential home owners," the developer said.

The families who decided during the Depression that home owning was a good investment were not the people Senator Reynolds had been seeking. They were mainly first generation working people of Irish, Italian, German, or Jewish descent. They were people frugal enough to have saved money for a down payment on a modest house, and after the election of Franklin D. Roosevelt in 1933, they could turn to the Homeowners Loan Corporation for help.

Potential home owners did not fail to notice that Laurelton was no longer restricted. The builders paid no attention to the ethnicity of names and asked no questions about religion. Neither did the buyers. They moved across the street, around the corner, or next door to each other without knowing the identity of their neighbors. They did not do much socializing, nor did they encourage their children to play together. They joined a church, a synagogue, or neither without comment from the neighbors. They waved to each other over their fences and kept the peace.

On Merrick Road, across from where the Twin Ponds Bakery building still stands, was the traditional white farmhouse of the Schmitt family. It had neither central heating nor running water. The Schmitts grew a wide variety of vegetables that they sold to stores on Merrick Road and carried by truck to the Wallabout Market in Brooklyn.

The Schmitt farmhouse was built by Albert Schmitt, whose family emigrated from Germany in 1849. He and Margarethe Kappelmaier were married in Saint Boniface Church in Fosters Meadow (later called Rosedale) on February 12, 1889. Three days later, he signed a contract to purchase a 28-acre farm for $3,400. The Schmitt family farmed this land until Albert's death in 1947.

At the age of 77, Albert was interviewed by a local newspaper. He said he had lived there "when Merrick was a plank one-way toll road to Jamaica, when those eastbound were forced to wait at muddy sidings for western traffic." During the mornings, "He led his cows all the way to . . . East New York and passed nothing but farms."

Next to the farm was the training academy of Capt. Ernest Engerer, who in addition to training police dogs also had a circus act. He claimed to have won his wild animals in a poker game and to have lost part of his left arm to a lion. He was a dashing figure, unconventional and theatrical, who sometimes took his show on the road and enlisted the help of his two children, Ernie and Barbara, for his act.

Captain Engerer's life and career came to a spectacularly tragic end in an amusement park in North Carolina in 1962. He was killed by his lion Monte before the eyes of a stunned audience. Police arrived and fired at the lion from outside the cage, and after a number of rounds were fired, they killed him.

"Before the animal was killed he alternately stalked then stood astraddle the body . . . for forty minutes," the newspaper reported. Engerer's assistant said he had no indication the attack was coming. "The animal was very deceptive," he said.

Bill Lederer's grandfather, Peter Gannon, built a house for his family on 231st Street in 1924. They did not have electricity for 10 more years. Like their neighbors the Schmitts, they had no running water. They had a hand pump in the kitchen and an outhouse in the yard. Bill still has one of the kerosene lamps by the light of which his mother, Peggy Gannon, did her homework.

For a long time, Laurelton has been known for the love and devotion of people who grew up there. Many Laurelton reunions have taken place in various parts of the country, but now the Internet makes it possible to reunite with old friends without going anywhere. The Laurelton Alumni page began with a wistful plea from Sue-Carol (Nussbaum) Ludacer to Skip Weinstock, who ran a Far Rockaway page, that the two of them team up and start a Laurelton page. Laurelton students had always had a choice of high schools—Jamaica, Andrew Jackson, or Far Rockaway. It usually happened that if your parents could afford the train fare, you went to Far Rockaway.

Almost instantly, the Laurelton page was overwhelmed by enthusiastic ex-Laureltonians. Most of them no longer lived there, but their glowing memories were astounding. Although the memories came from people who had come of age in different decades, from different religious and national backgrounds, and who had, by this time, lived most of their lives elsewhere, the message was always the same:

"What a wonderful way to grow up."

"How lucky we are to have been part of that wonderful experience."

"Growing up in Laurelton was a great experience."

"Life was terrific for a kid on our block."

"It was a perfect town, safe and friendly."

"They were the best years of my life."

The list goes on. The Laurelton Alumni website is now 184 pages long and growing. There are lists of friends, lists of beloved teachers (and a few not so beloved), and lists of stores on both sides of Merrick Road in the exact order in which they existed. (It is remarkable how many have fond memories of the stores at which they once hung out.) There are architectural discussions of the Laurelton Movie Theatre and linguistic disagreements about why it was called "the Itch." And there is a pervading tenderness overall, a sense that life can never again be that sweet and how lucky they were to have known it. Some historians think that the small town, as it was represented in the motion pictures of the 1930s and 1940s, may have influenced the feelings and behavior of those who grew up in them.

As Tom Smith, the archivist and historian of the Mentones, tells us, there was "a culture of subcultures," in which certain groups of young people, bound together by a religion, a certain school, a neighborhood, or a particular game they played in a certain area, would develop community structures and loyalties that almost constituted a "town within a town." The Mentones (named for Mentone Avenue near where they lived) were such a group, not only because of the large number of young people who belonged to it, but because its interests, values, and disciplines dominated their lives and affections for so many years. It was truly another way of living life in Laurelton.

In the 1960s and 1970s, Laurelton was victimized by the unscrupulous real estate practice of blockbusting. This practice struck at the heart of what most people hold dear—the homes in which they have invested a large part of their assets and the future of their children.

The picture is complicated. Laurelton, like other neighborhoods in the area, had been slowly integrating for some time. About 15 percent of the population was African American. They were accepted by their neighbors, the schools, and various churches.

Laurelton had no incidents of violence. The real estate industry had over 75 agents working in a tiny area, as Laurelton is only one square mile in circumference. They inundated the residents with bulletins, letters, and telephone calls predicting the transformation of Laurelton into a welfare ghetto within a matter of weeks. They sent trucks into quiet neighborhoods to broadcast predictions of doom accompanied by loud offers of instant cash. They even supplied funds to large welfare families to support the purchase of a house. To be fair, there were many factors at work in terms of Laurelton's demographic changes. The city and the nation faced widespread civil, racial, and economic unrest. Education also played a part in terms of zoning and business issues. The opening of Springfield Gardens High School in the mid-1960s used Merrick Boulevard as a dividing line when designating their geographical boundaries. This caused some families to move away as their children reached high school age.

Eleanor Holmes Norton, in an address to the City Club of New York, labeled real estate "the most irresponsible industry in New York City." She denied that Laurelton was bigoted. "There is no ugly attitude in Laurelton," she said.

People left for various reasons, but a substantial part of the population stayed, puzzled and confused yet willing to search for a solution.

Rabbi Howard Singer, the shy religious leader of the Laurelton Jewish Center, spent sleepless nights trying to figure out a solution. By his own admission, he was a scholar, more interested in religious literature than in real estate. Eventually, he came up with a solution so imaginative that a novelist could have dreamed it up, and his congregation decided to let him give it a try. They decided to open a free real estate agency in the synagogue, staffed by volunteers (mostly women), to guide and advise clients in the purchase of a house, thus achieving an integrated Laurelton. They were assisted by black members of the many block associations, like Bess DeBetham, a community activist who moved to Laurelton in 1971 and was angered by the tactics of the blockbusters. Like the scholar that he was, Rabbi Singer took a business course in real estate with some of the congregants to make sure they would not get into trouble. When a broker tried to shut them down on the grounds that they did not have a license, Rabbi Singer responded that because they did not charge for services, they did not fit the definition of a brokerage.

By the time the free agency had assisted in selling 500 houses to both blacks and whites, the population figures of Laurelton were split evenly between both races and the integrationists were ready to declare victory. Rabbi Howard Singer wrote a long article for the *Saturday Evening Post* called "How We Beat the Blockbusters" in 1968. In 1971, the *Long Island Press* released the series "The Saving of a Community: Residents Join Hands to Make Integration Work." But despite the sweet successes and the hard won victory, it turned out that integration was easier to achieve than to maintain. Laurelton remained integrated for only 15 years, then succumbed to the passage of time and painless attrition. A wave of prosperous West Indian immigrants discovered Laurelton and loved it.

When the trauma of blockbusting was finally over and the slow process of resegregation began, Laurelton, except for its change of population, was beginning to look much the same. The Laurelton Jewish Center, which had been the prime mover in the action to stop segregation, found that it could no longer afford to continue and sold its building to the Seventh-day Adventists. With respectful attention to its importance as a former synagogue, the Adventists refurbished it and brought it to its present-day splendor.

The Federation of Laurelton Block Associations continued the work it had been involved in with the Jewish Center—to provide advice to both buyers and sellers.

When old residents return to see what has become of the town they so dearly loved, they are often welcomed with enthusiasm. Invariably, they are impressed and delighted with the lack of changes they find. Over the years, the old redbrick Tudor and English houses have acquired a most extraordinary glow and seem to be on their way to becoming national treasures. The malls, or "islands" as the old residents called them, are blooming with prize-winning flowers. The whole town seems to have fallen into the hands of landscape artists. Beauty contests for the malls and gardens invite passionate competition and give substantial prizes in alternating years.

It is not possible to escape the feeling that Laurelton is in loving hands. There is much community interest and activity. The town has acquired some notable public assets. It boasts a community hospital for the first time ever. Churches and schools are flourishing. The library is no longer housed in a store but in its own brick building. On any afternoon, it is crowded with students and looks as if it could use an expansion. There is a movement afoot to refurbish the stores on Merrick Boulevard, and at long last, a real plan, now in the hands of engineers, to return the Twin Ponds to their former beauty while also solving some of the flooding problems in the streets.

Sometimes a young resident will happen upon the Laurelton Alumni page and add a few words to those of the old-timers who inhabit those pages. Often they remark, as if nobody had ever thought of it before, "Laurelton—it's like a magical town."

One

History of Laurelton

The town of Jamaica had been established as far back as 1655 by English settlers from Hempstead, Long Island, and became the county seat when Queens County was formed in 1683. At the time, the beautiful countryside running east from Jamaica (along what eventually became the Merrick Road) was little more than farmland, woodland, brooks, and ponds. The first settlers in the area arrived around 1660 and referred to their settlement as "the Spring Field," which later became Springfield Gardens. The British occupied Queens for seven years after the Battle of Long Island. They used it as a staging area for the disposition of loyalists and for feeding and sheltering their troops. When defeated in 1783, they left Queens to the slow rebuilding of its farms, villages, and ravished countryside. Laurelton remained unknown and unnamed until the early part of the 20th century.

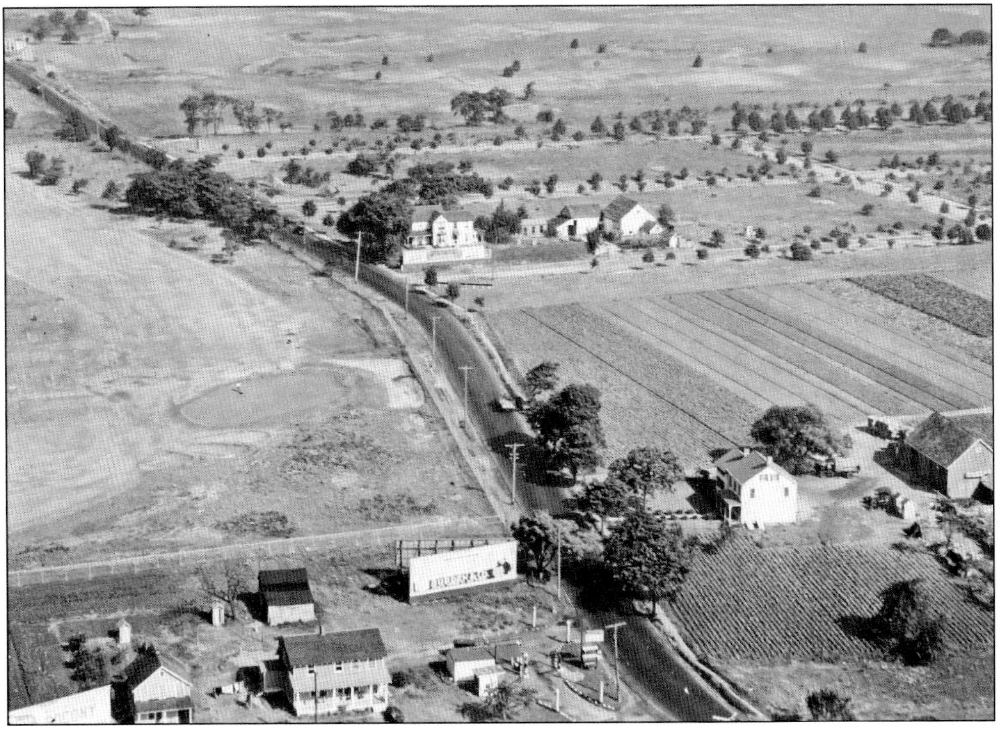

This 1928 aerial view of Merrick Road shows the Schmitt farm in bottom right and Capt. Ernest Engerer's Animal Training Academy in top right. Merrick Road is a simple one-way street where telephone poles had recently been installed. The airman who snapped this photograph was a customer of Captain Engerer and was later killed in a plane crash. (Courtesy of Ernest Engerer.)

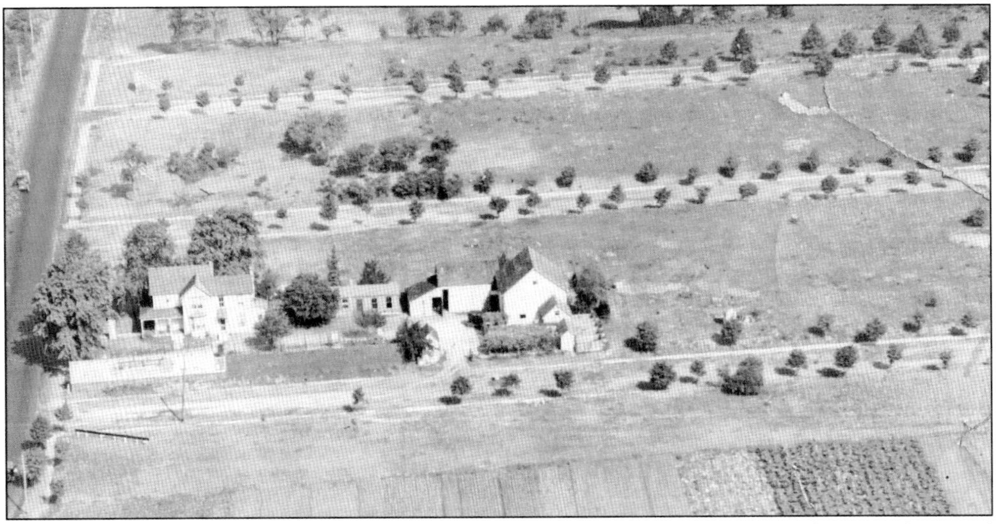

A closer aerial view of Captain Engerer's academy reveals various outbuildings and animal stalls. Captain Engerer was a dashing, colorful, and highly theatrical presence in an otherwise conventional farming community. Visiting the wild animal farm was a popular way to entertain children on weekends. It should be noted that the Engerer family's immigration to the United States was part of a wave of German immigration to the area who established a large farming community in the area, often called Fosters Meadow. (Courtesy of Ernest Engerer.)

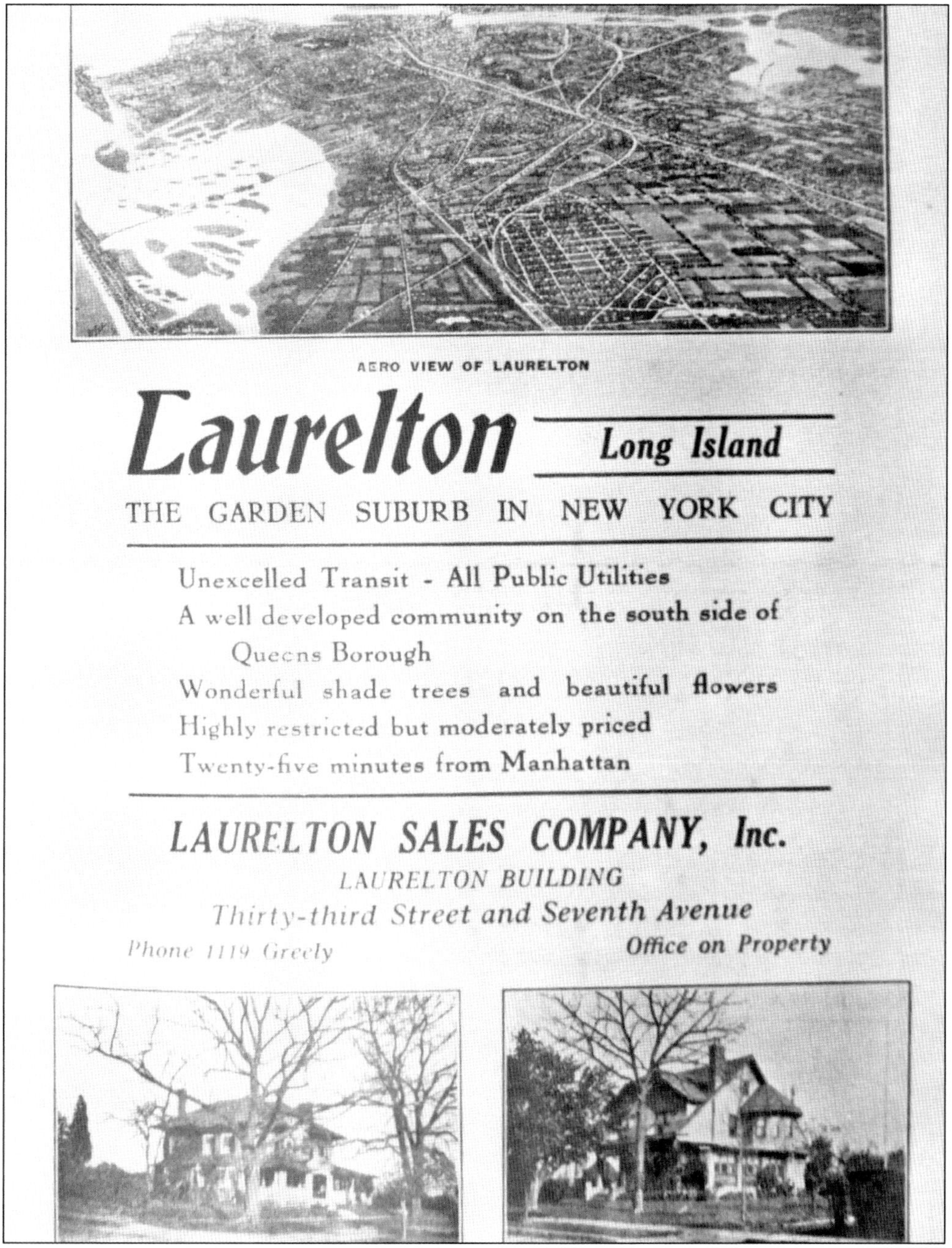

When this advertisement appeared in newspapers in 1906, it was the first attempt to develop Laurelton as an upscale, "highly restricted" community. It failed, but the description of Laurelton as a "garden suburb" lasted for many years and is still appropriate. (Courtesy of Queens Borough Public Library, Long Island Division.)

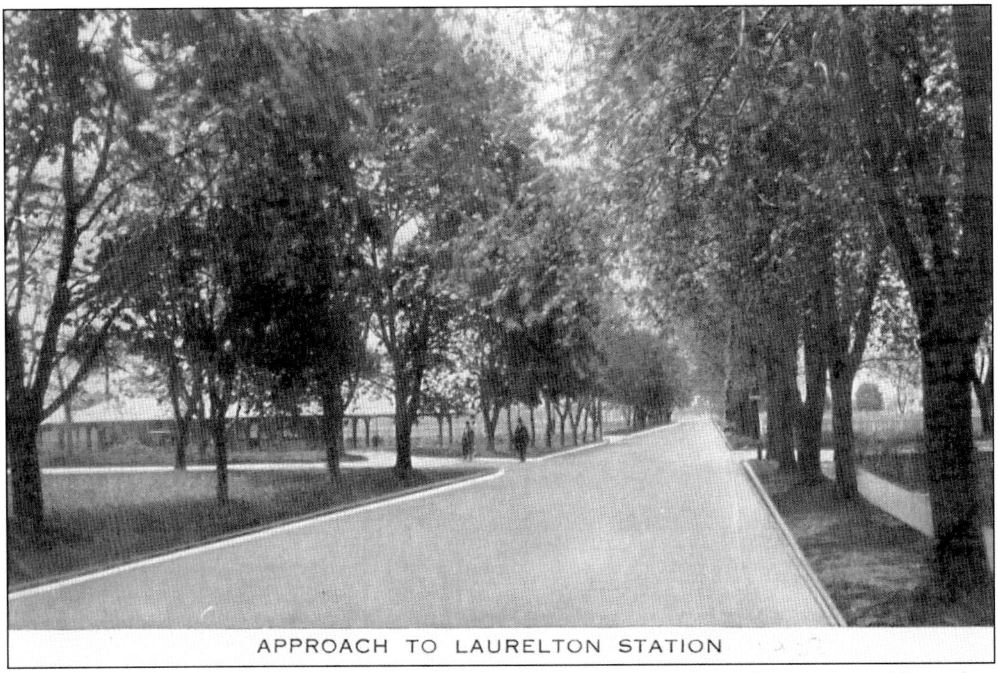

This postcard advertisement shows the bucolic approach to the Laurelton station. Note that there are no railroad tracks visible in the picture. (Courtesy of Queens Borough Public Library, Long Island Division.)

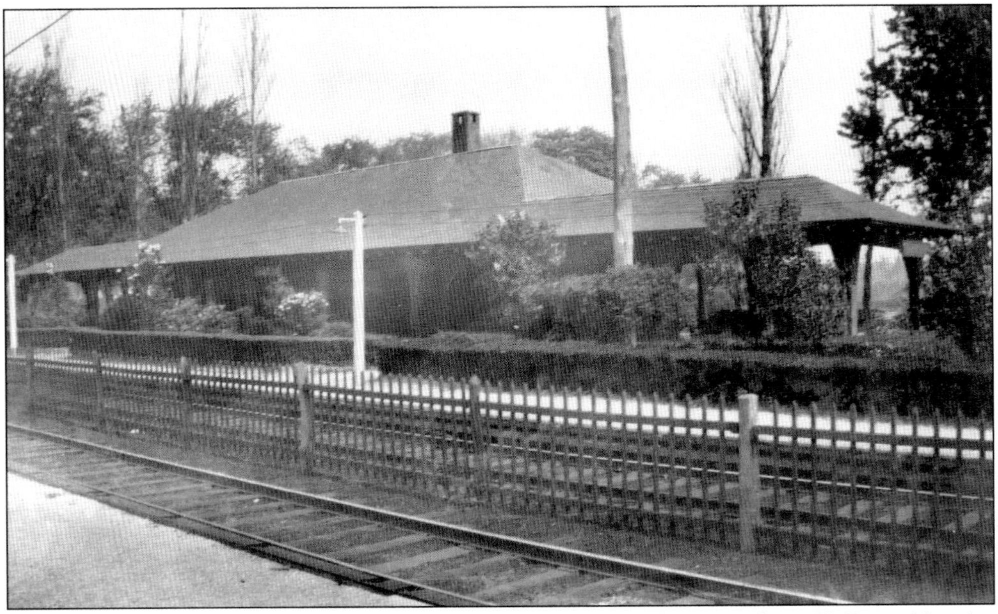

Laurelton did not have a stop on the Long Island Rail Road until Sen. William H. Reynolds, who wished to develop the town, paid the railroad $8,000 to build one. The station was the pride of Laurelton for a long time, often mentioned as the most beautiful on the line. This 1930 photograph shows the back of the station facing the westbound tracks. (Courtesy of Queens Borough Public Library, Long Island Division.)

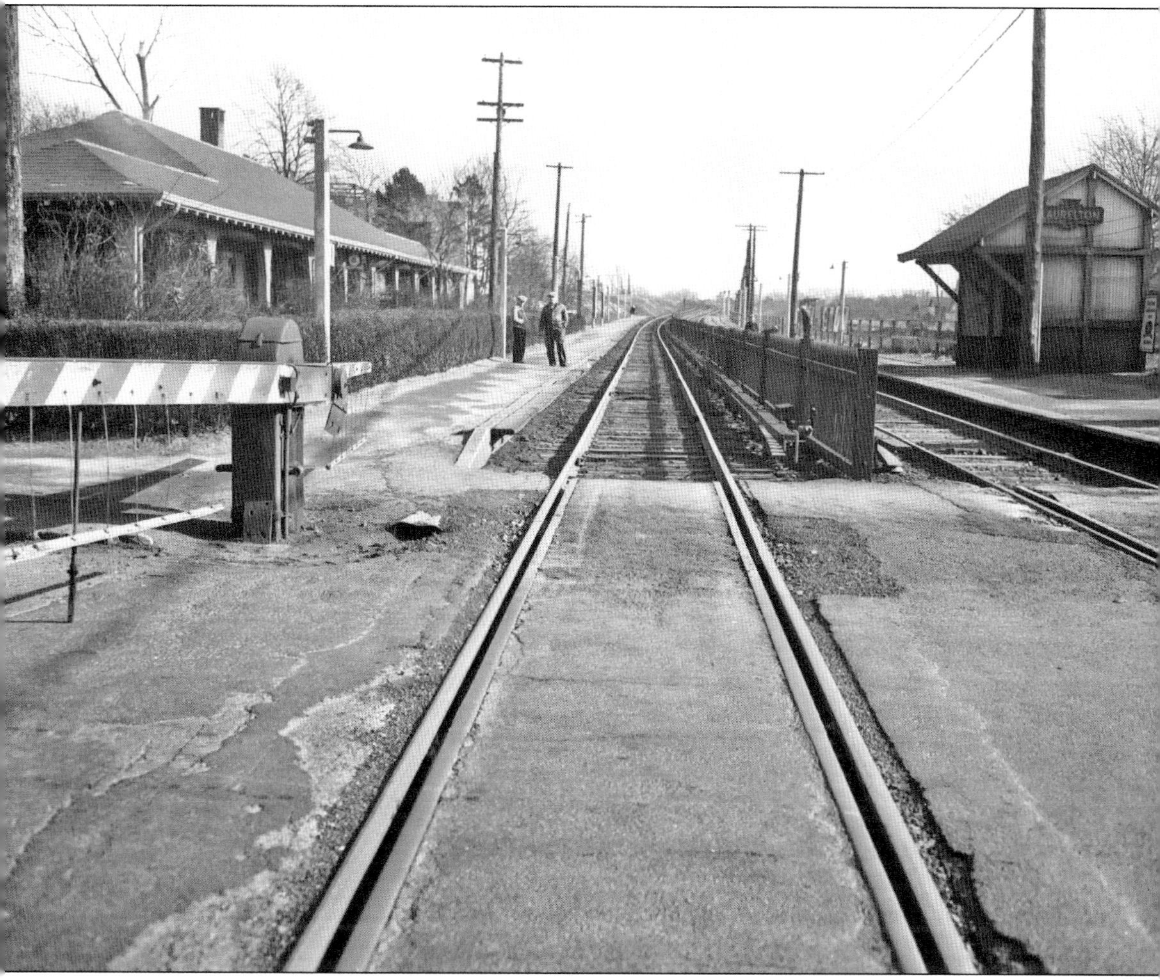

Seen above, two men wait for a westbound train a short distance from the railroad crossing. In the late 1940s and early 1950s, the Long Island Rail Road elevated its tracks, and the beautiful station house was demolished. (Courtesy of Queens Borough Public Library, Long Island Division.)

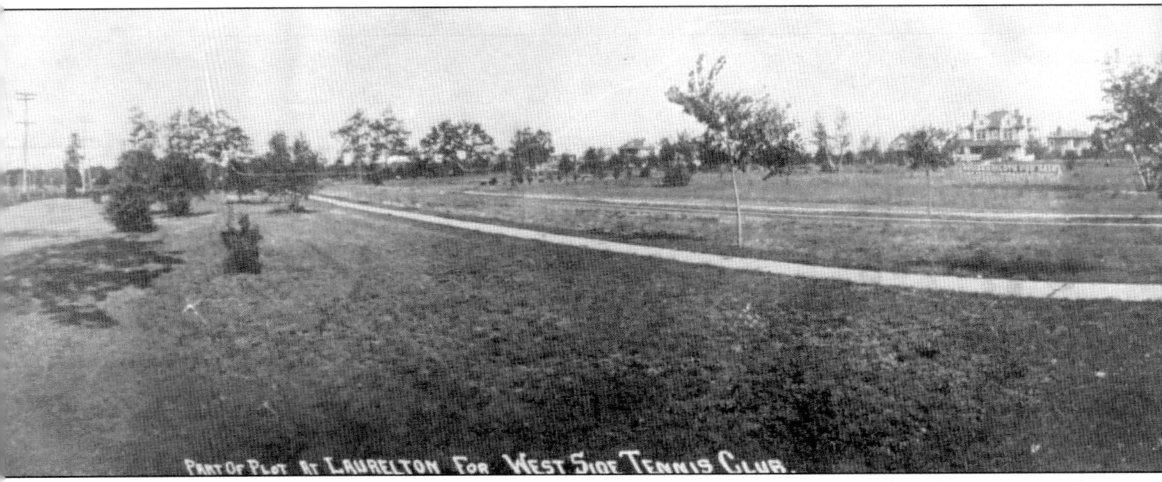

Laurelton was once under consideration as a site for the West Side Tennis Club, but Forest Hills was chosen instead. For a time, this was the home of the US Open. (Courtesy of Queens Borough Public Library, Long Island Division.)

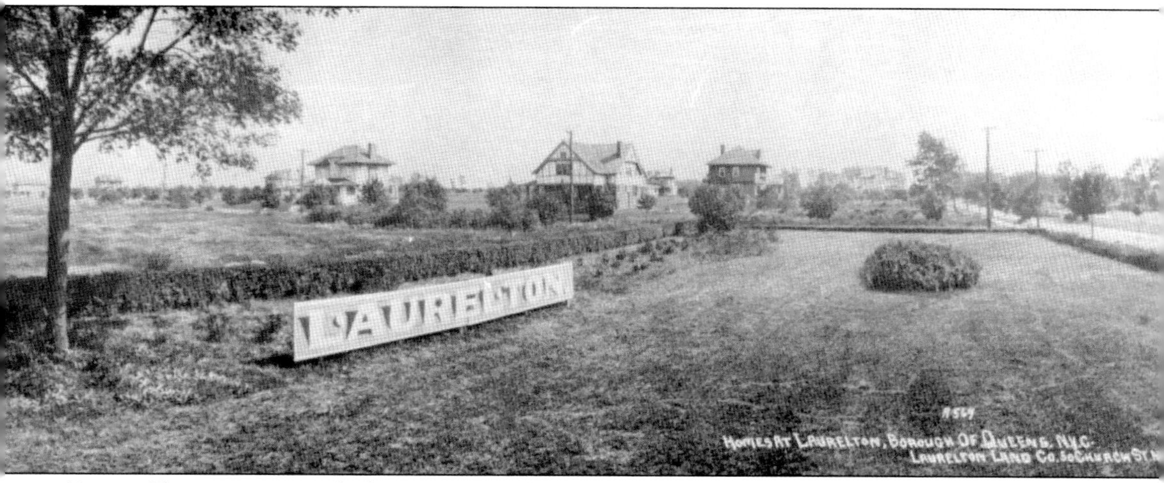

Pictured here is a postcard advertisement of beautiful Laurelton in the early 20th century. Some of Senator Reynold's "mansions" are seen in the background. (Courtesy of Queens Borough Public Library, Long Island Division.)

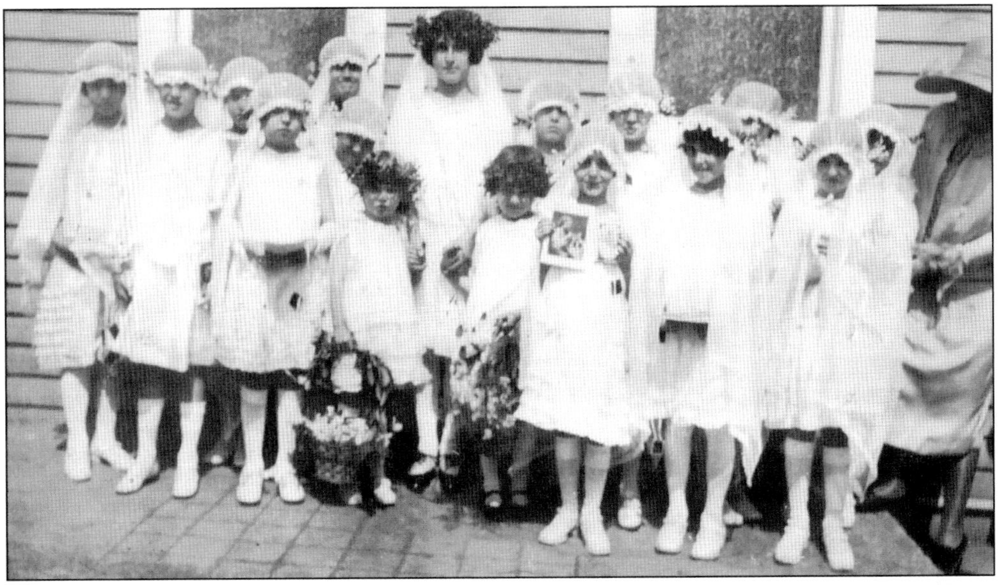

Margaret Gannon stands proudly with her communion class while displaying a picture of Jesus in 1928. The location of the church is unknown, but it is believed to be either St. Clare or Mary Magdalene. (Courtesy of Bill and Larry Lederer.)

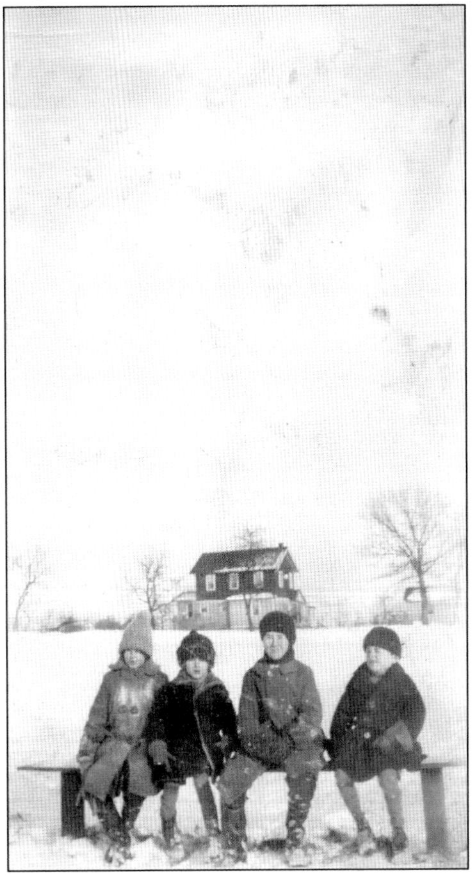

Four of the Gannon children sit in front of their house on a snowy day. Pictured from left to right are Loretta, Peggy, Edward, and Thomas. Note how barren and utterly rural southern Queens was at this time. (Courtesy of Bill and Larry Lederer.)

This lovely girl is Margaret "Peggy" Gannon, Bill and Larry Lederer's mother, posing in the eighth-grade graduation dress she sewed by hand at P.S. 156 in 1932. She is on the deck of the Gannon house, and in the background, the growing development of Laurelton can be seen. (Courtesy of Bill and Larry Lederer.)

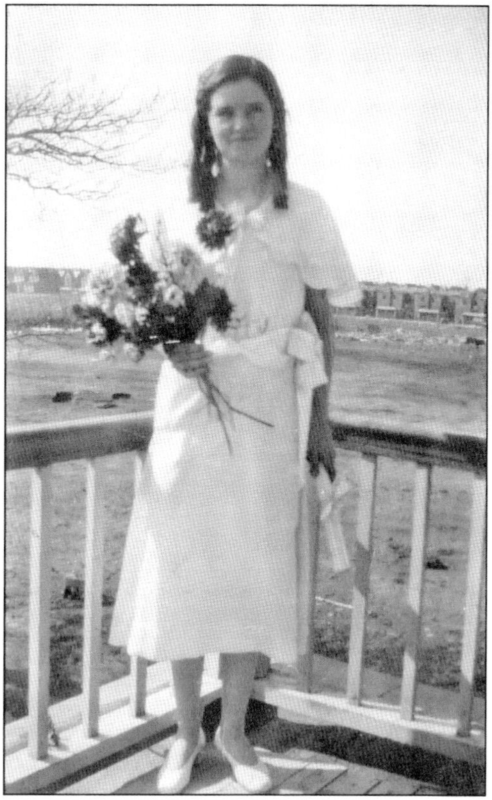

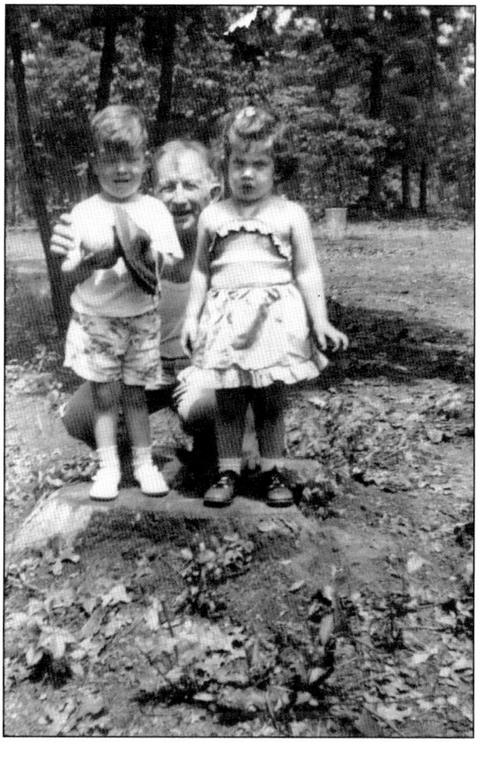

This photograph taken in 1950 shows, from left to right, Chuck Stein, with his catcher's mitt and softball; grandfather Sam Rosenberg; and Judy Rosenberg at Brookville Park. Brookville, near Laurelton, provided many families the opportunity to picnic.

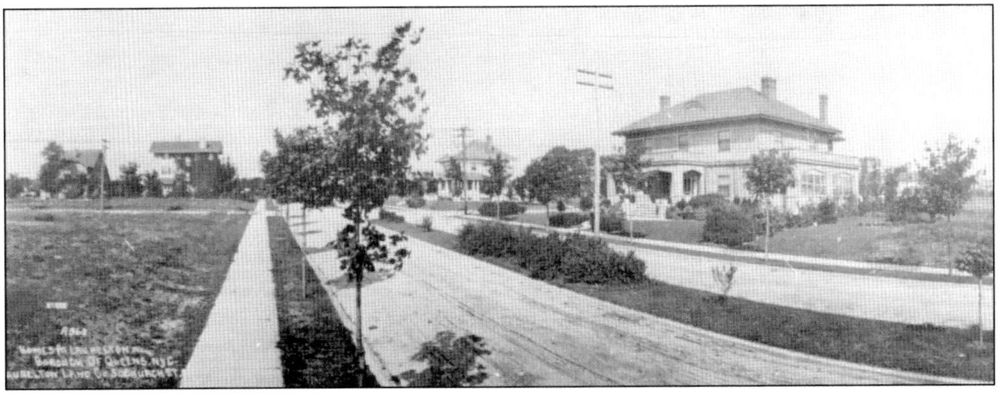

These are a few of the expensive houses built by Senator Reynolds's Laurelton Land Company at the beginning of the 20th century. Some of them exist today and are still considered desirable homes. Unfortunately for Senator Reynolds, the market for these houses proved to be thin. (Courtesy of Queens Borough Public Library, Long Island Division.)

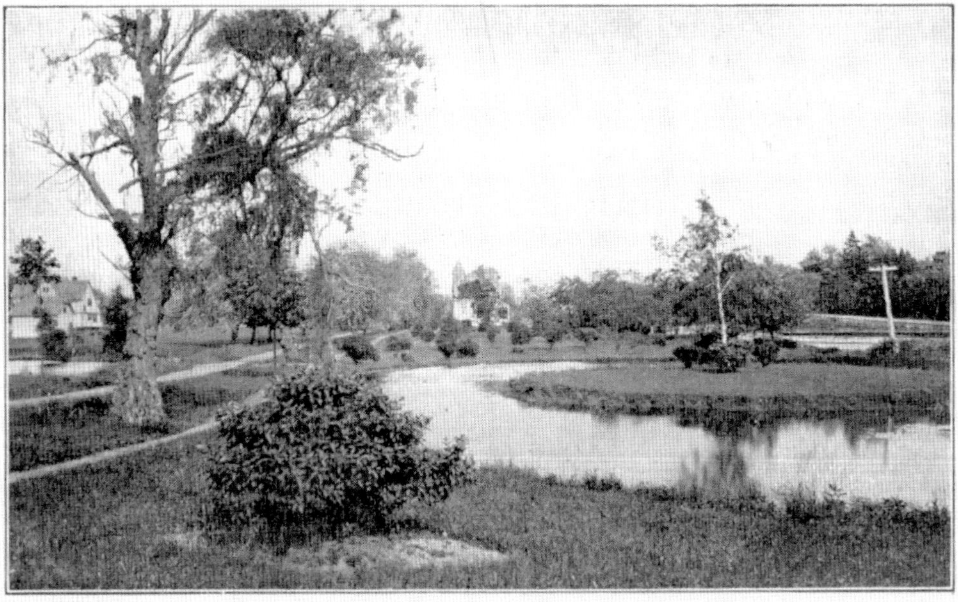

ONE OF THE BEAUTIFUL HOMES AT LAURELTON

This is another postcard advertisement displaying the developing community of Laurelton in the area around what is 141st Avenue today. (Courtesy of Queens Borough Public Library, Long Island Division.)

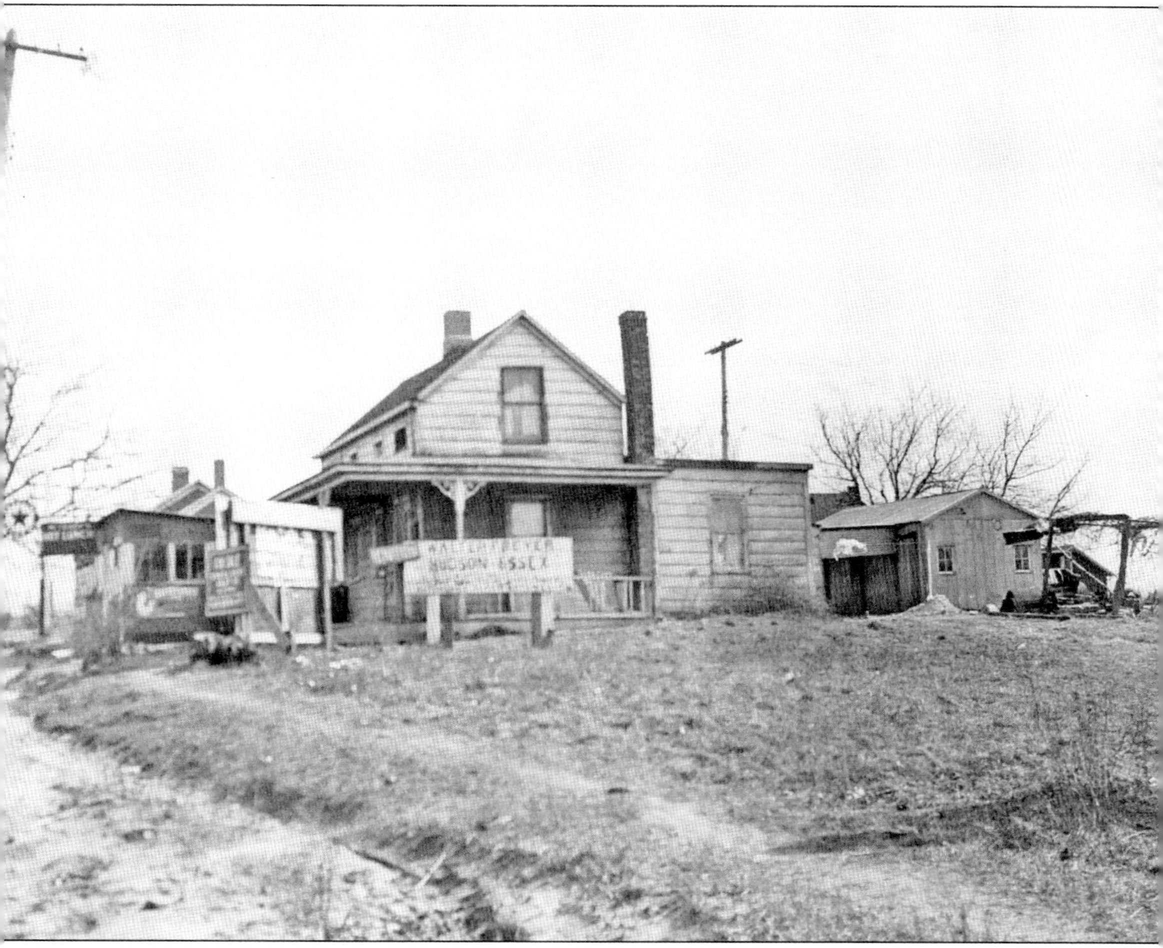

In 1927, this building stood on the east corner of 223rd Street and Merrick Road. It offered "Walter Freyer's Repairs," in addition to a "Hot Lunch." (Courtesy of Queens Borough Public Library, Long Island Division.)

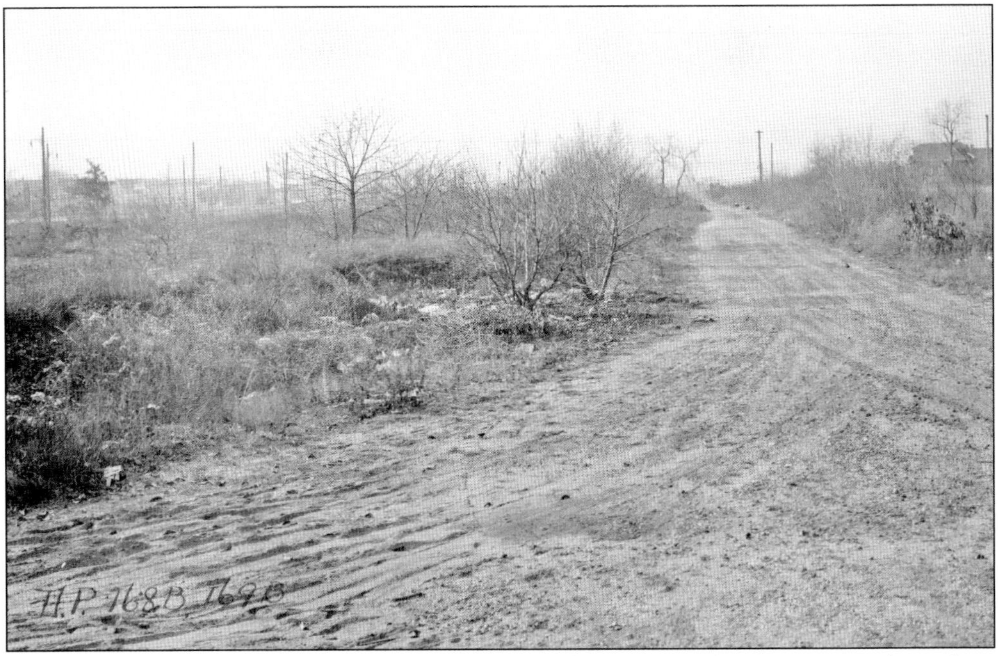

In 1934, this was a view of the waterworks property on the north side of Sunrise Highway from 224th Street. It was the proposed route of North Conduit Avenue. (Courtesy of Queens Borough Public Library, Long Island Division.)

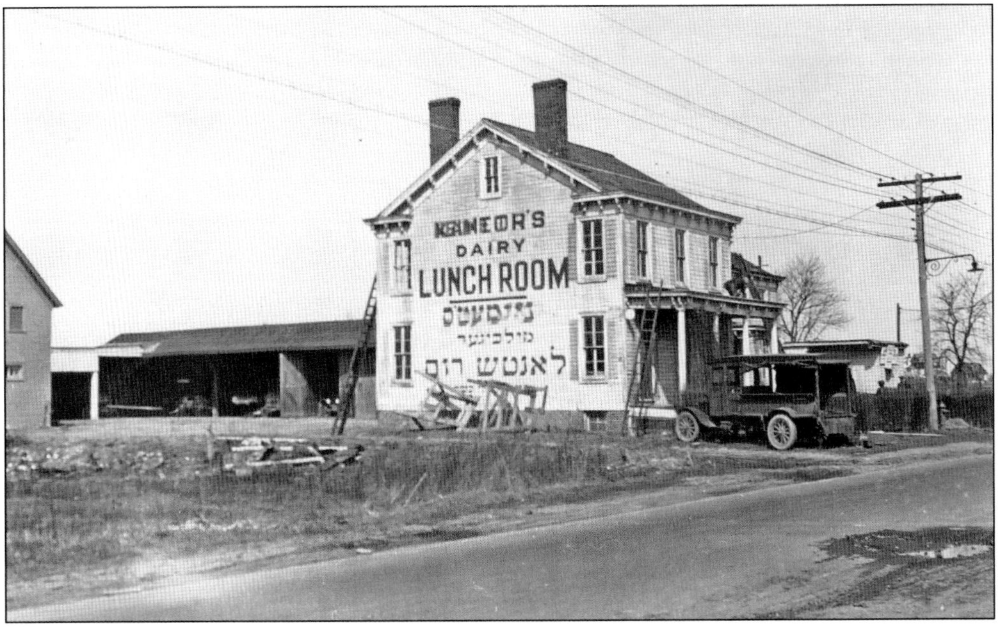

This is Kantor's Dairy Lunch Room in 1928, which offered a dairy lunch to those who might be visiting Montifiore Cemetery, located nearby on Springfield Boulevard. The Hebrew writing is a translation of the English sign. Montifiore Cemetery today is well known as the Ohel of the Lubavitcher Rebbe Menachem Mendel Schneerson. The Ohel cemetery maintains an office that is open 24 hours a day, six days a week. (Courtesy of Queens Borough Public Library, Long Island Division.)

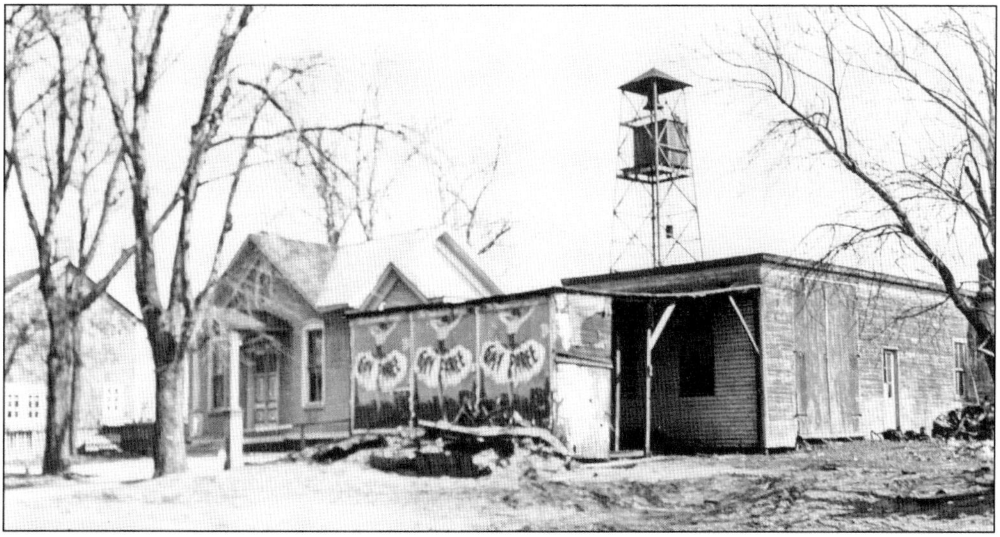

This view of a frame Episcopal church and the adjacent firehouse of the Springfield Hose Company No. 1 sharing one bell between them is indicative of the rural nature of the Springfield-Laurelton area in 1927. The entertainment being offered at the firehouse is called "Gay Paree." This was most likely a variety show featuring vaudevillian acts as well as showgirls. (Courtesy of Queens Borough Public Library, Long Island Division.)

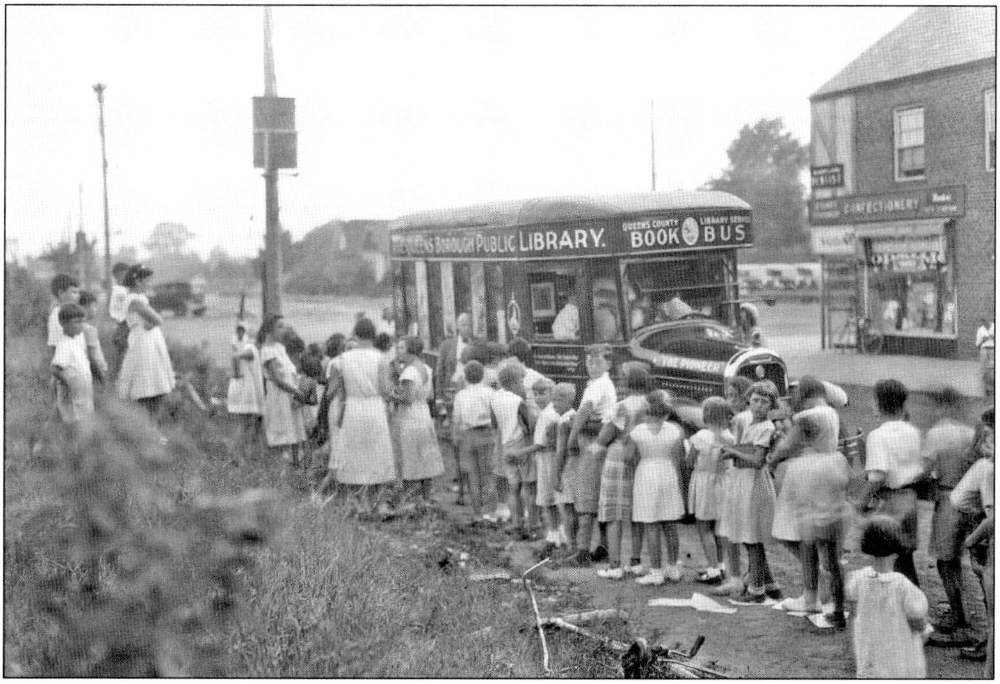

In this delightful 1934 photograph, a large group of Laurelton children wait for their chance to choose books from an exciting new acquisition, the Book Bus. Until this time, Laurelton did not have a public library and many children walked through the woods or across the overpass to the Rosedale Public Library while carrying heavy loads of books both ways. One wonders how many library books may have fallen into the streams or been left unheeded beneath a tree. (Courtesy of Queens Borough Public Library.)

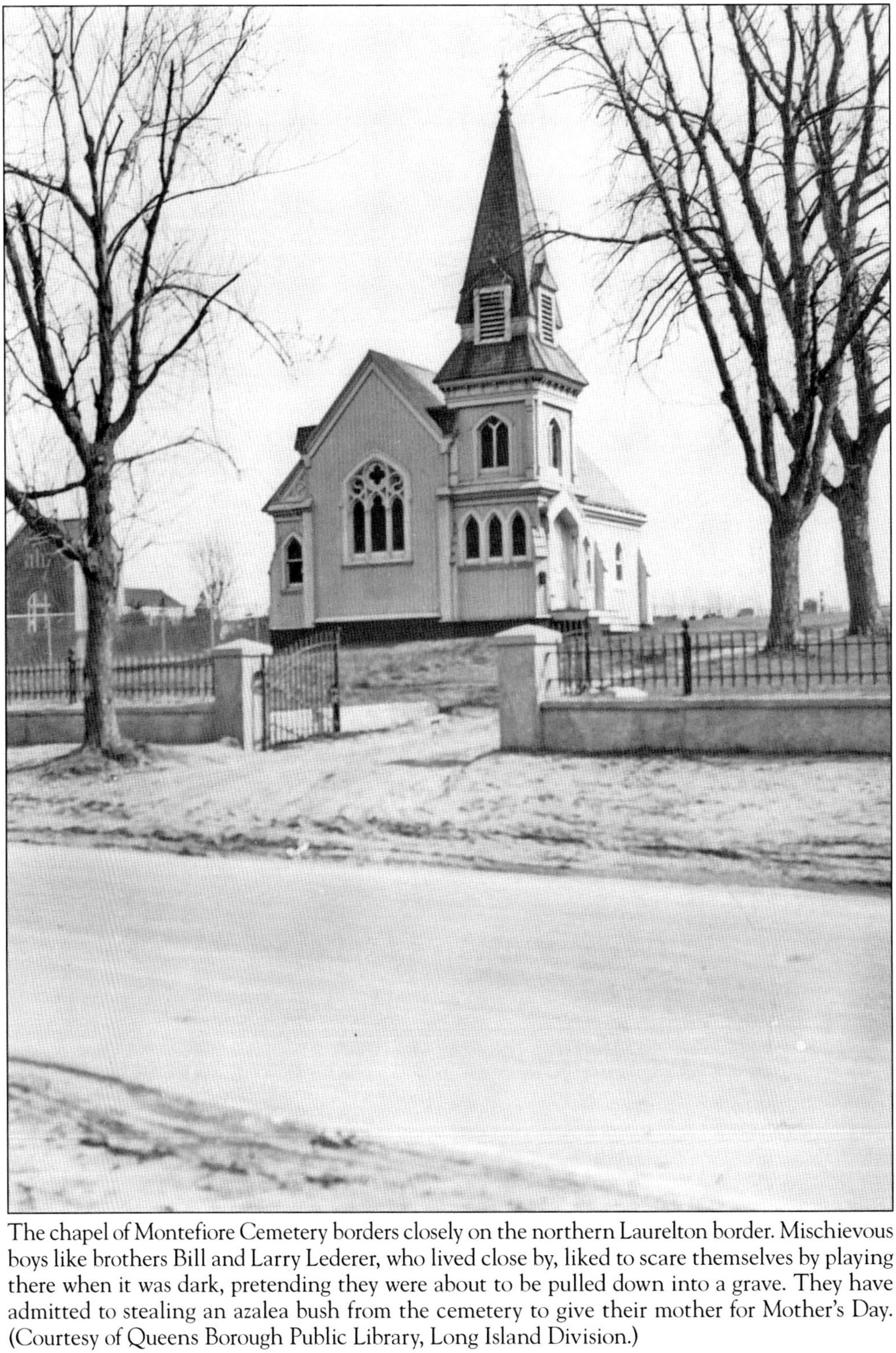

The chapel of Montefiore Cemetery borders closely on the northern Laurelton border. Mischievous boys like brothers Bill and Larry Lederer, who lived close by, liked to scare themselves by playing there when it was dark, pretending they were about to be pulled down into a grave. They have admitted to stealing an azalea bush from the cemetery to give their mother for Mother's Day. (Courtesy of Queens Borough Public Library, Long Island Division.)

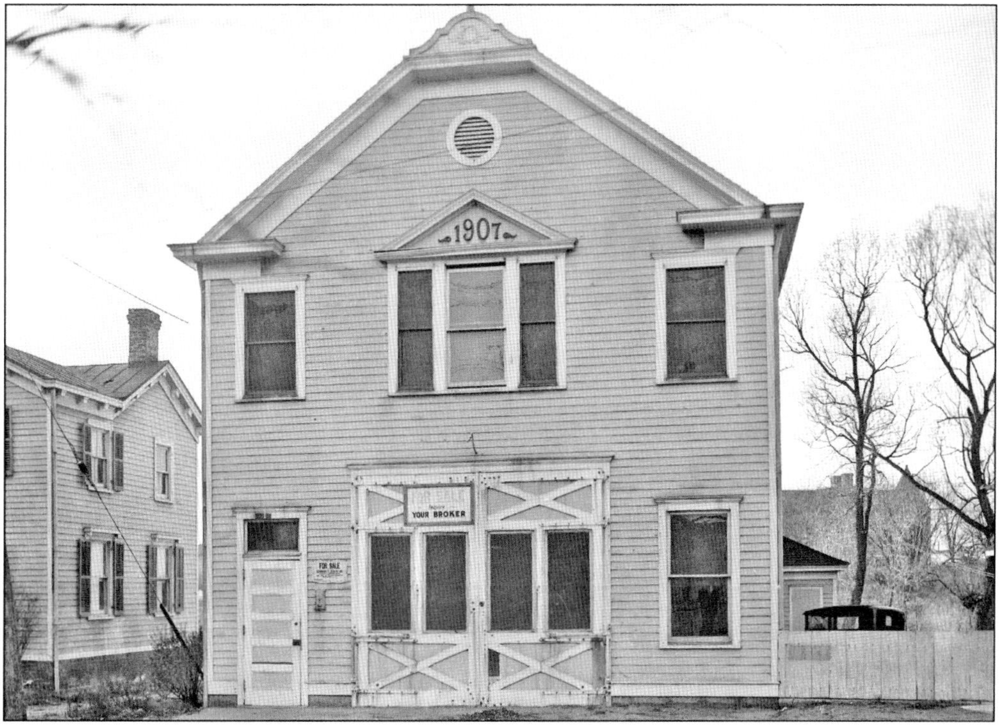

The old Springfield Gardens Firehouse, built in 1907 and pictured here in 1933, was used as a community space for Scout meetings until its demolition. (Courtesy of Queens Borough Public Library, Long Island Division.)

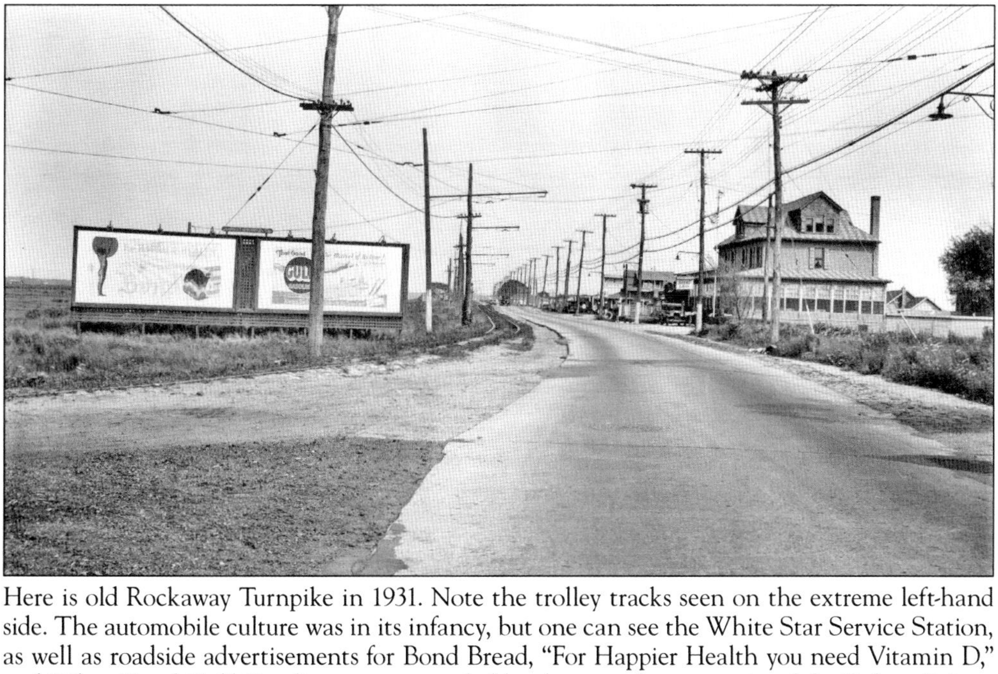

Here is old Rockaway Turnpike in 1931. Note the trolley tracks seen on the extreme left-hand side. The automobile culture was in its infancy, but one can see the White Star Service Station, as well as roadside advertisements for Bond Bread, "For Happier Health you need Vitamin D," and "That Good Gulf Gasoline, recommended by the steamboat captain of the Robert E. Lee, the marvel of its time."

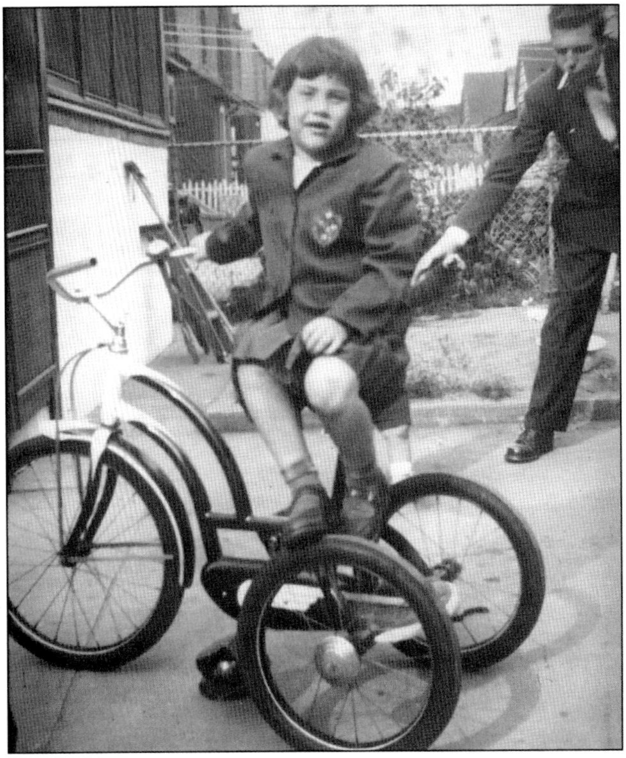

Judy Garber (née Rosenberg), age four, in 1952 sits on her train driver Murray tricycle in her driveway in Laurelton. She and her parents and brother (whose dimpled leg can be seen in the background) lived at 134-27 229th Street in Laurelton. Her cousin Jack Stein, who lived with his family at 134-31 229th Street, can be seen trying to direct traffic.

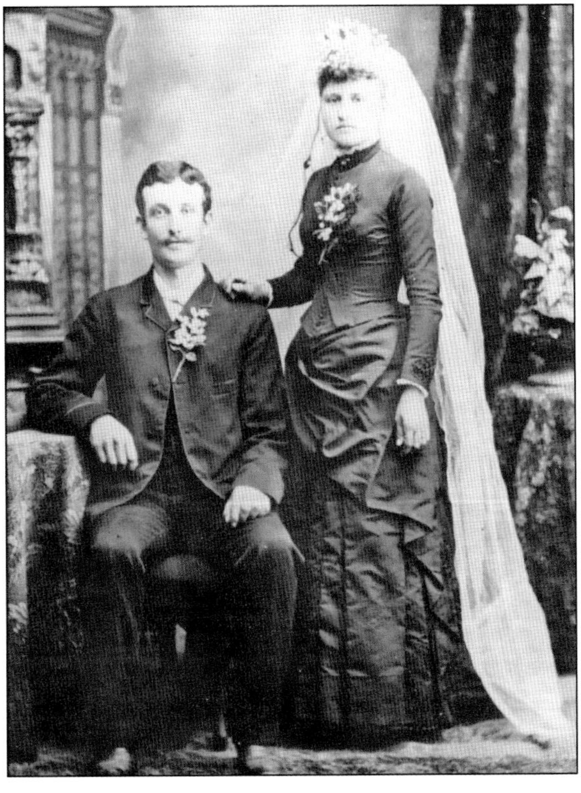

This charming photograph is the wedding picture of Albert Schmitt and Margaretha Kappelmaier, Jean Schmitt's grandparents. They were married in St. Boniface Church in Fosters Meadow (later named Rosedale) on February 12, 1889. Three days later, they signed a contract to purchase a 23-acre farm on Merrick Road for $3,400. The farm, just west of the Twin Ponds, remained in the Schmitt family's possession until 1947. (Courtesy of Jean Schmitt Garvey.)

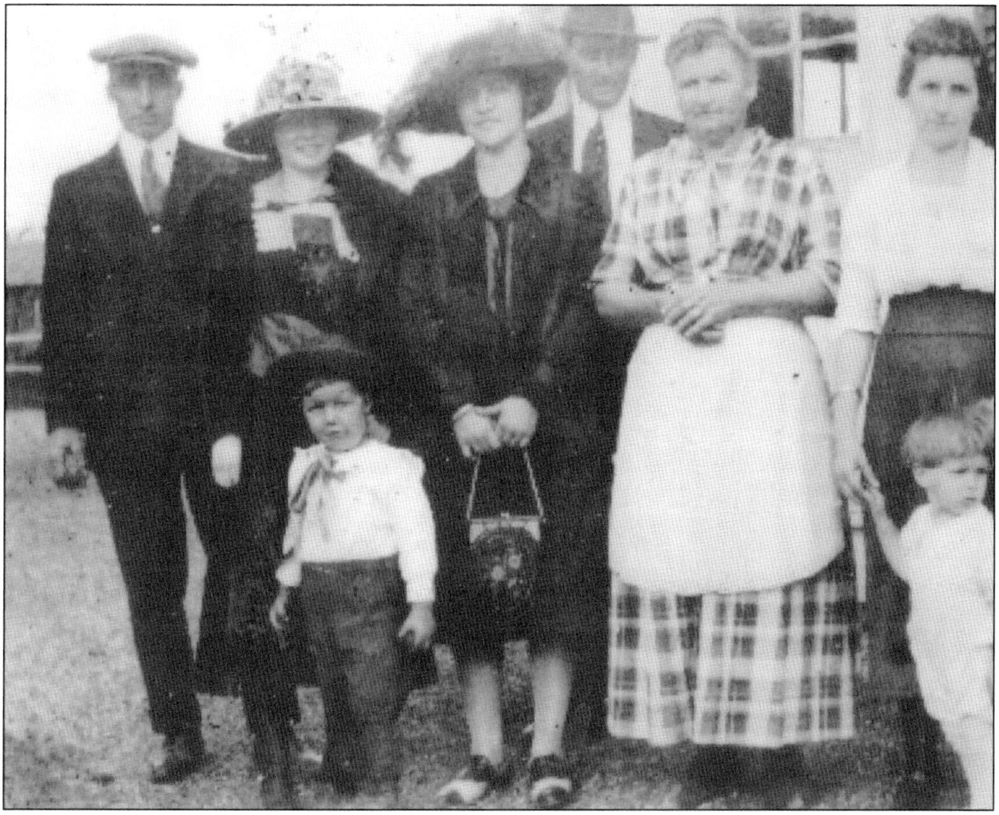

Members of the Schmitt family (some shown above) were children Edwin Kumenacher and Johnny Kumenacher, Ferdinand Schmitt, Mary Schmitt, Margie Schmitt, Margaret (Margaretha) Schmitt, Clara Kumenacher, Louise Kappelmaier, John Kumenacher, and Albert Schmitt Jr. (Courtesy of Jean Schmitt Garvey.)

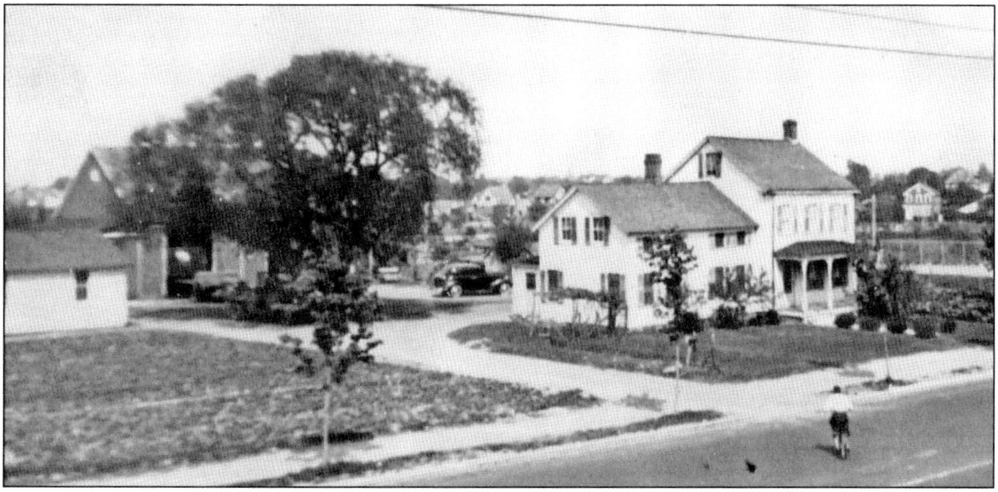

The owner of Twin Ponds Bakery took this lovely photograph of the Schmitt farmhouse from the second story of the bakery building on the opposite side of Merrick Road. Note that Merrick Road has been widened and paved. This image is possibly from the 1940s. (Courtesy of Jean Schmitt Garvey.)

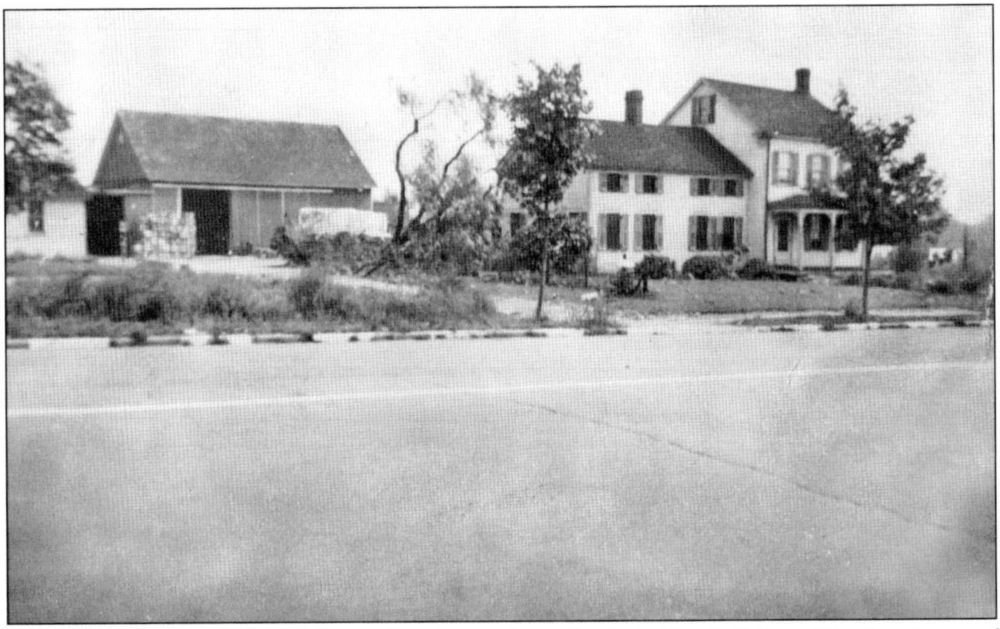

This is another view of the Schmitt farmhouse from the Twin Ponds Bakery. The hurricane of 1944 did tremendous damage, as can be seen by the large tree in the front yard that was blown over. At that time, the National Weather Service did not give storms official names. (Courtesy of Jean Schmitt Garvey.)

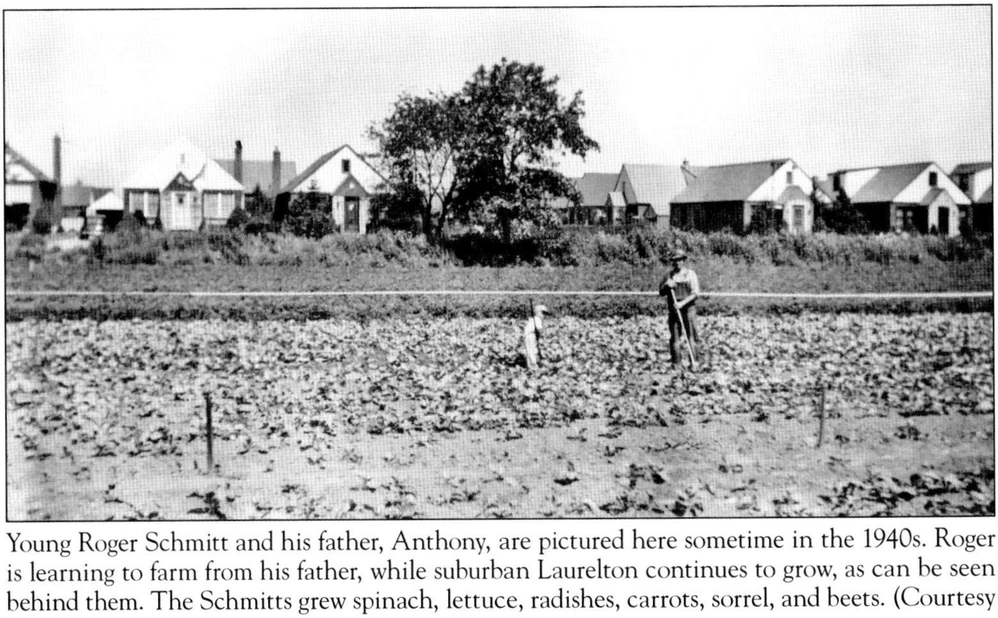

Young Roger Schmitt and his father, Anthony, are pictured here sometime in the 1940s. Roger is learning to farm from his father, while suburban Laurelton continues to grow, as can be seen behind them. The Schmitts grew spinach, lettuce, radishes, carrots, sorrel, and beets. (Courtesy of Jean Schmitt Garvey.)

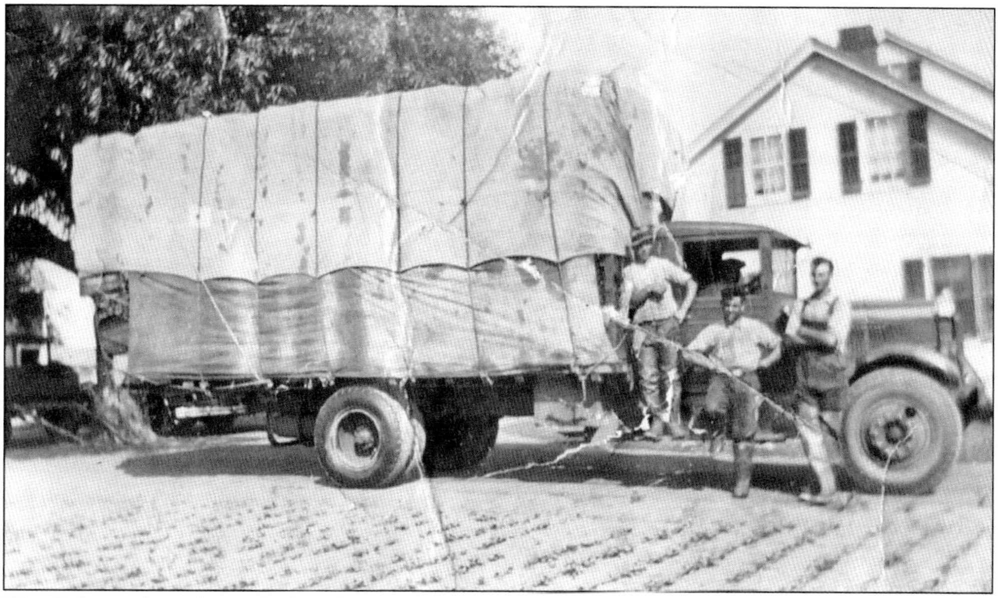

The Schmitts' truck, packed with produce, is being readied to deliver products to Brooklyn and Queens. The Schmitts' farm was considered a truck farm because they took their crops to the Wallabout Market in Carnarsie, where other trucks bearing produce would also gather. This enabled local produce merchants to stock their stores with fresh local goods. (Courtesy of Jean Schmitt Garvey.)

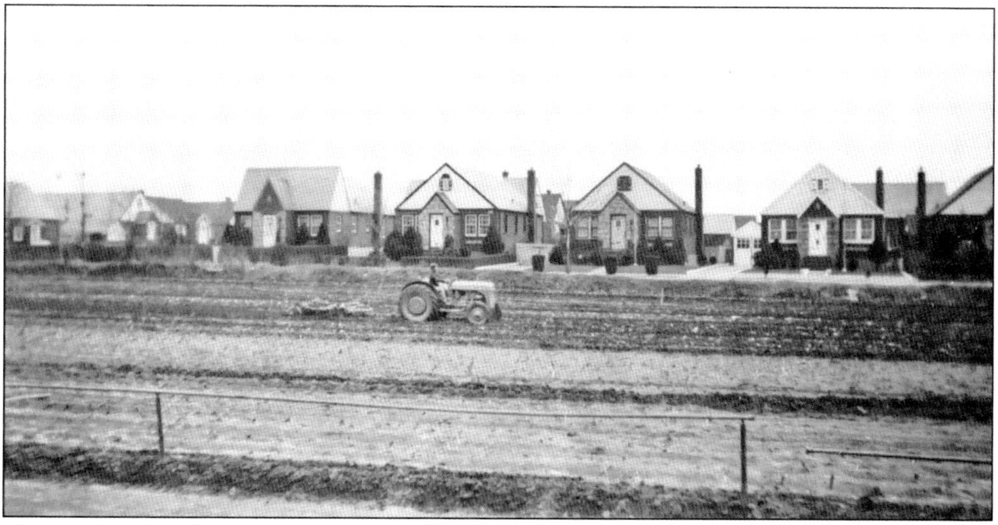

The neighborhood continues to grow as Rodger Schmitt works the back 40 in 1942. (Courtesy of Jean Schmitt Garvey.)

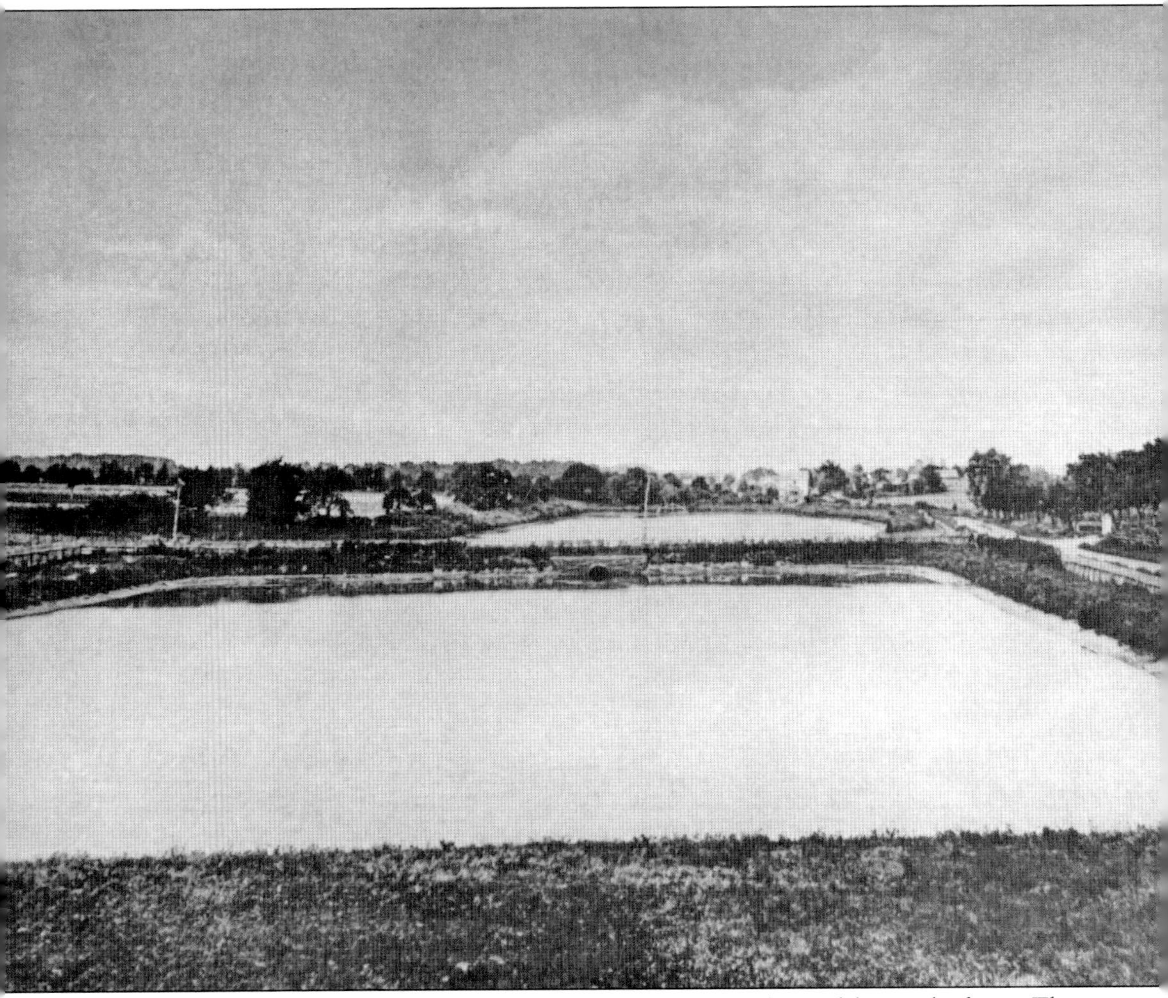

In 1896, the Twin Ponds, shown here neatly squared, was a supply pond for nearby farms. There was an aqueduct under Merrick Road, dividing the pond in two. The aqueduct and the Twin Ponds have been the objects of much tampering since then, which sometimes resulted in a change for the better, but not always. The ponds are scheduled for a major improvement in 2011, which may also benefit neighborhoods subject to flooding. (Courtesy of the Queens Borough Public Library, Long Island Division.)

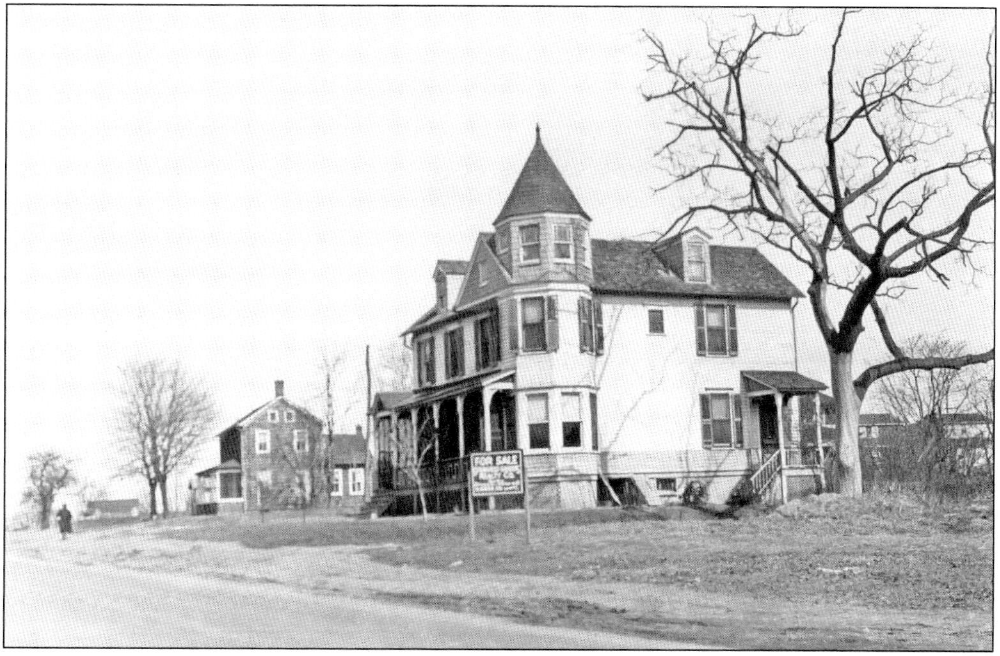

This is an example of the kind of older home that had been built in Laurelton, then in Rosedale, at the end of the 19th century. It is a typical clapboard home with a front porch and shuttered windows. The "for sale" sign may indicate that the owners have heard about the new developments slated for their area. (Courtesy of Queens Borough Public Library, Long Island Division.)

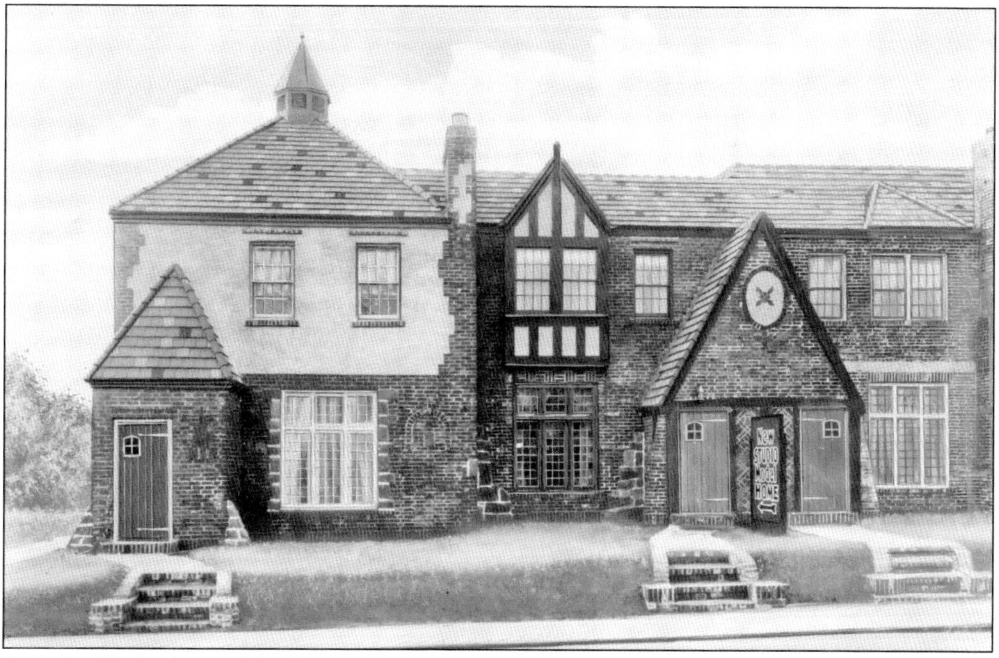

Attached Tudor houses like these were built in several parts of Laurelton. Somewhat frowned upon at first because they seemed too citified, they came to be much admired during modern times and are often used as illustrations in articles about the beauty of Laurelton. The home on the right is a model house. (Courtesy of Queens Borough Public Library, Long Island Division.)

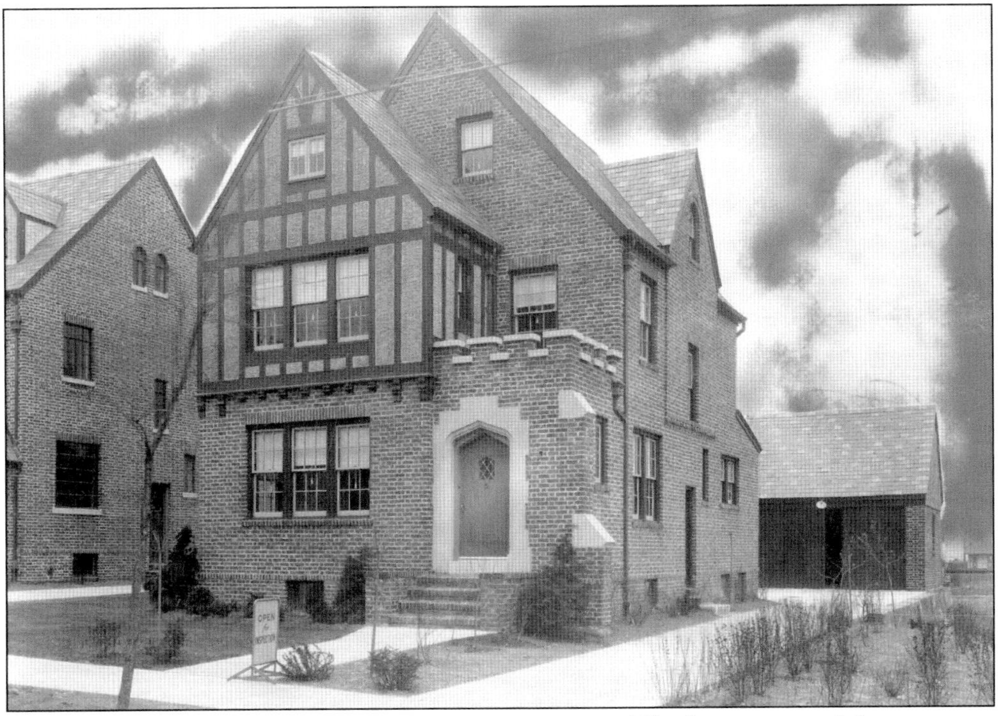

This home is one of the conventional varieties of detached houses built in Laurelton in the 1920s and 1930s. A house like this often had a sun parlor and room in the attic for extra bedrooms. This one appears to have a double garage. (Courtesy of Queens Borough Public Library, Long Island Division.)

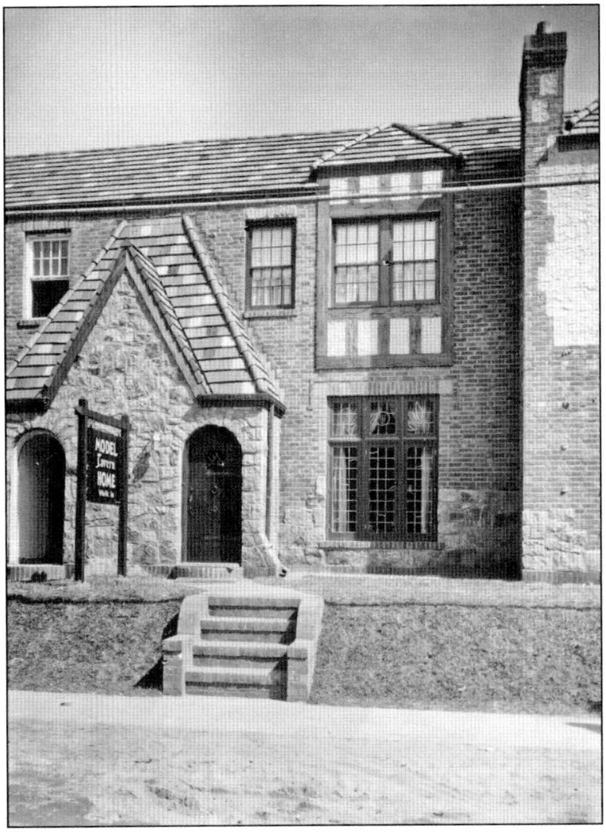

This model house is another example of the tavern or Tudor style of architecture that was popular with the builders of these and many other homes throughout the borough of Queens, the Gross Morton Company. This lovely home featured two fireplaces, one in the living room and the other in the finished basement. (Courtesy of Queens Borough Public Library.)

In March 1934, the draining of the Twin Ponds made for big news, as it had been a particularly severe winter, impairing construction work on the Laurelton Parkway. (Courtesy of Jean Schmitt Garvey.)

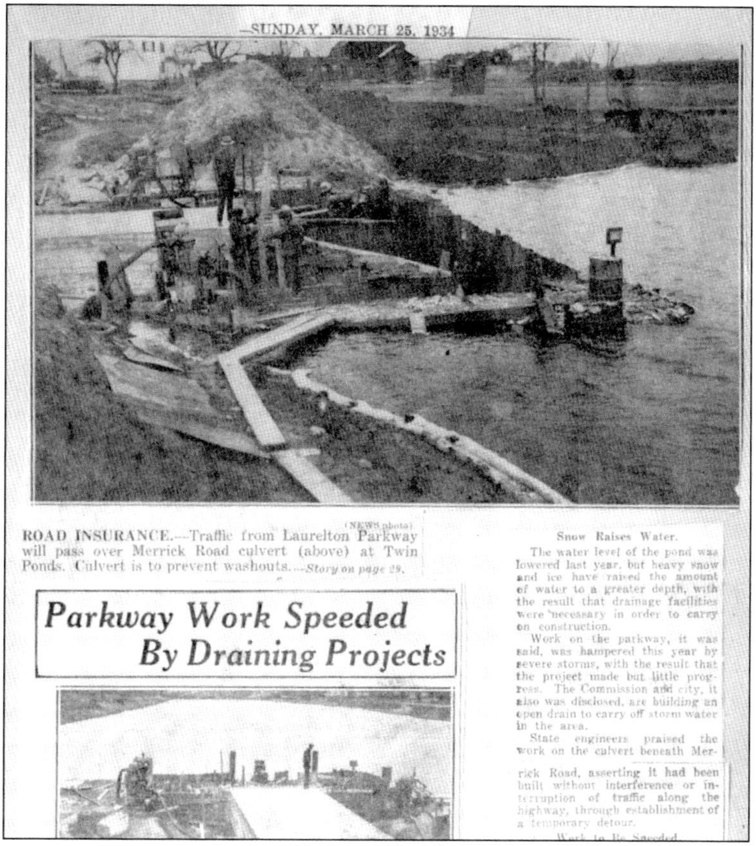

—SUNDAY, MARCH 25, 1934

(NEWS photo)

ROAD INSURANCE.—Traffic from Laurelton Parkway will pass over Merrick Road culvert (above) at Twin Ponds. Culvert is to prevent washouts.—*Story on page 29.*

Parkway Work Speeded By Draining Projects

Snow Raises Water.

The water level of the pond was lowered last year, but heavy snow and ice have raised the amount of water to a greater depth, with the result that drainage facilities were necessary in order to carry on construction.

Work on the parkway, it was said, was hampered this year by severe storms, with the result that the project made but little progress. The Commission and city, it also was disclosed, are building an open drain to carry off storm water in the area.

State engineers praised the work on the culvert beneath Merrick Road, asserting it had been built without interference or interruption of traffic along the highway, through establishment of a temporary detour.

Work to Be Speeded

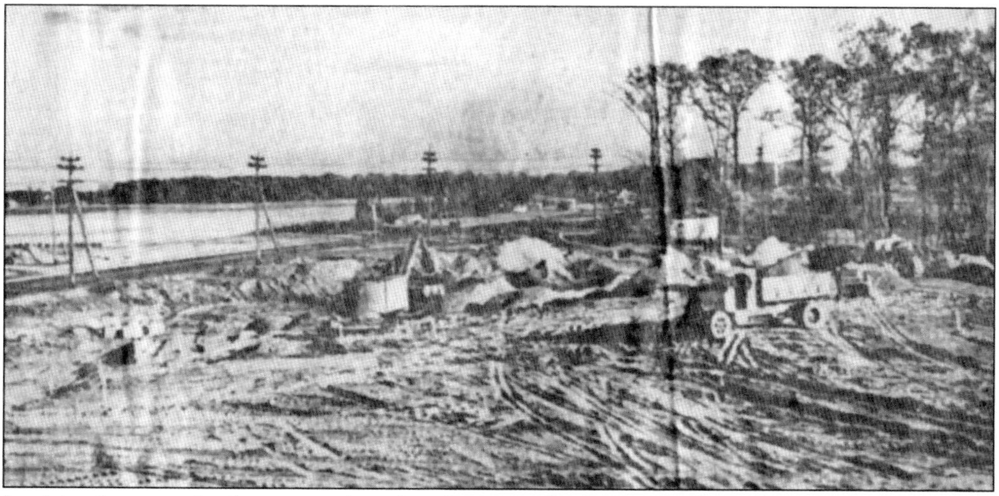

In this photograph, the steam shovel is draining the Twin Ponds as the Laurelton Parkway construction progresses. (Courtesy of Jean Schmitt Garvey.)

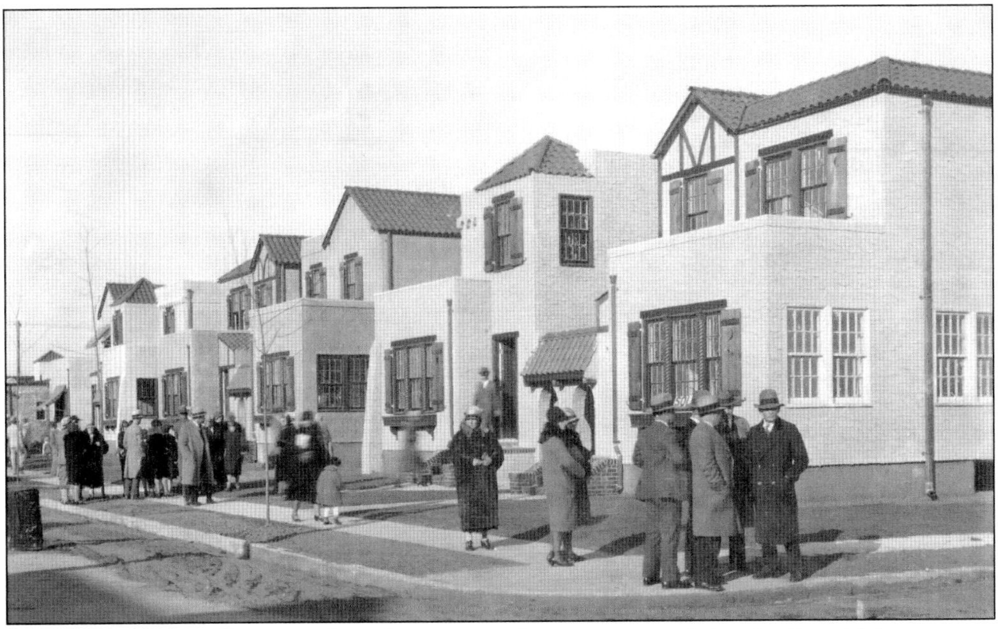

In this photograph, a large number of prospective buyers are examining the Spanish homes on a cold winter day in the late 1920s or early 1930s. In 1928, an announcement was made that there would be 900 houses altogether on what had once been the Laurelton Golf Club. (Courtesy of Queens Borough Public Library, Long Island Division.)

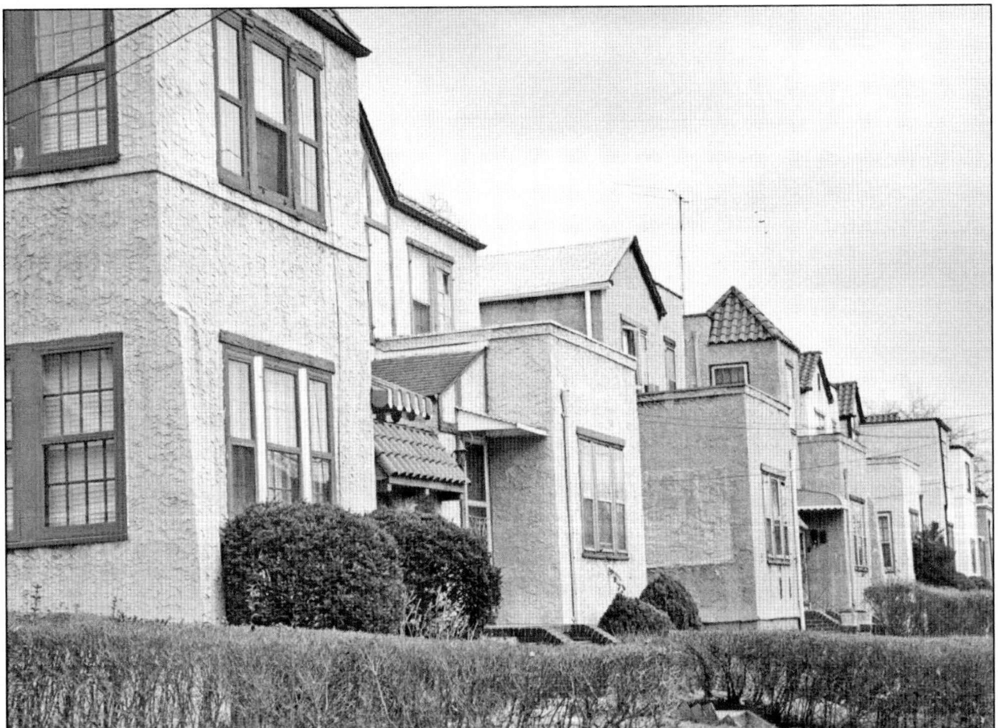

As shown in this 1953 photograph, the Spanish-style homes grow lovelier as they age, just like most of Laurelton. (Courtesy of Queens Borough Public Library, Long Island Division.)

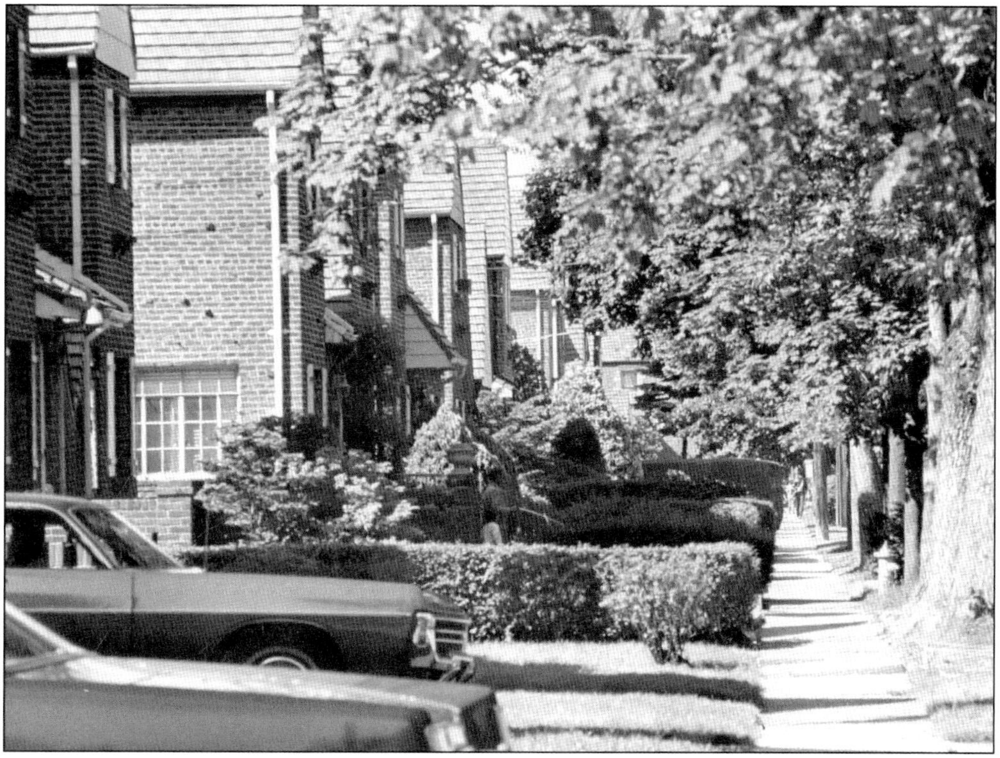

This beautiful 1972 streetscape was taken on 229th Street facing north towards Merrick Road. (Courtesy of Queens Borough Public Library, Long Island Division.)

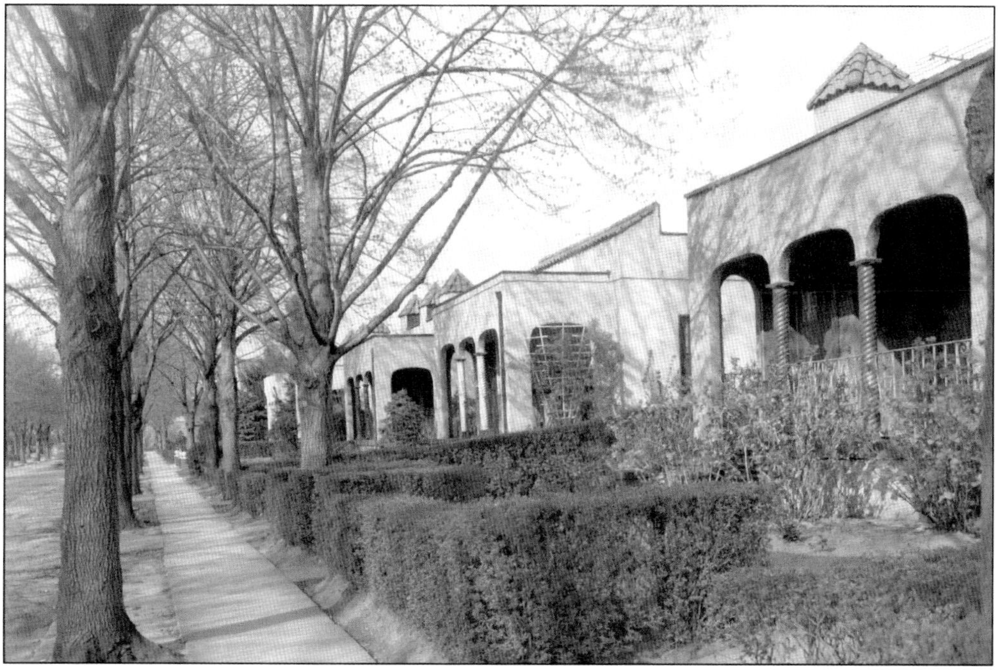

Another streetscape, this is 232nd Street in 1953, where the Spanish-style homes are south of Merrick Road. (Courtesy of Queens Borough Public Library, Long Island Division.)

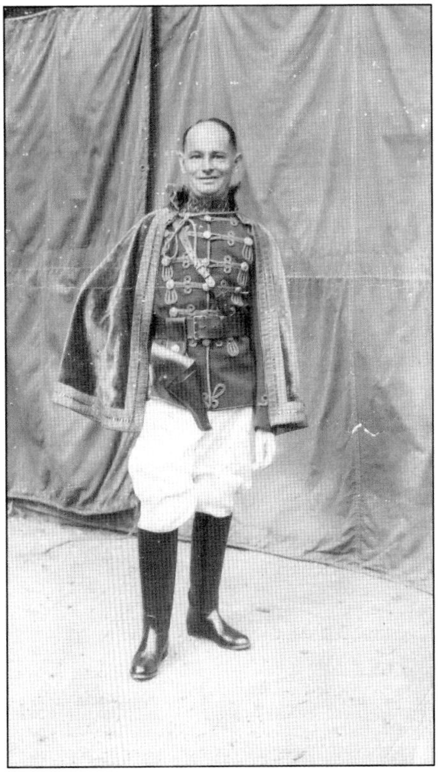

Capt. Ernest Engerer, here posing theatrically in his cape and holster, looked every bit the lion tamer. He trained many animals besides dogs; he claimed to have the world's only trained lamb. (Courtesy of Ernest Engerer.)

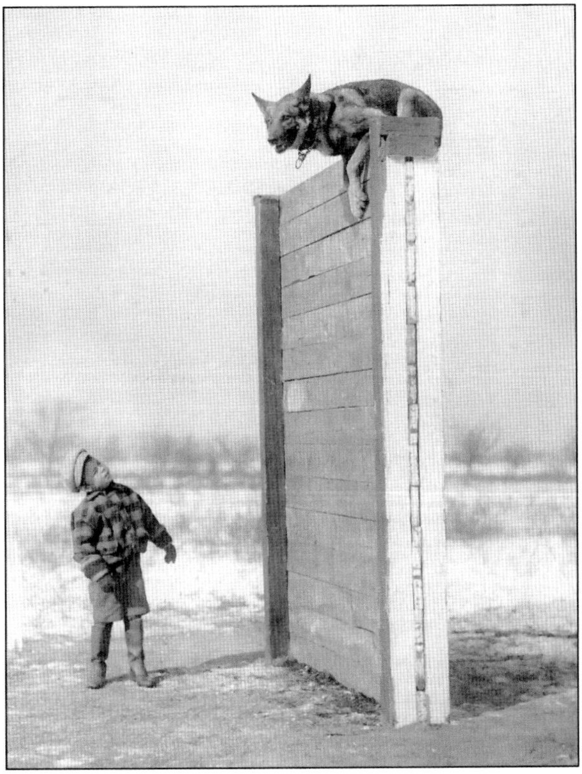

Taken in 1928, a young Ernie Engerer looks up as one of Captain Engerer's German shepherds scales a wall for a publicity photograph. (Courtesy of Ernest Engerer.)

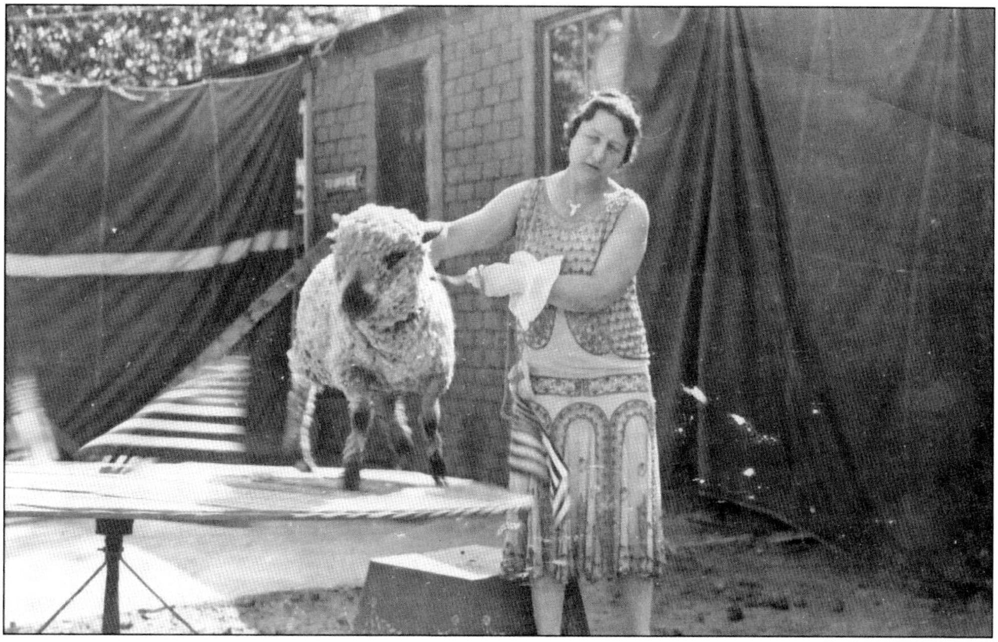

Pictured here is Mimi, "the world's only trained lamb," with her handler. (Courtesy of Ernest Engerer.)

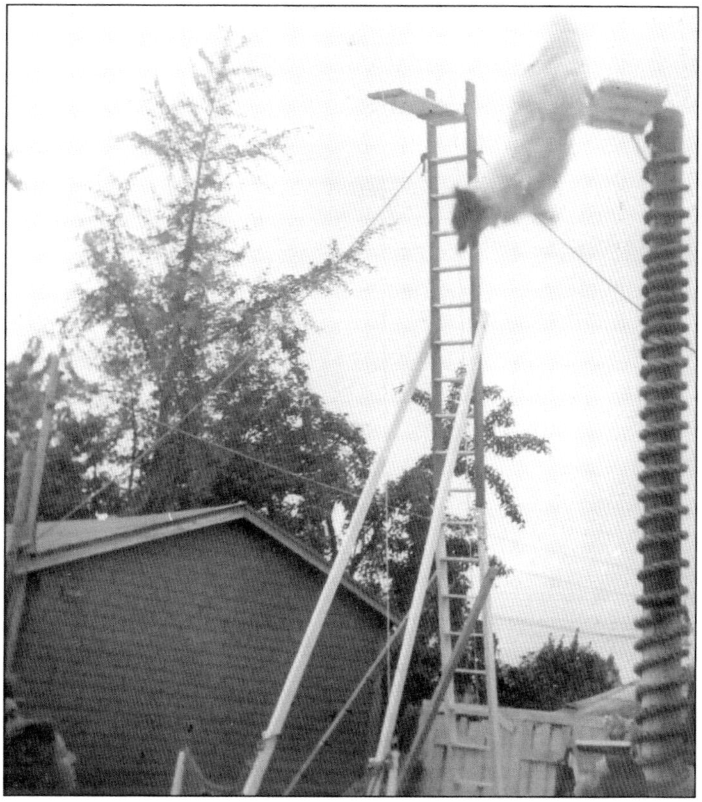

Mixie the Leaping Dog jumps from her perch after climbing the pole while spectators anxiously watch from below at a performance of the Captain Engerer Trained Dog Show. (Courtesy of Ernest Engerer.)

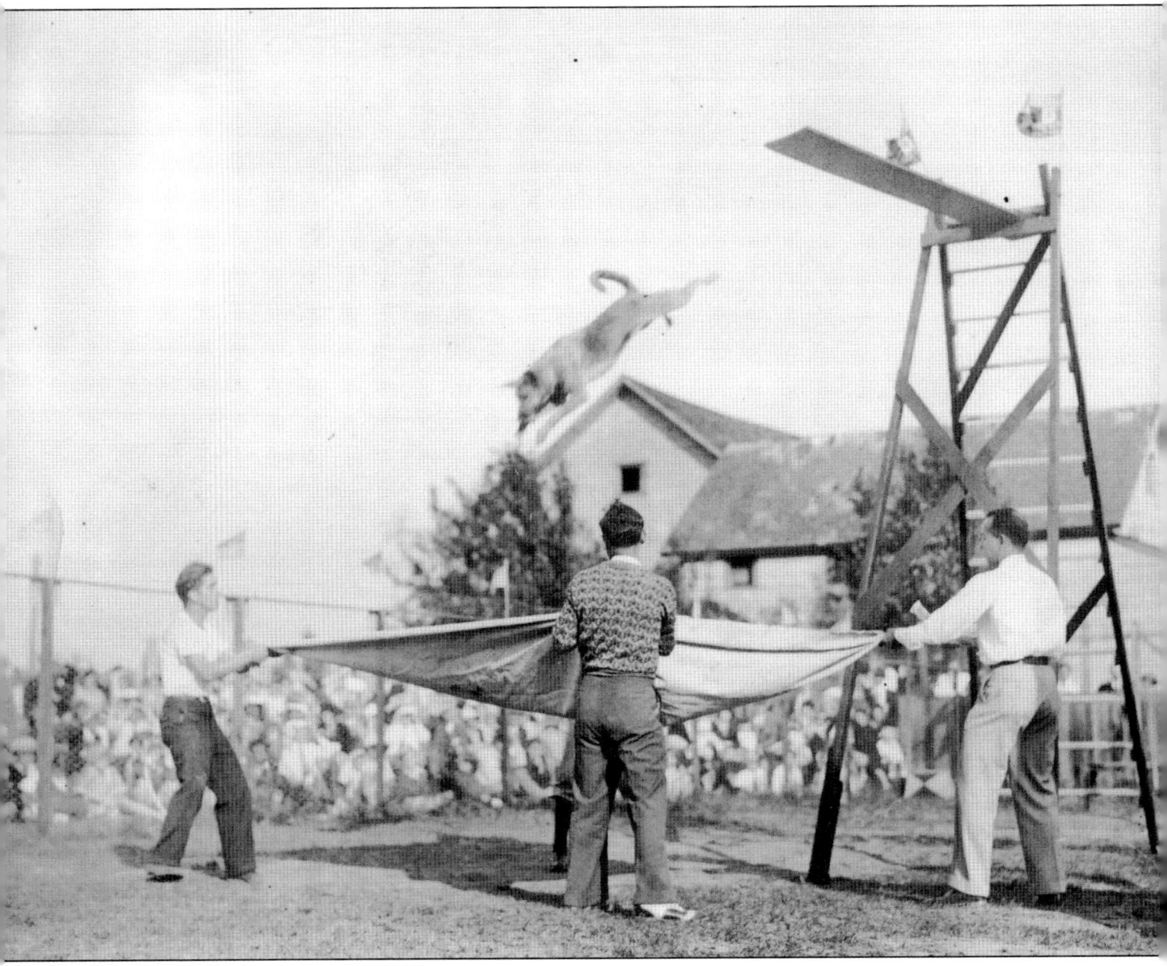

One of the trained police dogs is diving into a blanket from the diving board mounted on the ladder. This act was part of the well-attended exhibitions that the training academy performed on the weekends. (Courtesy of Ernest Engerer.)

For quite some time, Laurelton, Springfield Gardens, and Rosedale addresses were not carefully defined. Captain Engerer apparently thought his academy was in Springfield Gardens, though it was actually located in Laurelton. It was customary in those days to refer to Queens as "Long Island." (Courtesy of Ernest Engerer.)

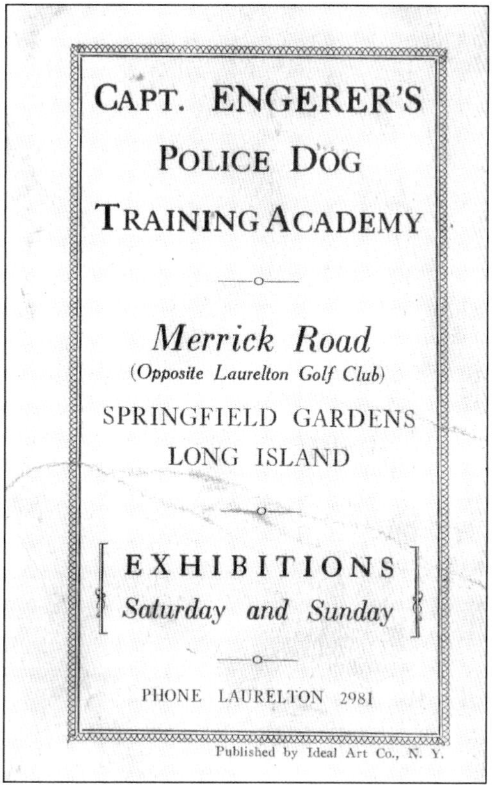
CAPT. ENGERER'S

POLICE DOG

TRAINING ACADEMY

Merrick Road

(Opposite Laurelton Golf Club)

SPRINGFIELD GARDENS

LONG ISLAND

EXHIBITIONS

Saturday and Sunday

PHONE LAURELTON 2981

Published by Ideal Art Co., N. Y.

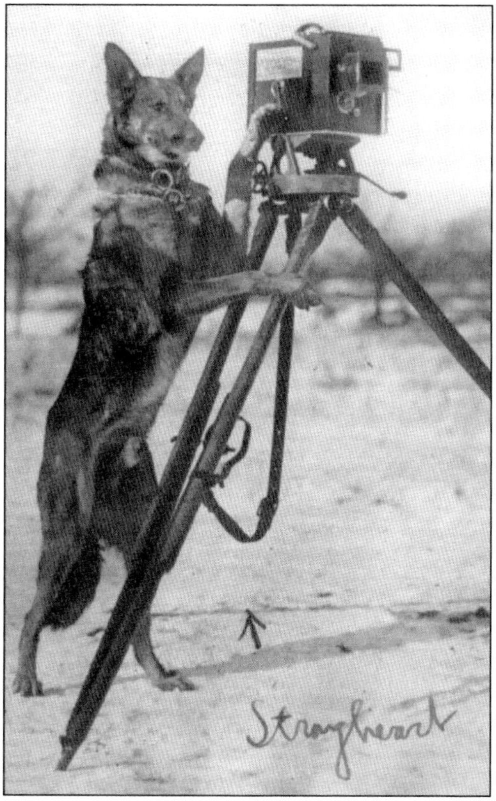

Although the captain advertised that he trained police dogs, he also trained lions, tigers, and other wild animals. The dog featured in the photograph at left is Tuetal Grimbaczky, "America's best known trained police dog," who only answered to commands spoken in German. (Courtesy of Ernest Engerer.)

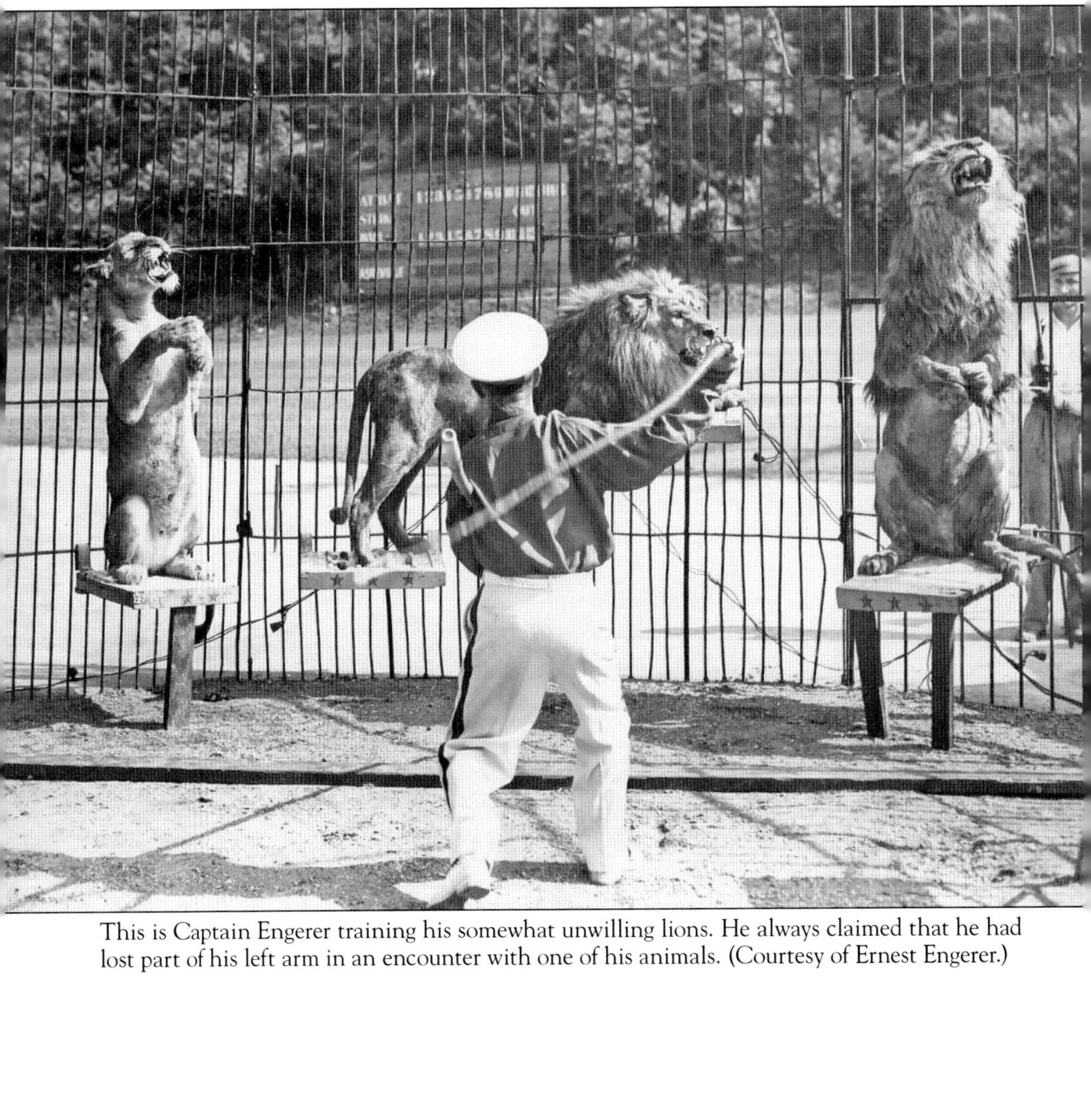

This is Captain Engerer training his somewhat unwilling lions. He always claimed that he had lost part of his left arm in an encounter with one of his animals. (Courtesy of Ernest Engerer.)

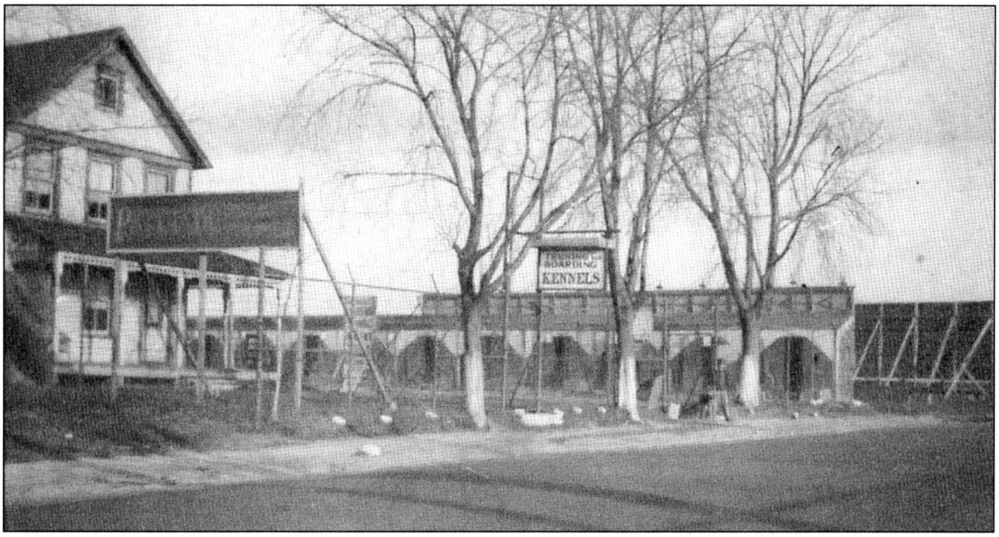

This is the academy as seen from Merrick Road. It consisted of the Engerer home and a number of outbuildings, which housed the animals, as well as training and performance areas. (Courtesy of Ernest Engerer.)

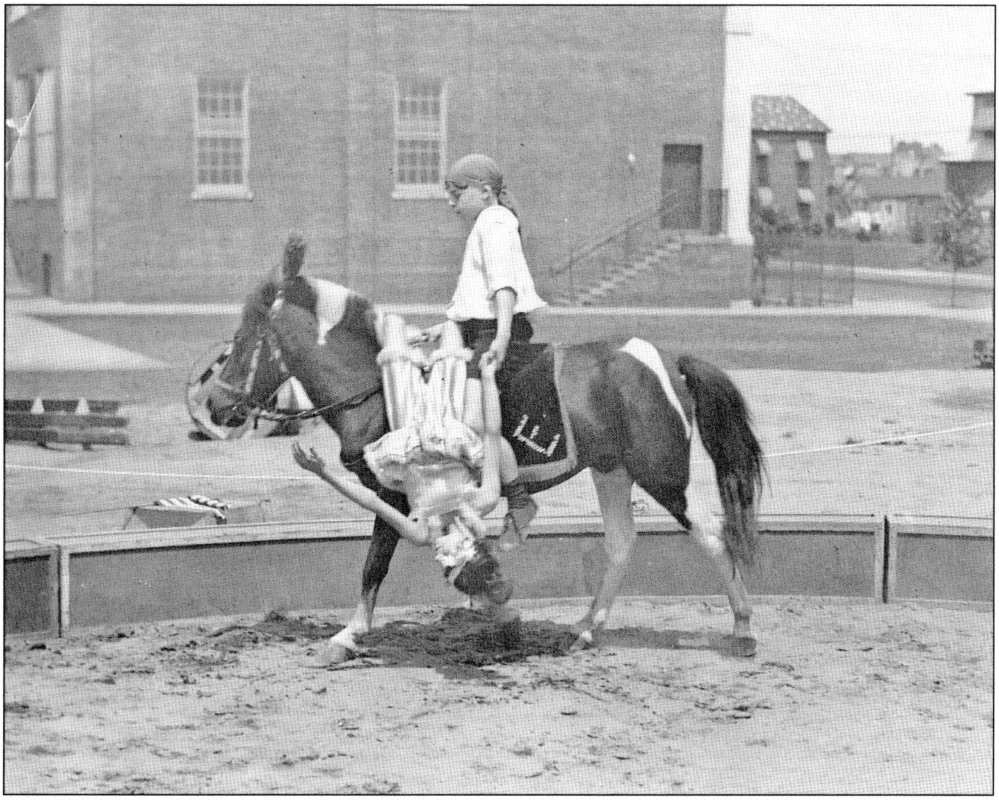

This extraordinary photograph is of Captain Engerer's children, Ernie and Barbara, as they perform their act at P.S. 156 in 1930. One of the captain's fondest mementoes was the thank-you letter he received from Principal Joseph Baron of P.S. 156 as a result of this benefit performance by his children, who were also students. (Courtesy of Ernest Engerer.)

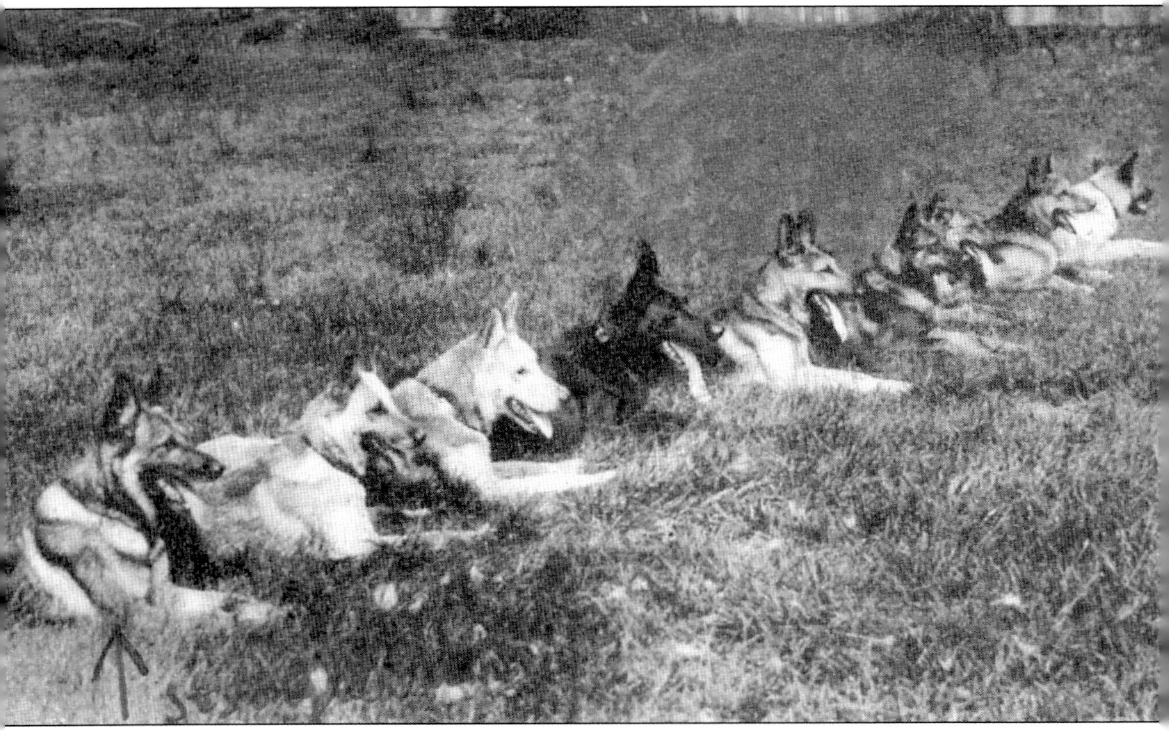

These are some of Captain Engerer's canine students posing for a photograph. The captain believed that his business of training police dogs had been given a considerable impetus by the kidnapping of the Lindbergh baby in 1932. (Courtesy of Ernest Engerer.)

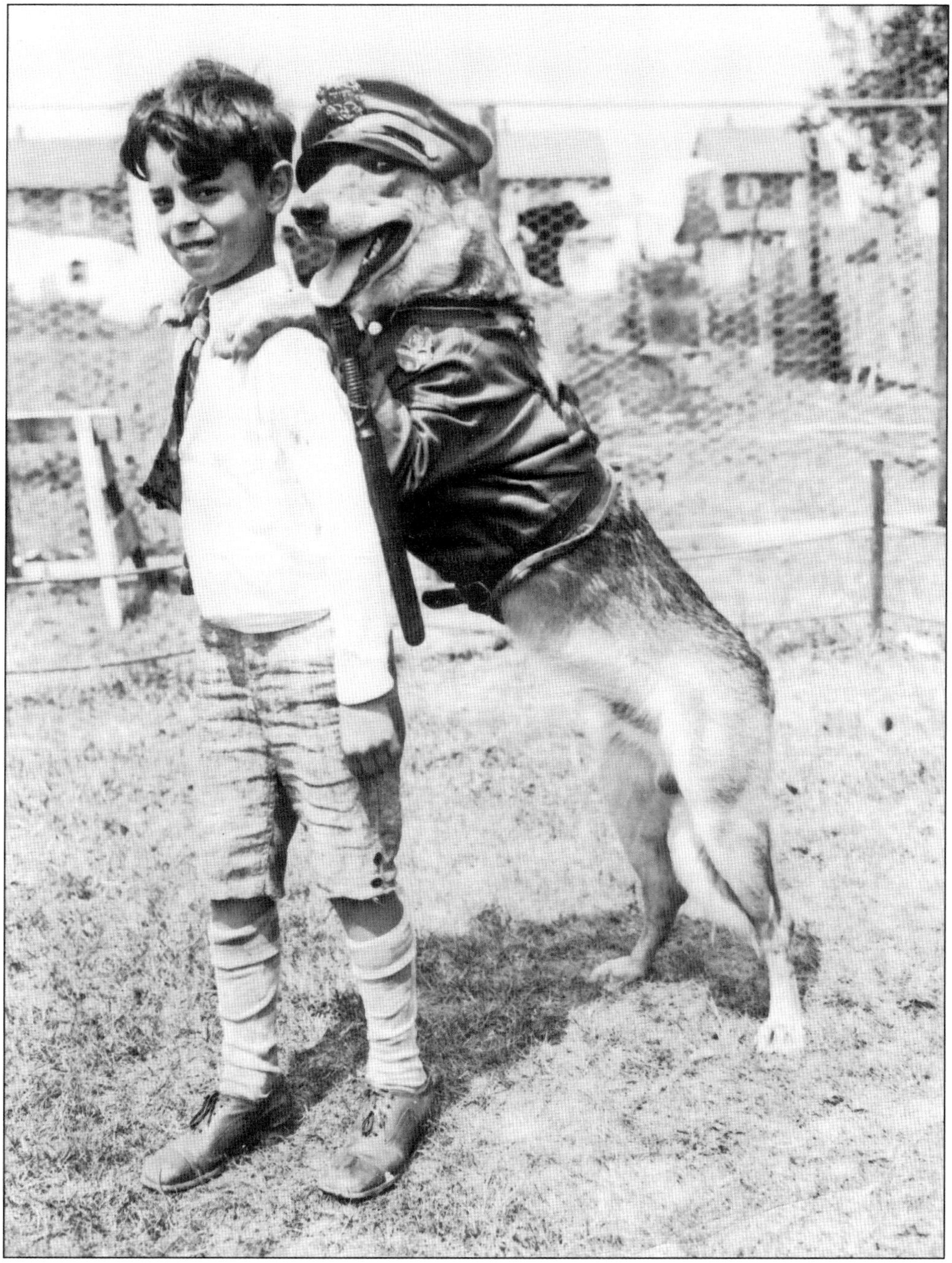
In this image, Ernie Engerer is posing with the famous Tuetal Grimbaczky, who is masquerading as a cop. (Courtesy of Ernest Engerer.)

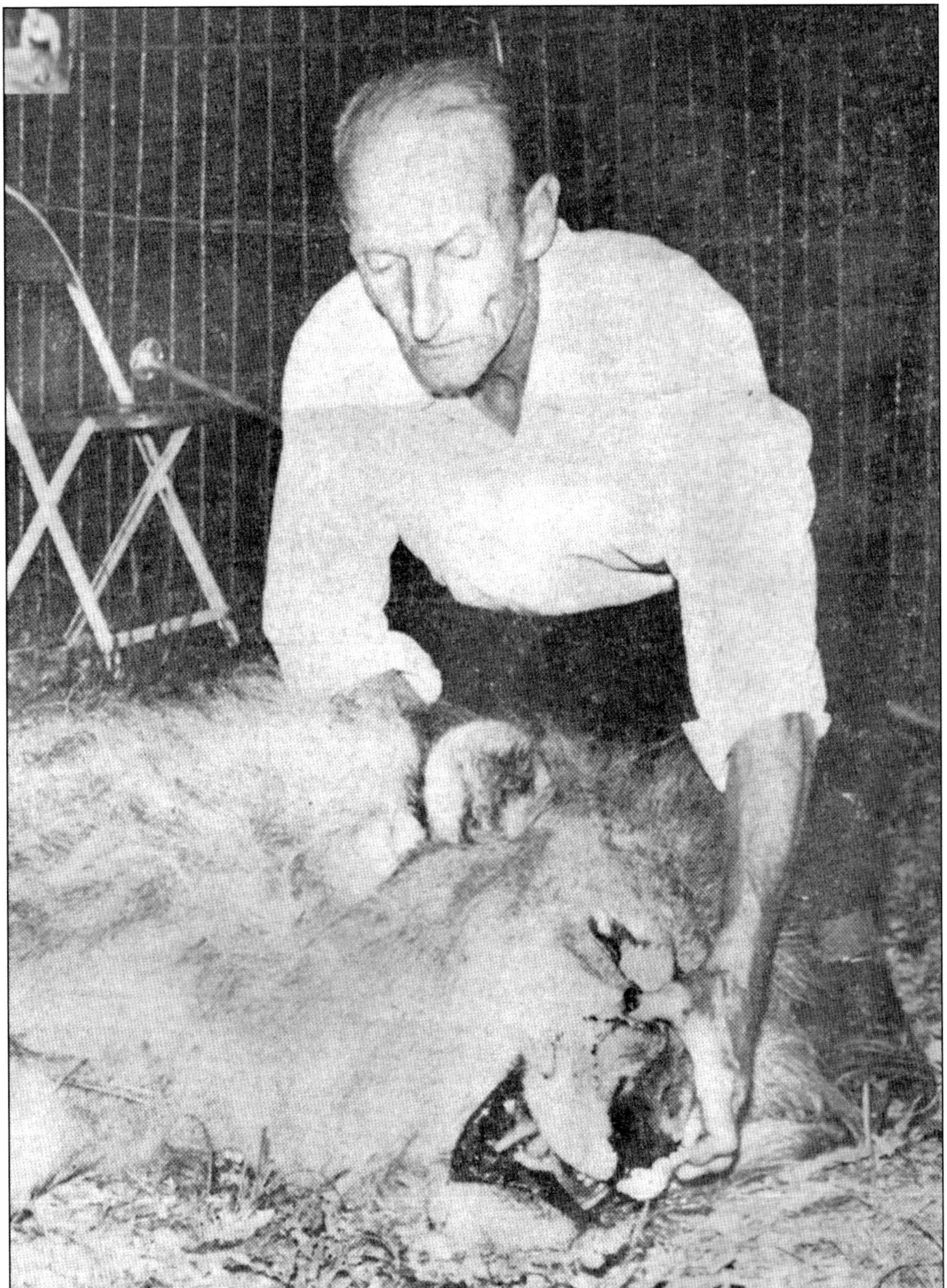

Edgar Gresham, assistant trainer to Captain Engerer, is seen here with the lifeless body of Monte, the lion who attacked and killed Captain Engerer in full sight of the audience at his performance in Winston-Salem, North Carolina, in August 1962. It took three rounds of ammunition to finally subdue the animal that had been raised from a cub by Captain Engerer's wife. (Courtesy of Ernest Engerer.)

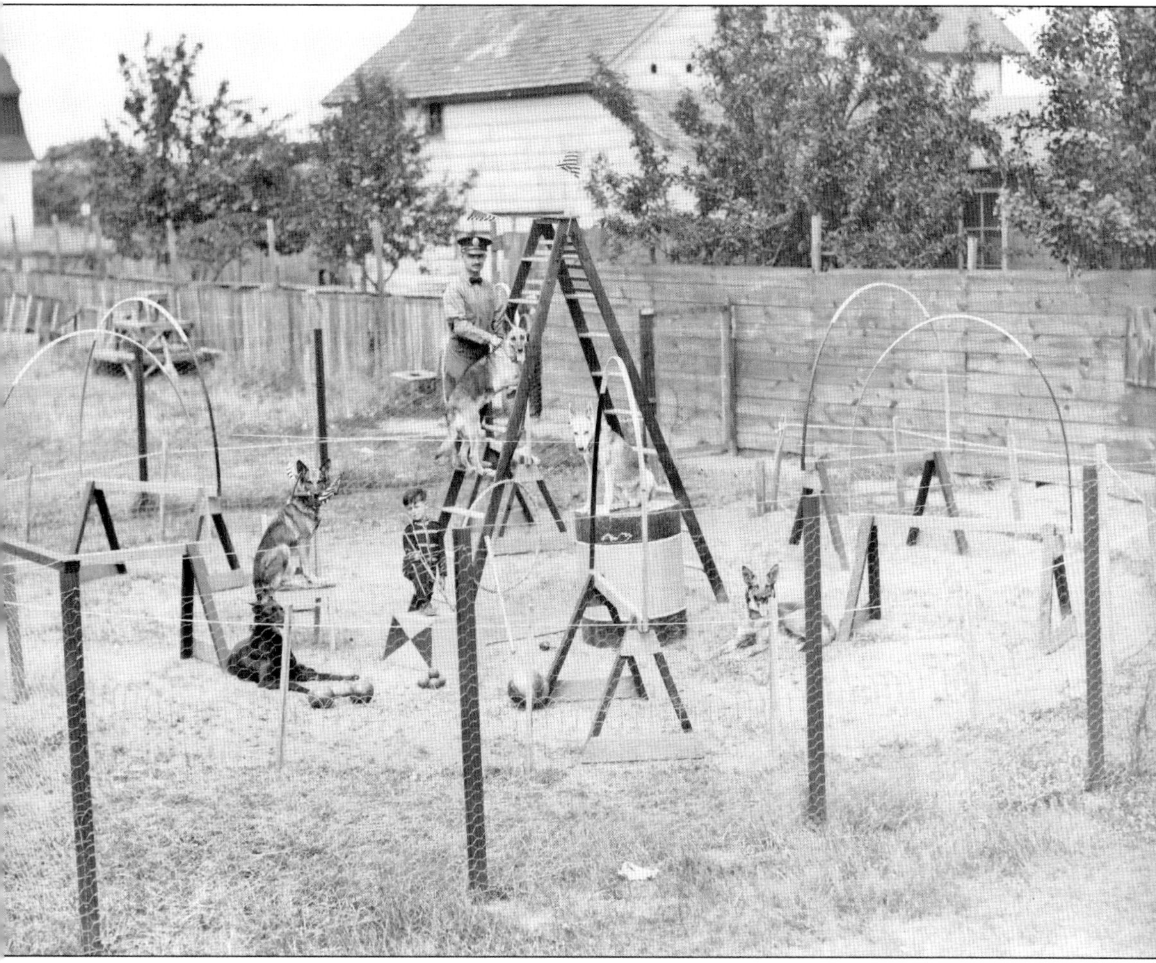

This is a photograph of the captain, his son, and the police dogs in the training arena on the grounds of the academy. Note the American flags in the dog's mouth. (Courtesy of Ernest Engerer.)

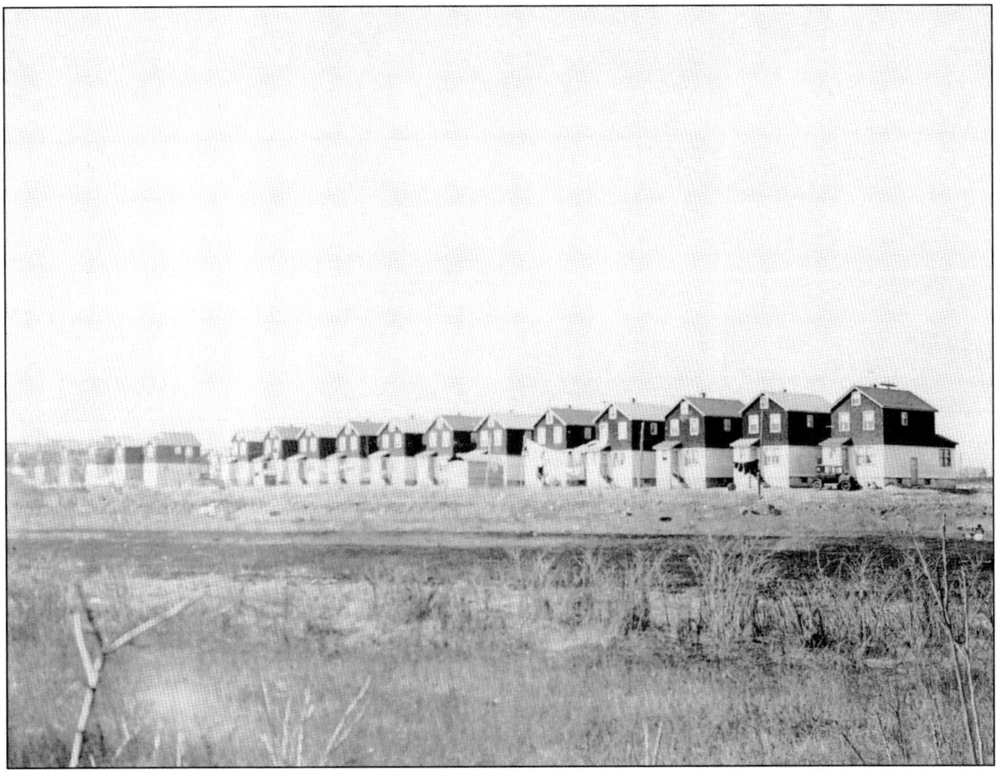

This view of Laurelton from Montefiore Cemetery illustrates the beginnings of a suburban development. (Courtesy of Ernest Engerer.)

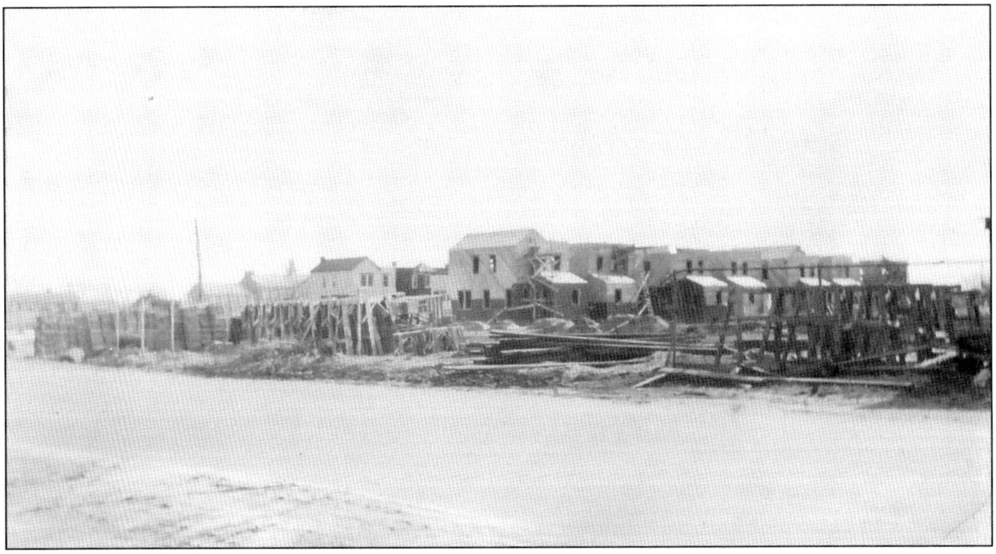

These are the detached brick homes going up on the northern side of Merrick Road in the area of 227th Street. The date is unknown. (Courtesy of Bill and Larry Lederer.)

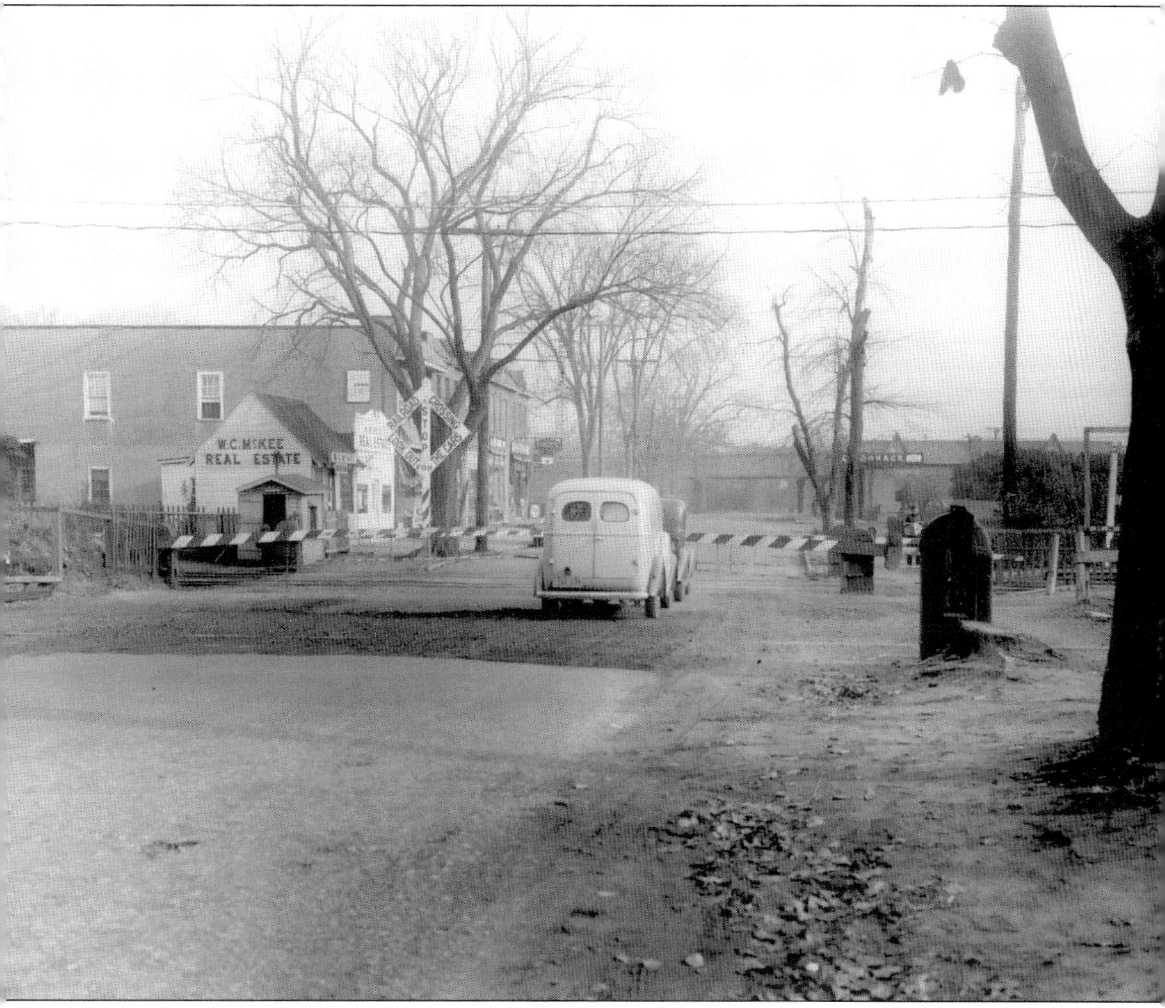

This photograph of the Long Island Rail Road station street crossing was taken in 1941. A couple of blocks to the north, the tracks of the Babylon line, which have been already elevated, can be seen. The elevation of the rest of the tracks was delayed when the country entered World War II in 1942 and was not completed until after the war was over. (Courtesy of Queens Borough Public Library, Long Island Division.)

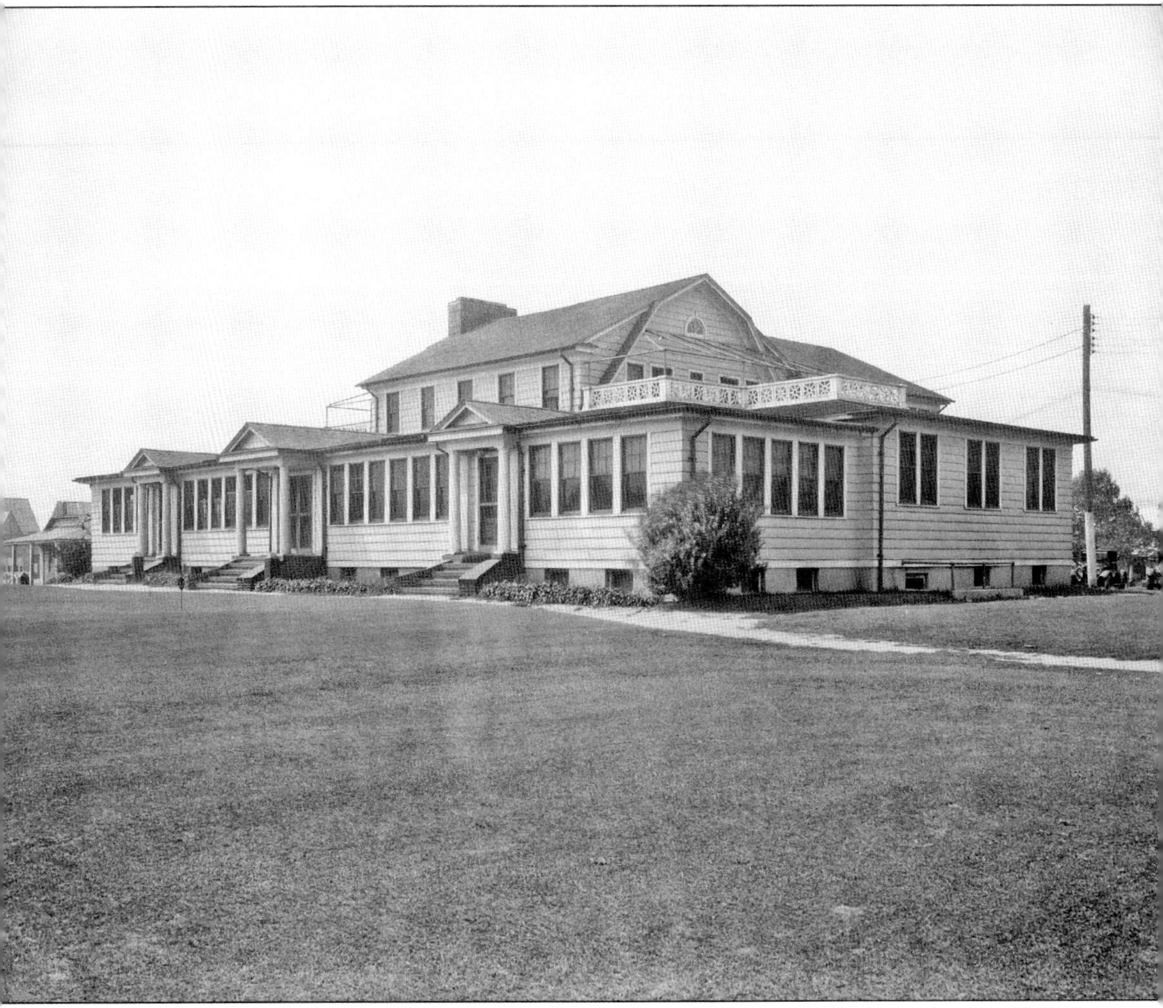

This handsome building, still in use in 1928, was the clubhouse of the Laurelton Golf Club. (Courtesy of Queens Borough Public Library, Long Island Division.)

Sometime during World War II, the little Lederer boys played in a wagon with wooden wheels, as rubber had to be conserved for the war effort. (Courtesy of Bill and Larry Lederer.)

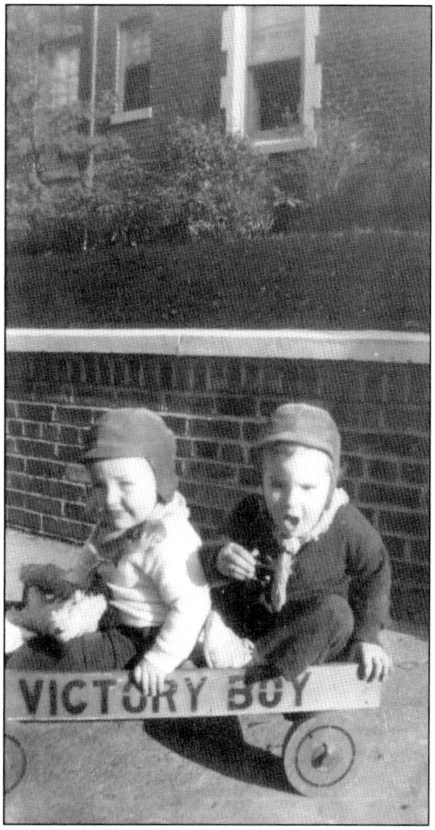

The Rosenberg clan picnics at Brookville Park in 1950. From left to right are Ruth Stein, Artie Rosenberg, and Judy Rosenberg. Artie convinced his sister Ruth to move from Brighton Beach Brooklyn to Laurelton after she had spent many weekends visiting her brother in "the country," as Laurelton was known then to people who were living in more densely populated parts of the city.

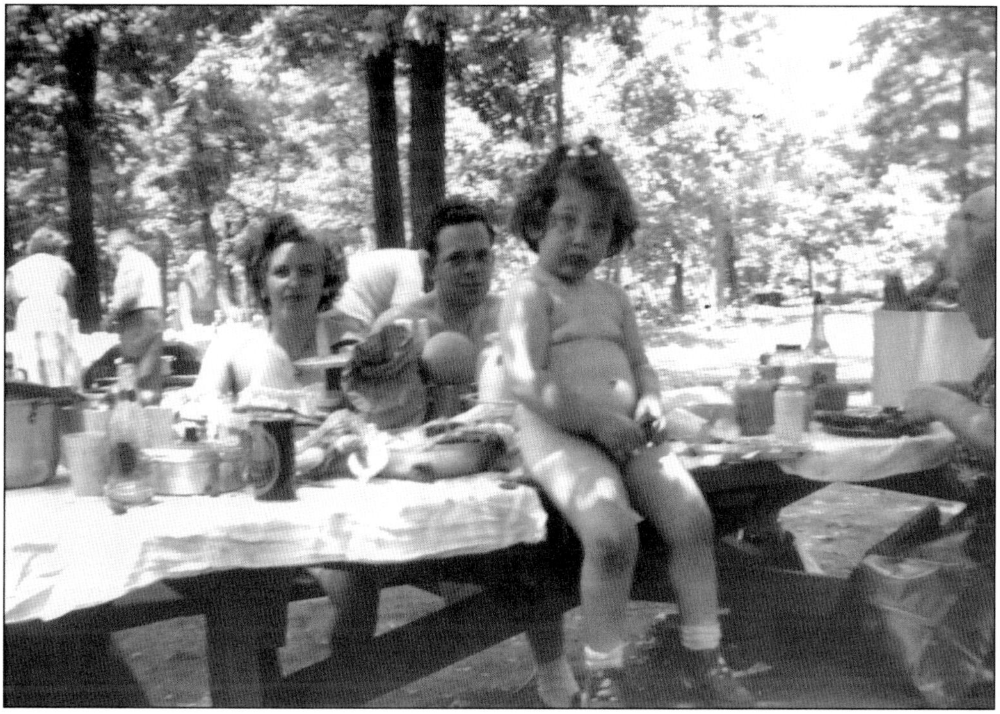

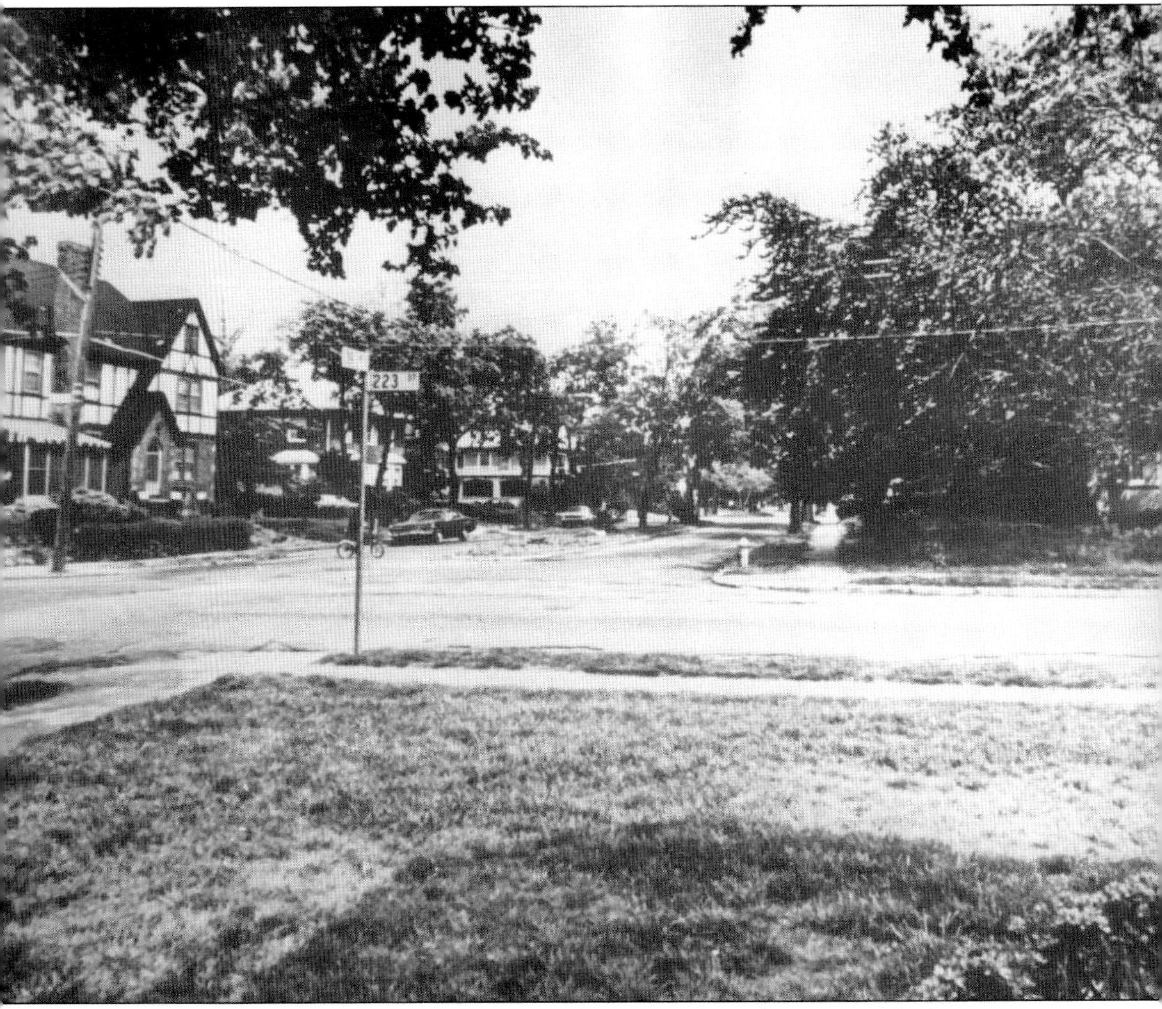

This is a view of beautiful Laurelton at 223rd Street and 139th Avenue. The loving care and attention given to the magnificent trees and splendid lawns is apparent in all of these gardens. (Courtesy of Queens Borough Public Library, Long Island Division.)

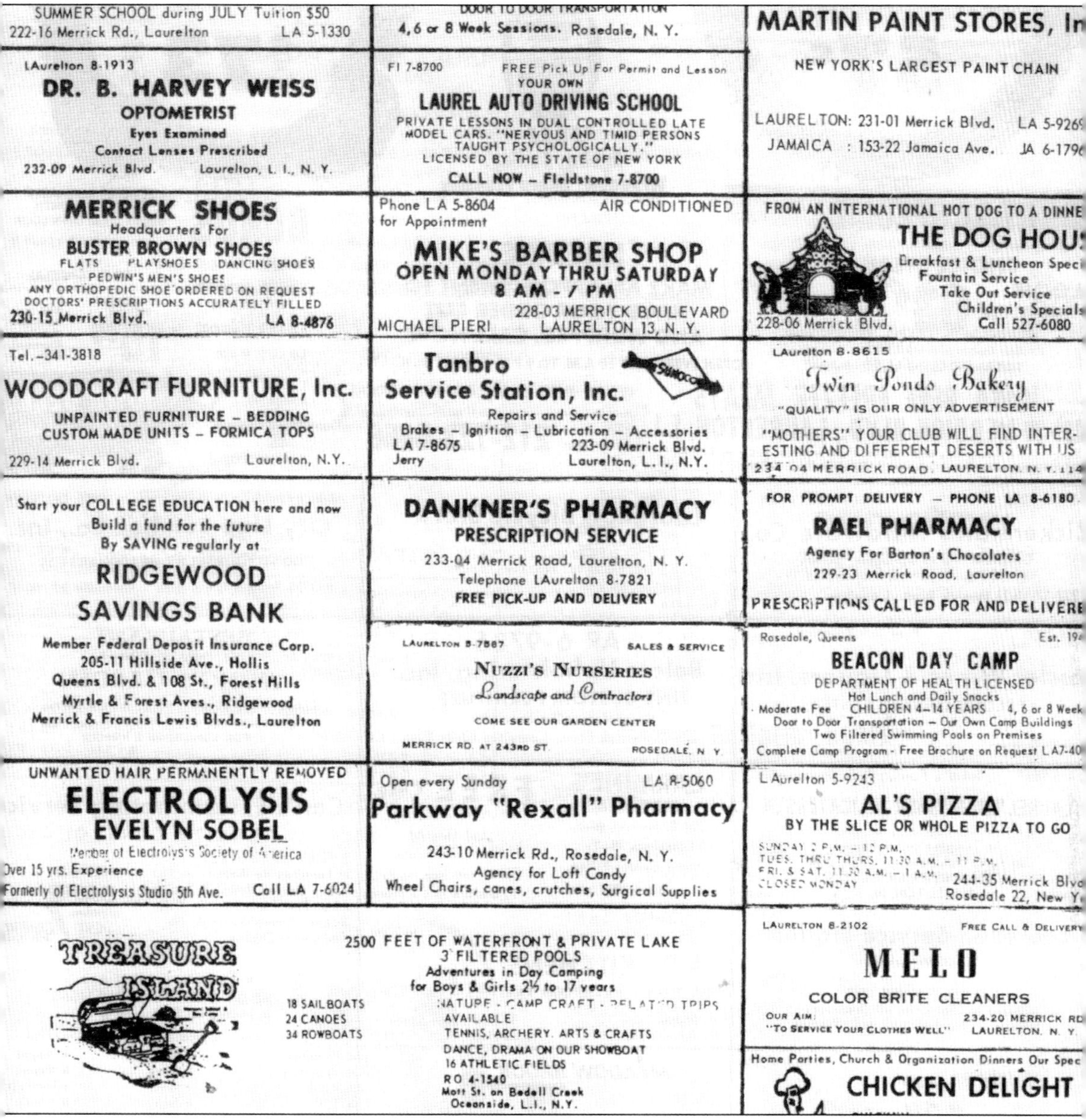

SUMMER SCHOOL during JULY Tuition $50
222-16 Merrick Rd., Laurelton LA 5-1330

DOOR TO DOOR TRANSPORTATION
4, 6 or 8 Week Sessions. Rosedale, N. Y.

MARTIN PAINT STORES, In
NEW YORK'S LARGEST PAINT CHAIN
LAURELTON: 231-01 Merrick Blvd. LA 5-926
JAMAICA : 153-22 Jamaica Ave. JA 6-179

LAurelton 8-1913
DR. B. HARVEY WEISS
OPTOMETRIST
Eyes Examined
Contact Lenses Prescribed
232-09 Merrick Blvd. Laurelton, L. I., N. Y.

FI 7-8700 FREE Pick Up For Permit and Lesson
YOUR OWN
LAUREL AUTO DRIVING SCHOOL
PRIVATE LESSONS IN DUAL CONTROLLED LATE MODEL CARS. "NERVOUS AND TIMID PERSONS TAUGHT PSYCHOLOGICALLY."
LICENSED BY THE STATE OF NEW YORK
CALL NOW – Fieldstone 7-8700

MERRICK SHOES
Headquarters For
BUSTER BROWN SHOES
FLATS PLAYSHOES DANCING SHOES
PEDWIN'S MEN'S SHOES
ANY ORTHOPEDIC SHOE ORDERED ON REQUEST
DOCTORS' PRESCRIPTIONS ACCURATELY FILLED
230-15 Merrick Blvd. LA 8-4876

Phone LA 5-8604 AIR CONDITIONED
for Appointment
MIKE'S BARBER SHOP
OPEN MONDAY THRU SATURDAY
8 AM - 7 PM
228-03 MERRICK BOULEVARD
MICHAEL PIERI LAURELTON 13, N. Y.

FROM AN INTERNATIONAL HOT DOG TO A DINNE
THE DOG HOU
Breakfast & Luncheon Spec
Fountain Service
Take Out Service
Children's Specials
228-06 Merrick Blvd. Call 527-6080

Tel.-341-3818
WOODCRAFT FURNITURE, Inc.
UNPAINTED FURNITURE – BEDDING
CUSTOM MADE UNITS – FORMICA TOPS
229-14 Merrick Blvd. Laurelton, N.Y.

Tanbro
Service Station, Inc.
SUNOCO
Repairs and Service
Brakes – Ignition – Lubrication – Accessories
LA 7-8675 223-09 Merrick Blvd.
Jerry Laurelton, L. I., N.Y.

LAurelton 8-8615
Twin Ponds Bakery
"QUALITY" IS OUR ONLY ADVERTISEMENT
"MOTHERS" YOUR CLUB WILL FIND INTERESTING AND DIFFERENT DESERTS WITH US
234-04 MERRICK ROAD, LAURELTON, N. Y. 11

Start your COLLEGE EDUCATION here and now
Build a fund for the future
By SAVING regularly at
RIDGEWOOD
SAVINGS BANK
Member Federal Deposit Insurance Corp.
205-11 Hillside Ave., Hollis
Queens Blvd. & 108 St., Forest Hills
Myrtle & Forest Aves., Ridgewood
Merrick & Francis Lewis Blvds., Laurelton

DANKNER'S PHARMACY
PRESCRIPTION SERVICE
233-04 Merrick Road, Laurelton, N. Y.
Telephone LAurelton 8-7821
FREE PICK-UP AND DELIVERY

FOR PROMPT DELIVERY – PHONE LA 8-6180
RAEL PHARMACY
Agency For Barton's Chocolates
229-23 Merrick Road, Laurelton
PRESCRIPTIONS CALLED FOR AND DELIVERE

LAURELTON 8-7887 SALES & SERVICE
NUZZI'S NURSERIES
Landscape and Contractors
COME SEE OUR GARDEN CENTER
MERRICK RD. AT 243RD ST. ROSEDALE, N. Y.

Rosedale, Queens Est. 19
BEACON DAY CAMP
DEPARTMENT OF HEALTH LICENSED
Hot Lunch and Daily Snacks
Moderate Fee CHILDREN 4–14 YEARS 4, 6 or 8 Week
Door to Door Transportation – Our Own Camp Buildings
Two Filtered Swimming Pools on Premises
Complete Camp Program - Free Brochure on Request LA7-40

UNWANTED HAIR PERMANENTLY REMOVED
ELECTROLYSIS
EVELYN SOBEL
Member of Electrolysis Society of America
Over 15 yrs. Experience
Formerly of Electrolysis Studio 5th Ave. Call LA 7-6024

Open every Sunday LA 8-5060
Parkway "Rexall" Pharmacy
243-10 Merrick Rd., Rosedale, N. Y.
Agency for Loft Candy
Wheel Chairs, canes, crutches, Surgical Supplies

LAurelton 5-9243
AL'S PIZZA
BY THE SLICE OR WHOLE PIZZA TO GO
SUNDAY 2 P.M. – 12 P.M.
TUES. THRU THURS. 11:30 A.M. – 11 P.M.
FRI. & SAT. 11:30 A.M. – 1 A.M.
CLOSED MONDAY
244-35 Merrick Blv
Rosedale 22, New Y

TREASURE ISLAND
2500 FEET OF WATERFRONT & PRIVATE LAKE
3 FILTERED POOLS
Adventures in Day Camping
for Boys & Girls 2½ to 17 years
18 SAILBOATS
24 CANOES
34 ROWBOATS
NATURE - CAMP CRAFT - RELATED TRIPS AVAILABLE
TENNIS, ARCHERY, ARTS & CRAFTS
DANCE, DRAMA ON OUR SHOWBOAT
16 ATHLETIC FIELDS
RO 4-1540
Mott St. on Bedell Creek
Oceanside, L.I., N.Y.

LAURELTON 8-2102 FREE CALL & DELIVERY
MELO
COLOR BRITE CLEANERS
OUR AIM: "TO SERVICE YOUR CLOTHES WELL"
234-20 MERRICK RD
LAURELTON, N. Y.

Home Parties, Church & Organization Dinners Our Spec
CHICKEN DELIGHT

Classified advertisements from the back pages of the P.S. 156 student newspaper, the *Laurelite*, illustrate how local merchants helped to support the newspaper. This issue of the *Laurelite* dates to 1967. (Courtesy of Bernard Kavaler.)

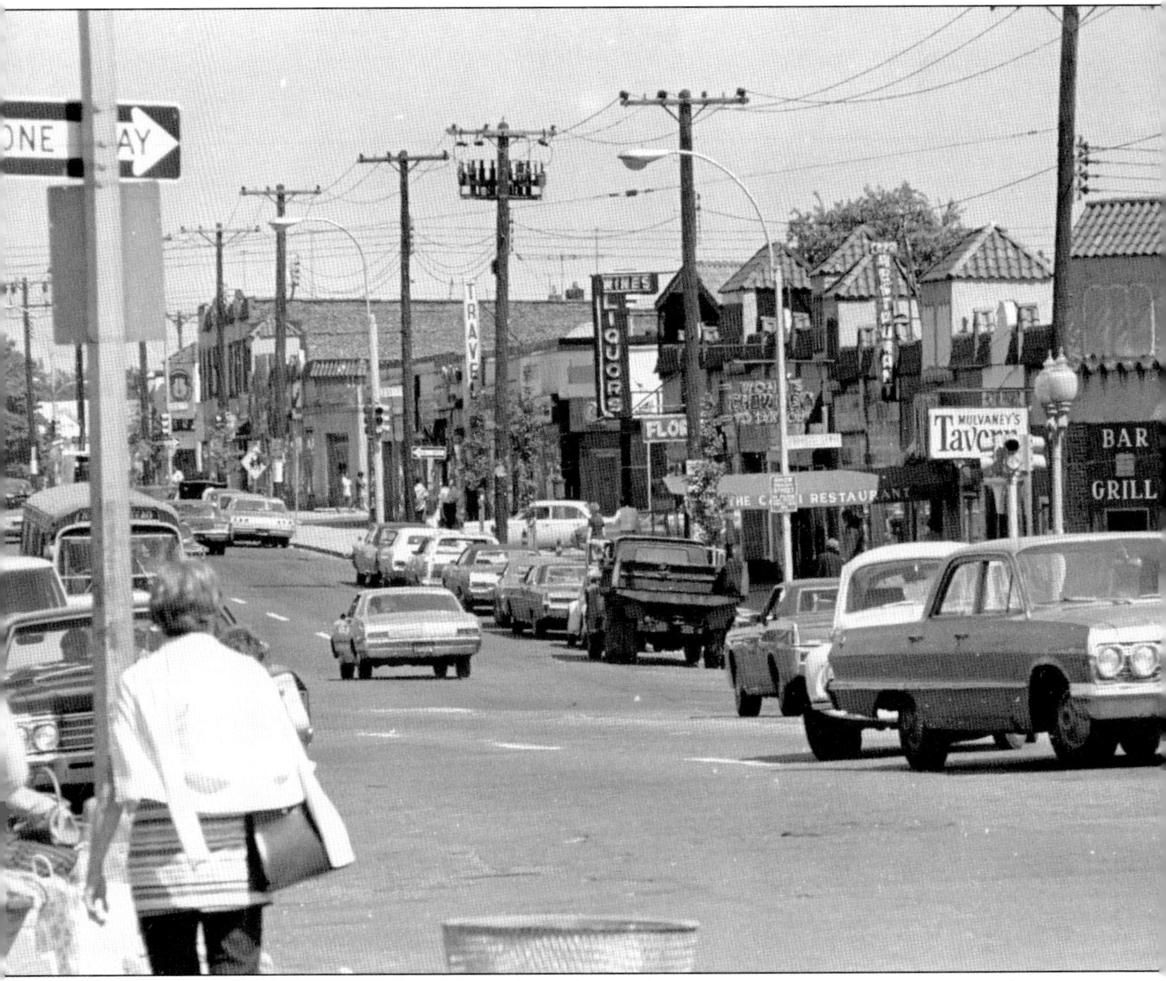

This photograph faces southwest on Merrick Road in 1971. On the corner of Francis Lewis Boulevard and 231st Street are Mulvaney's Tavern, the Capri Restaurant (famous for their pizza), and Wong's Chinese Restaurant (famous for their egg rolls). The stucco facades and terra-cotta roofs match the Tudor architecture of the surrounding homes. Urban planners in later years developed the idea of uniformity between residential and commercial areas, which early Laurelton developers seemed to understand instinctively. (Courtesy of Queens Borough Public Library, Long Island Division.)

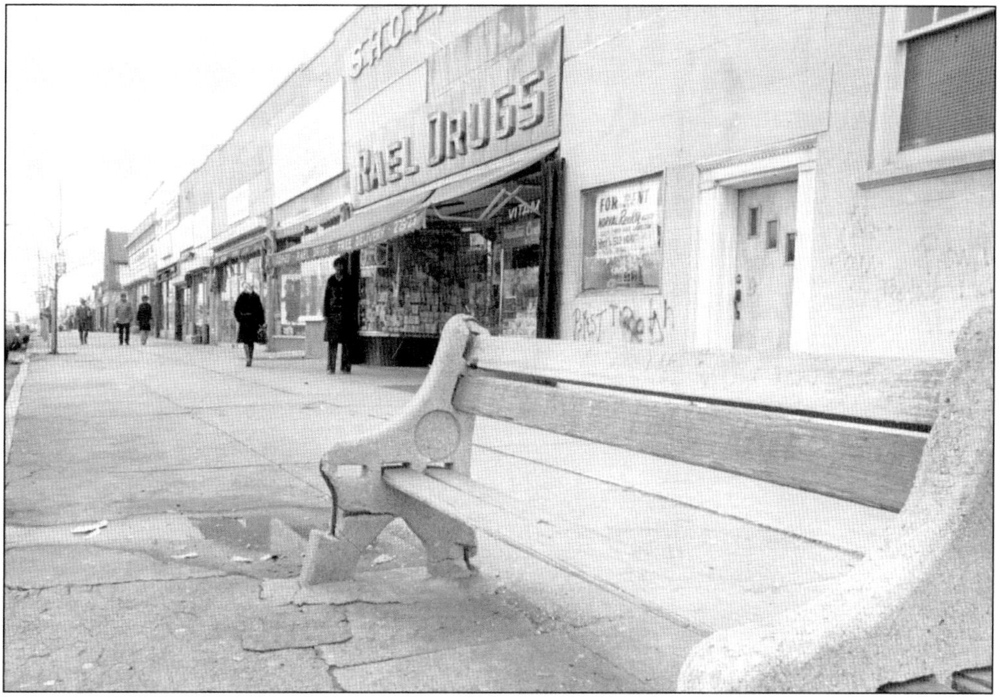

This 1971 photograph of Merrick Road near 229th Street is a good representation of New York City in the 1970s. There are vacant stores, graffiti, and cracking sidewalks. Visible here is Rael Drugs and the awning for Sharry's Bakery; today, this area is home to a Charlotte Russe clothing store. (Courtesy of Queens Borough Public Library, Long Island Division.)

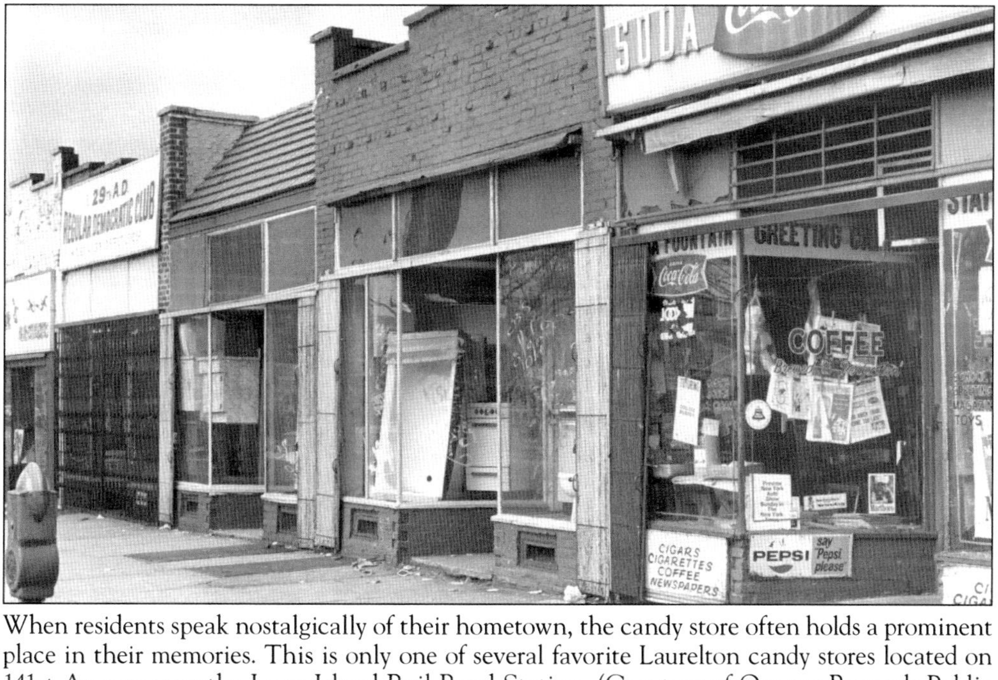

When residents speak nostalgically of their hometown, the candy store often holds a prominent place in their memories. This is only one of several favorite Laurelton candy stores located on 141st Avenue near the Long Island Rail Road Station. (Courtesy of Queens Borough Public Library, Long Island Division.)

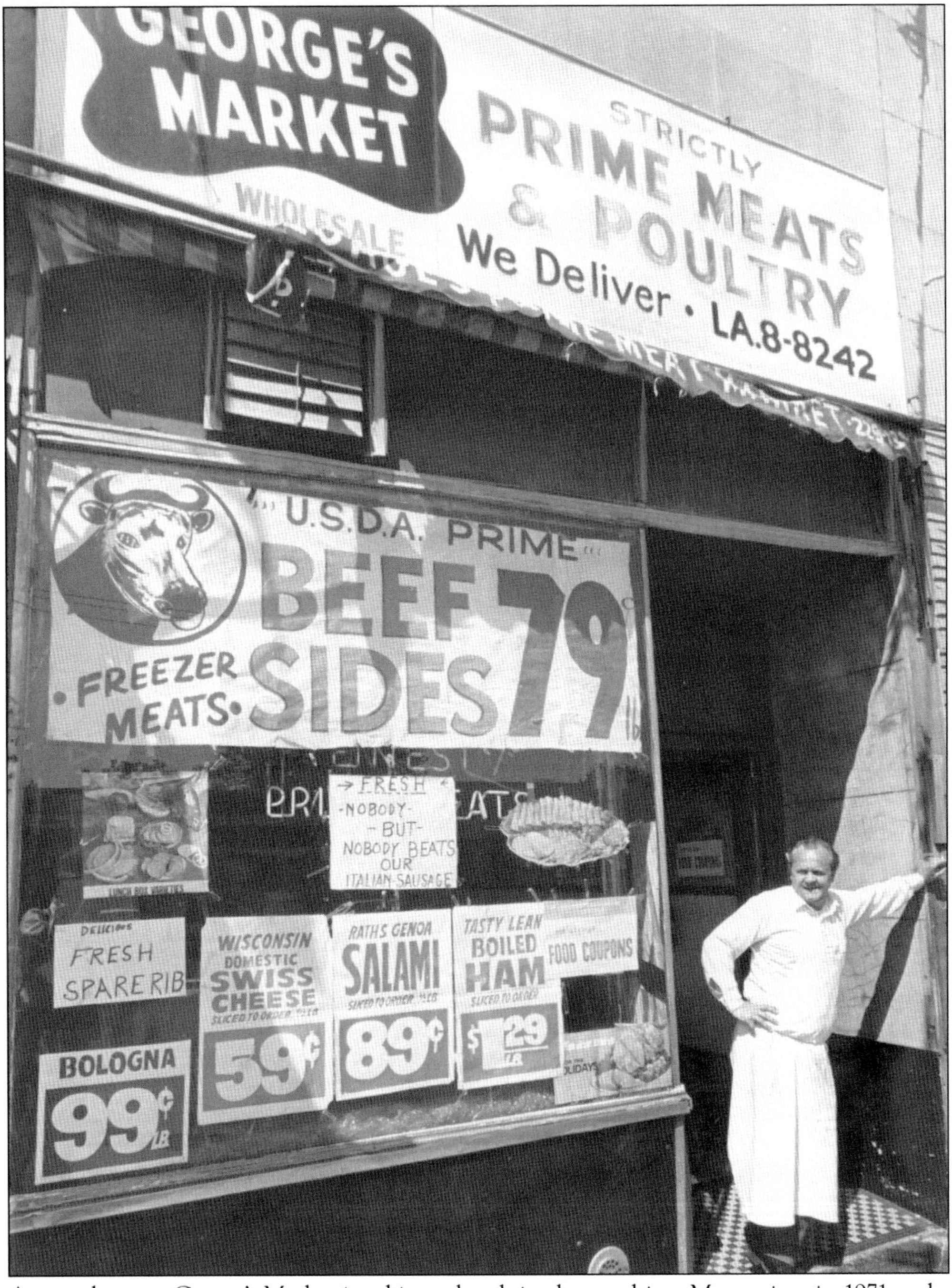

An employee at George's Market is taking a break in the sunshine. Meat prices in 1971 make a interesting contrast to today's prices. (Courtesy of Queens Borough Public Library, Long Island Division.)

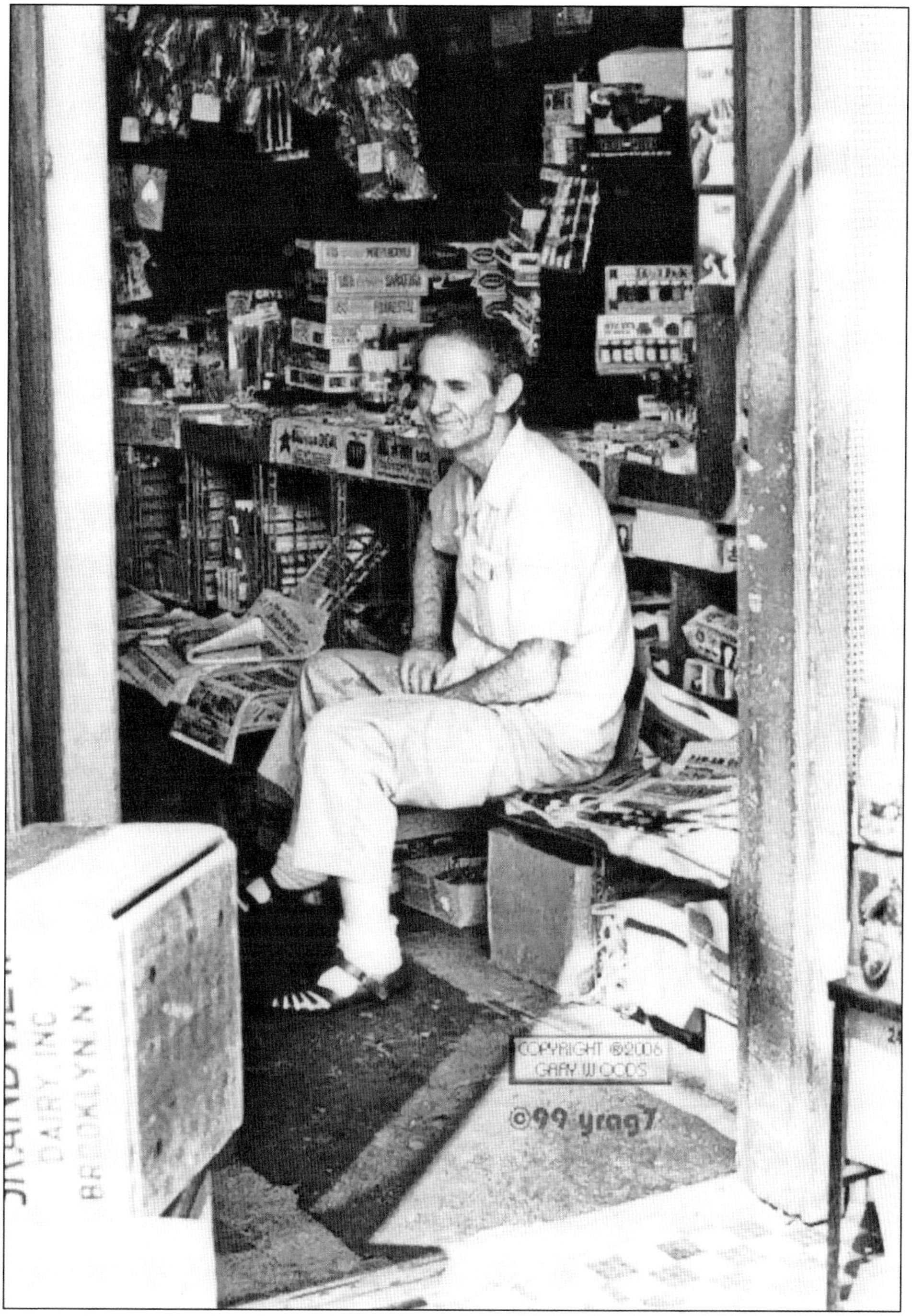

This is a photograph of the famous Irving Rausch, owner of Stanley's Stationery Store. In 1975, Stanley's was burglarized and Rausch was killed in an ensuing scuttle. The store was then set on fire to hide the murder. Many remember Stanley's as a store that could be relied on for school supplies, Pensy Pinky or Spaulding balls, baseball cards, and many other essential childhood items. The store was also home to an intimidating dog. (Courtesy of Queens Borough Public Library, Long Island Division.)

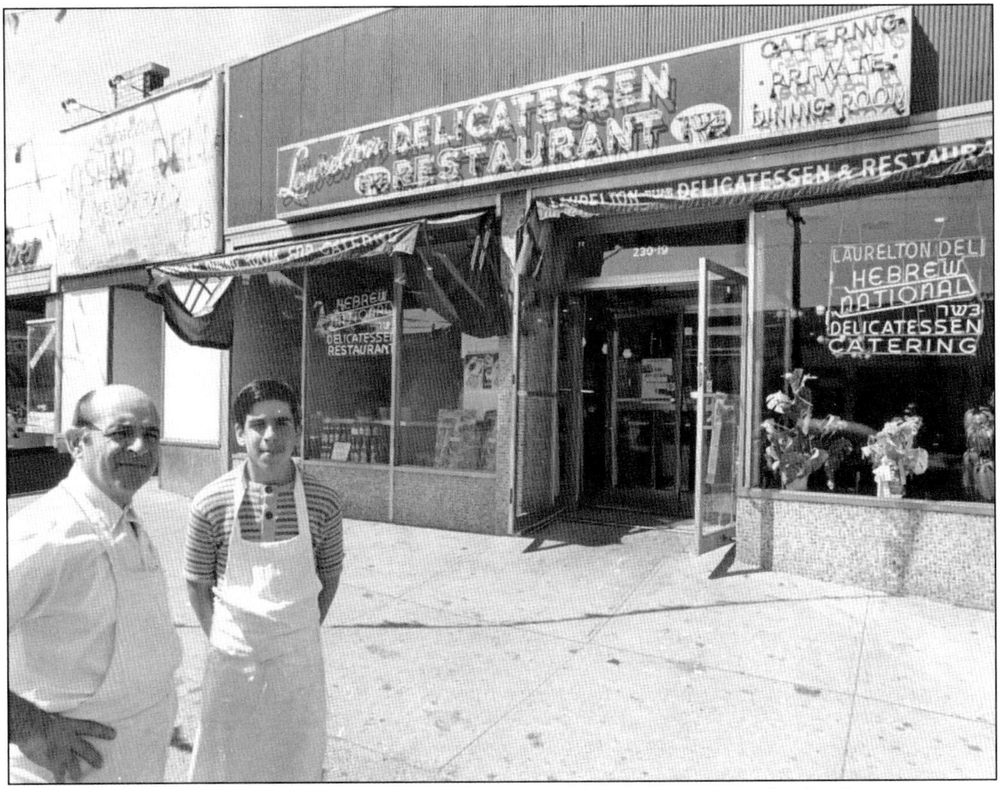

Sol Fishman, the proprietor of this kosher delicatessen, poses here with his nephew Mark in 1971. (Courtesy of Queens Borough Public Library, Long Island Division.)

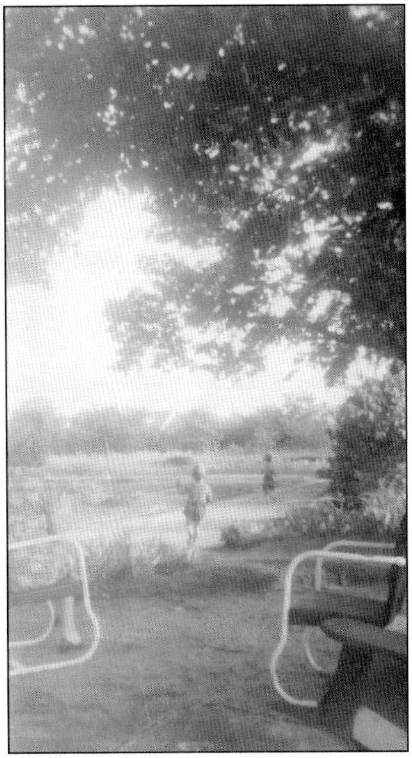

This bucolic setting is the backyard of Peter Gannon, whose two grandsons Bill and Larry can be seen running as their mother, Peggy Lederer, supervises. (Courtesy of Bill and Larry Lederer.)

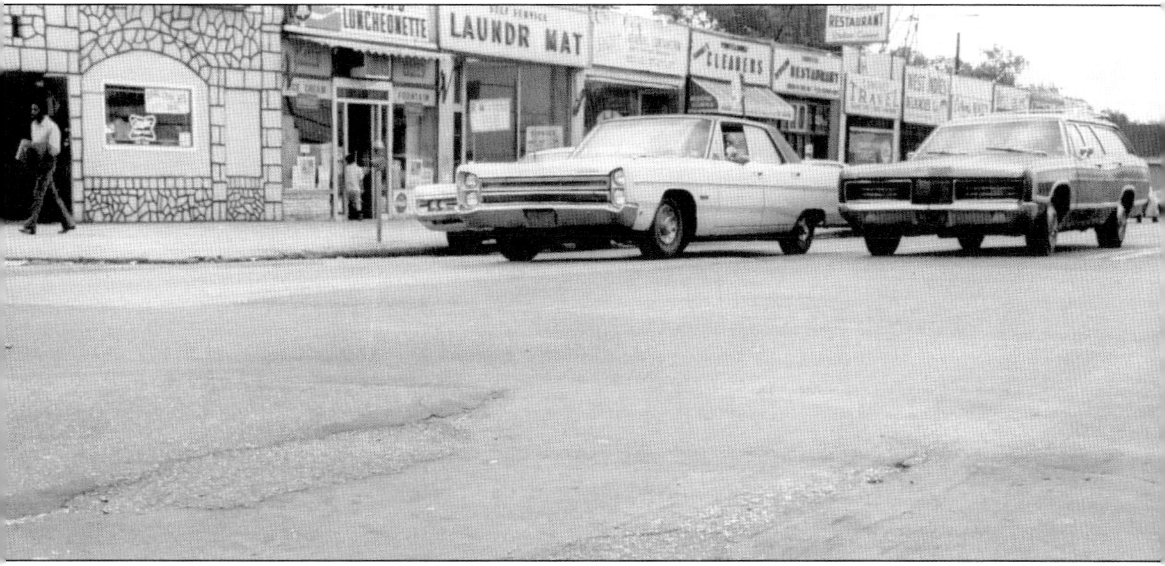

This is a typical Merrick Road traffic scene in 1973. The road seems to be in need of some repairing. (Courtesy of Queens Historical Society.)

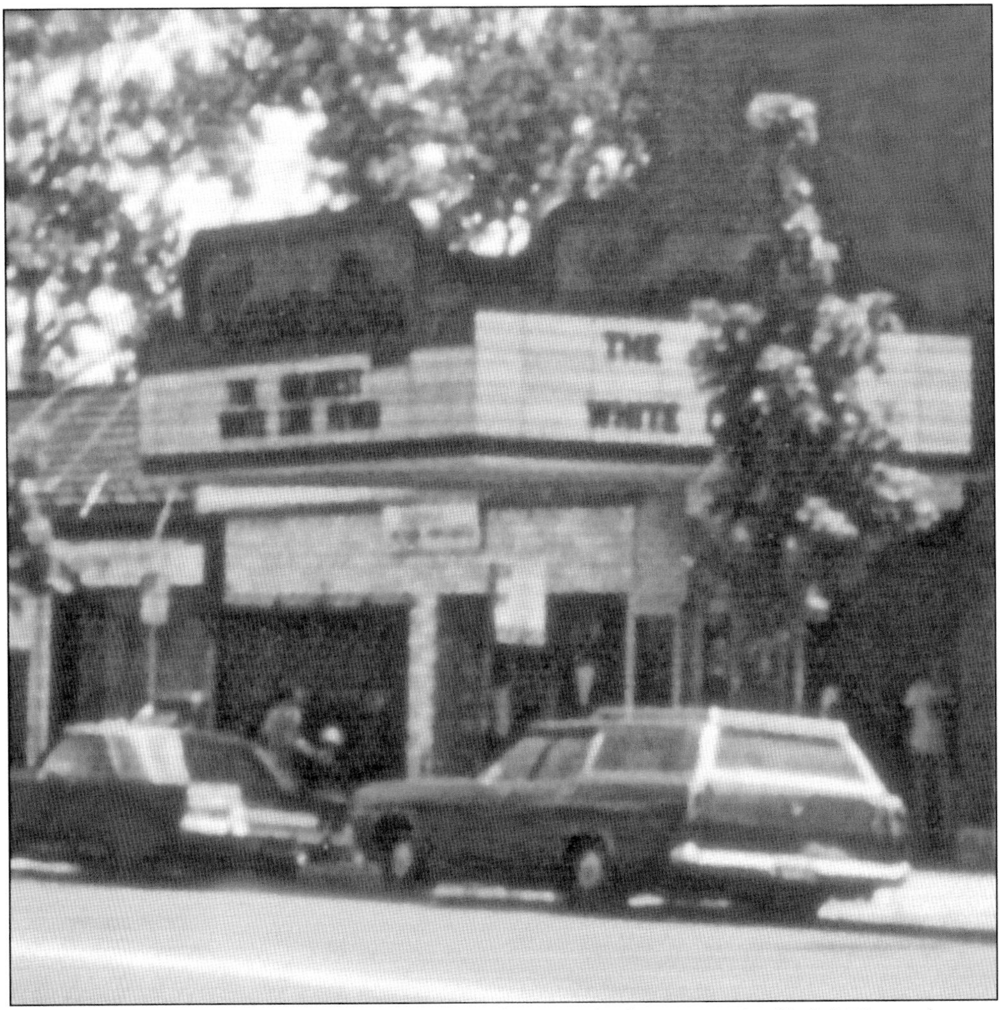

Pictured here is Laurelton's beloved Laurelton Theatre, also known as the "Itch." The nickname is a source of much speculation, but many suggest the "Itch" was named for the feeling one experiences while watching the newsreels and coming attractions in anticipation of the main feature. (Courtesy of Emile Schaffer.)

Judy Rosenberg celebrates her Sweet Sixteen at the Lamplighter Nightclub in Valley Stream. The Lamplighter was the place for such a celebration in 1964 for the teenagers of Laurelton. Pictured are Harvey and Marilyn Saunders, cousins; Harvey Wolf; Betty Sherman; Barry Salter; and Sandy Ettinger, Judy's neighbor since both girls were three. All were from Laurelton; Joanne Schwartz and Judy Rosenberg attended kindergarten together.

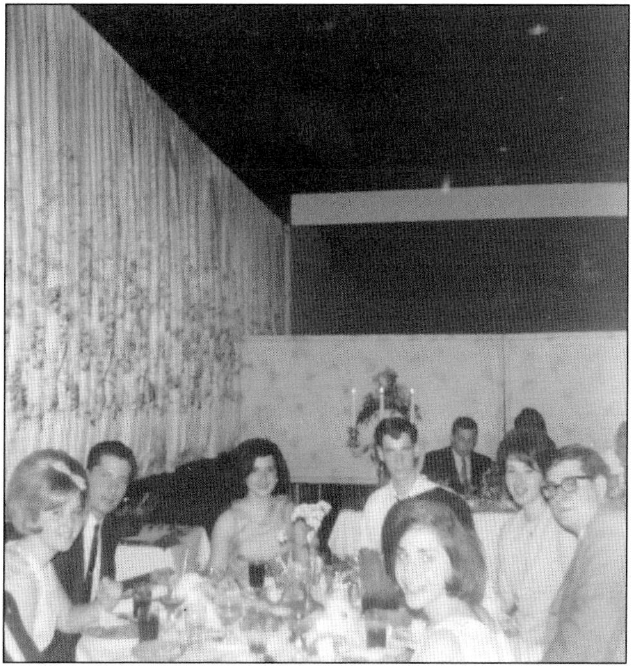

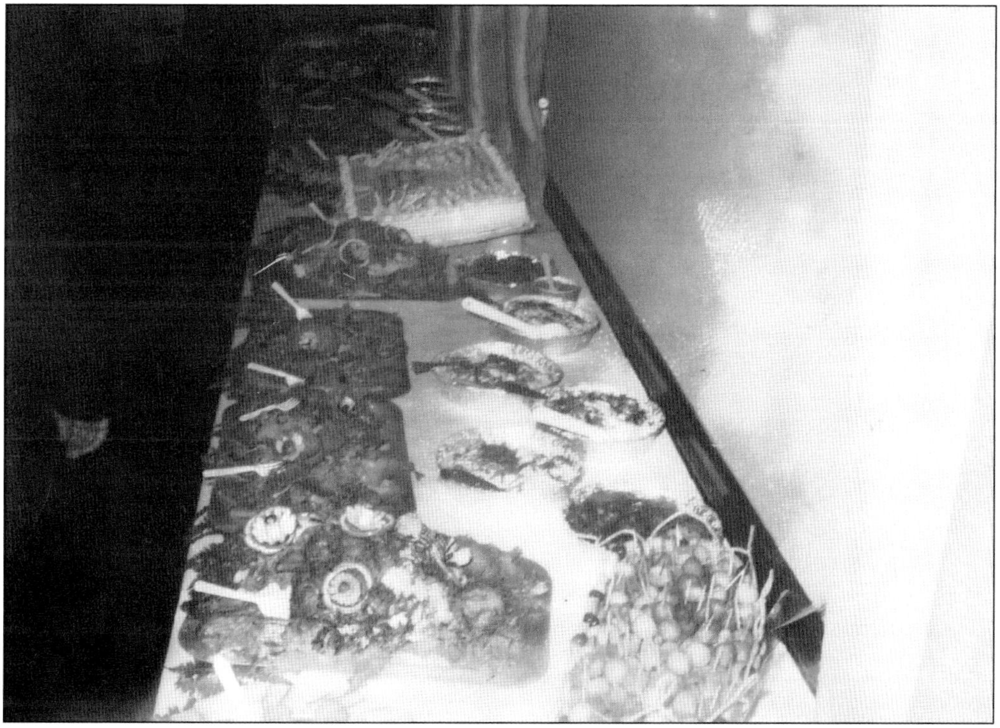

This is a photograph of the spread of food as prepared by Laurelton Deli for the surprise anniversary party for Arthur and Martha Rosenberg in 1966. In addition to the mounds of delicatessen meats such as pastrami and corn beef, there was also a 1950s-style fruit bowl, with decorative toothpicks placed in each chunk of fruit. The event was held at the Jewish War Veteran's Hall , next to the Laurelton Jewish Center.

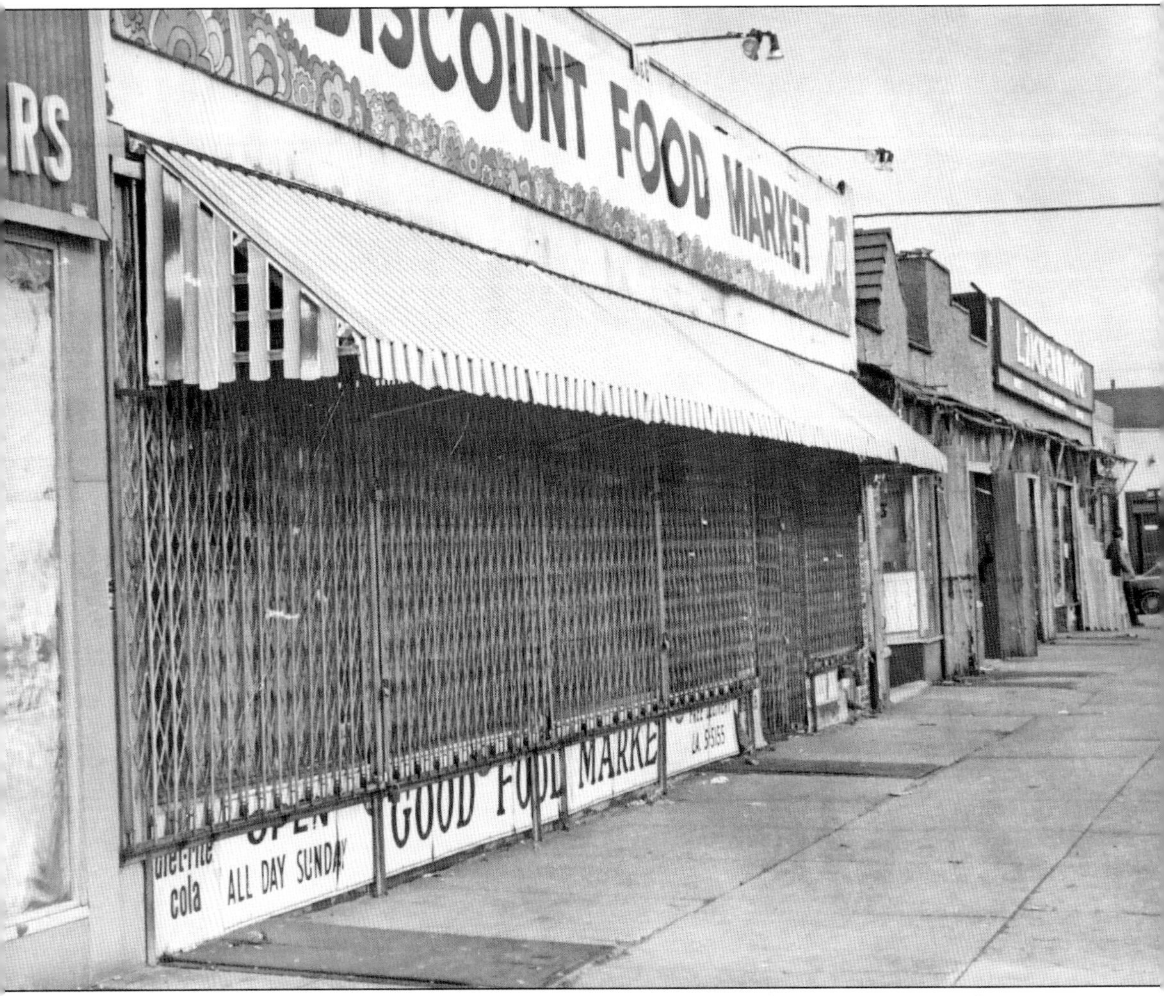

The Good Food Market was primarily a kosher food emporium whose owner, Morris Gruenstein, was a Holocaust survivor. Gruenstein's forearm bore the infamous tattooed number and was the first introduction to the Holocaust for many young Laureltonians. (Courtesy of Queens Borough Public Library, Long Island Division.)

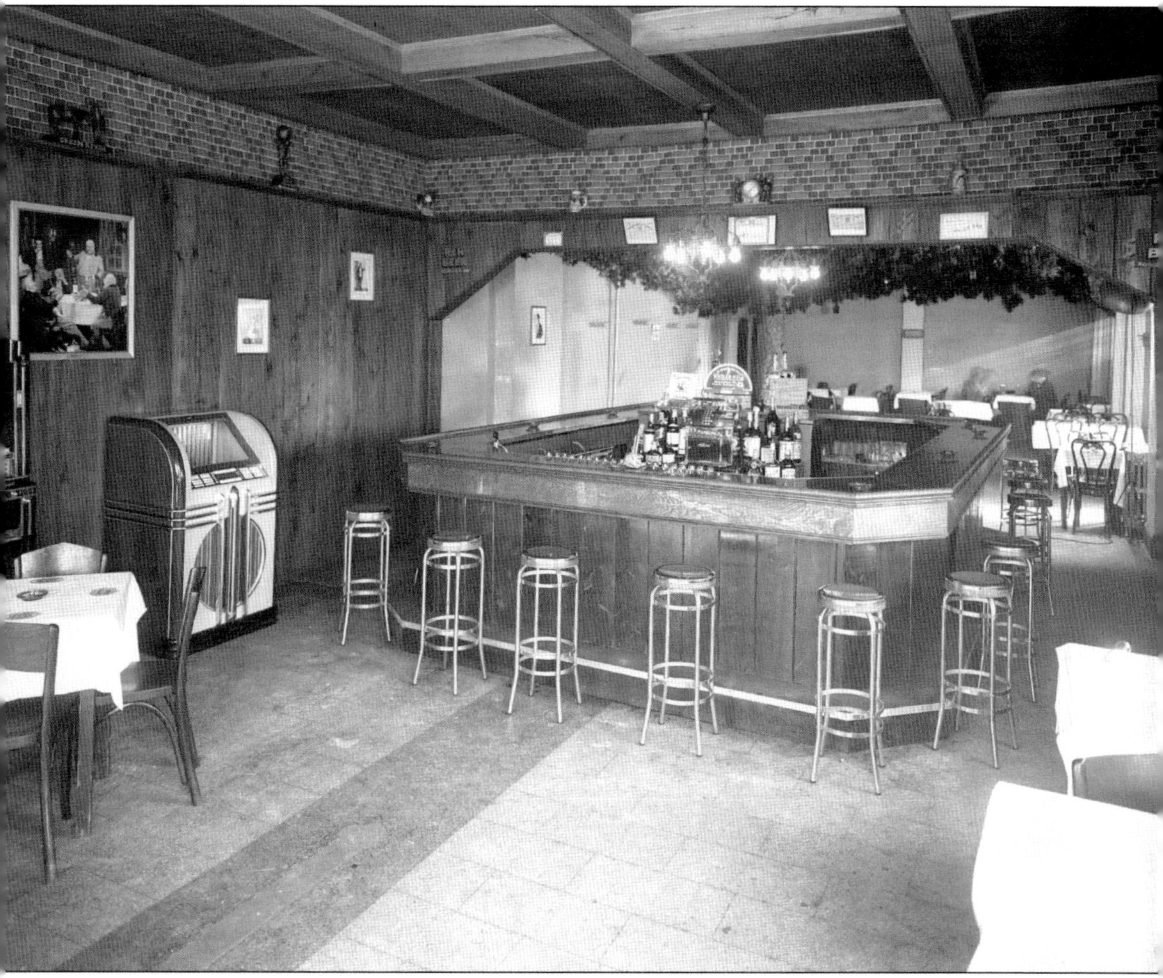

Seen above in 1938 is the homey interior of Sterry's Bar and Grill, reminiscent of a British neighborhood pub. Sterry's was a popular place for drink and conversation. (Courtesy of Queens Borough Public Library, Long Island Division.)

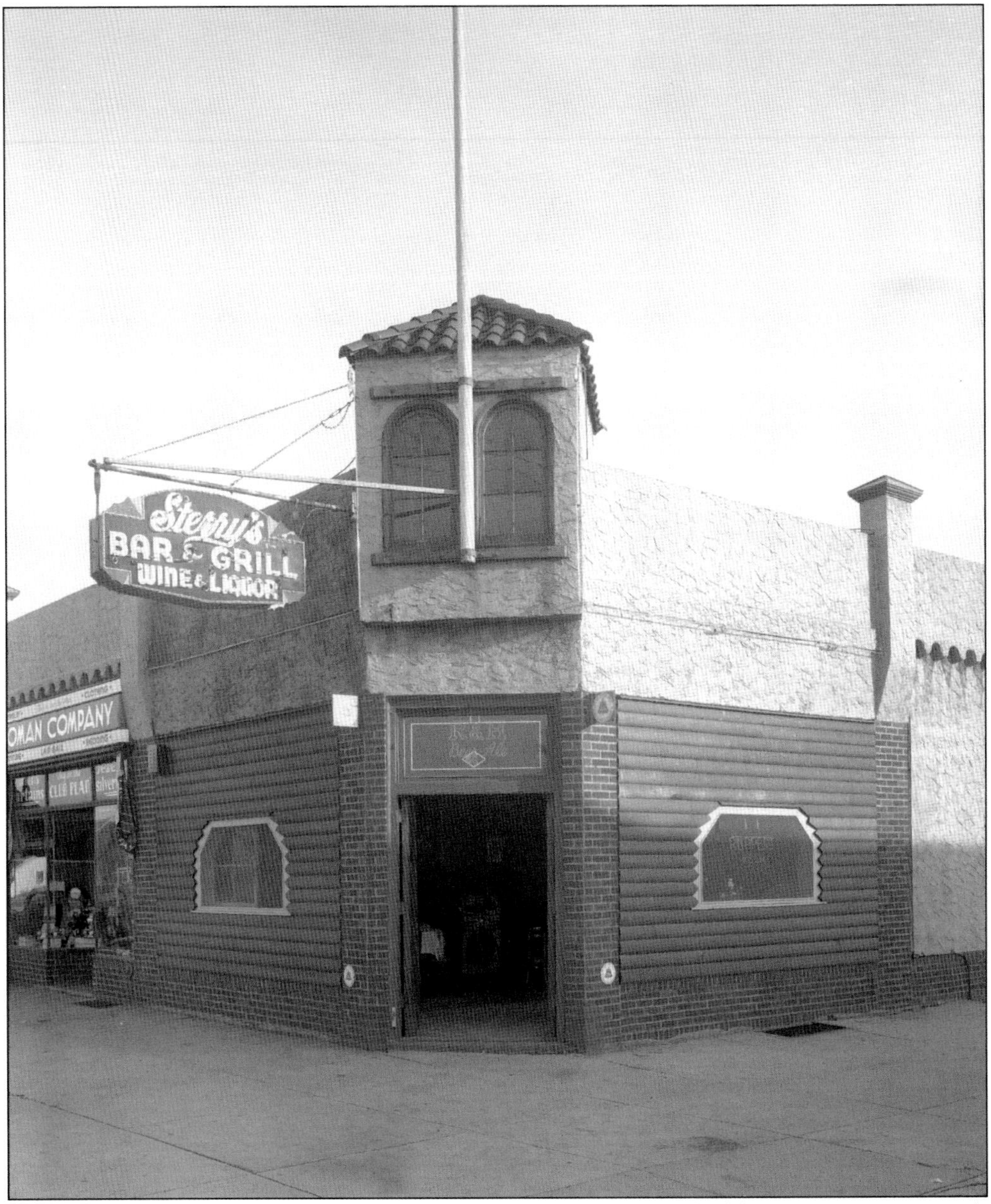

This is the exterior of Sterry's Bar on Merrick Road in 1938. This building was consistent with the rest of the architecture in the neighborhood. (Courtesy of Queens Borough Public Library, Long Island Division.)

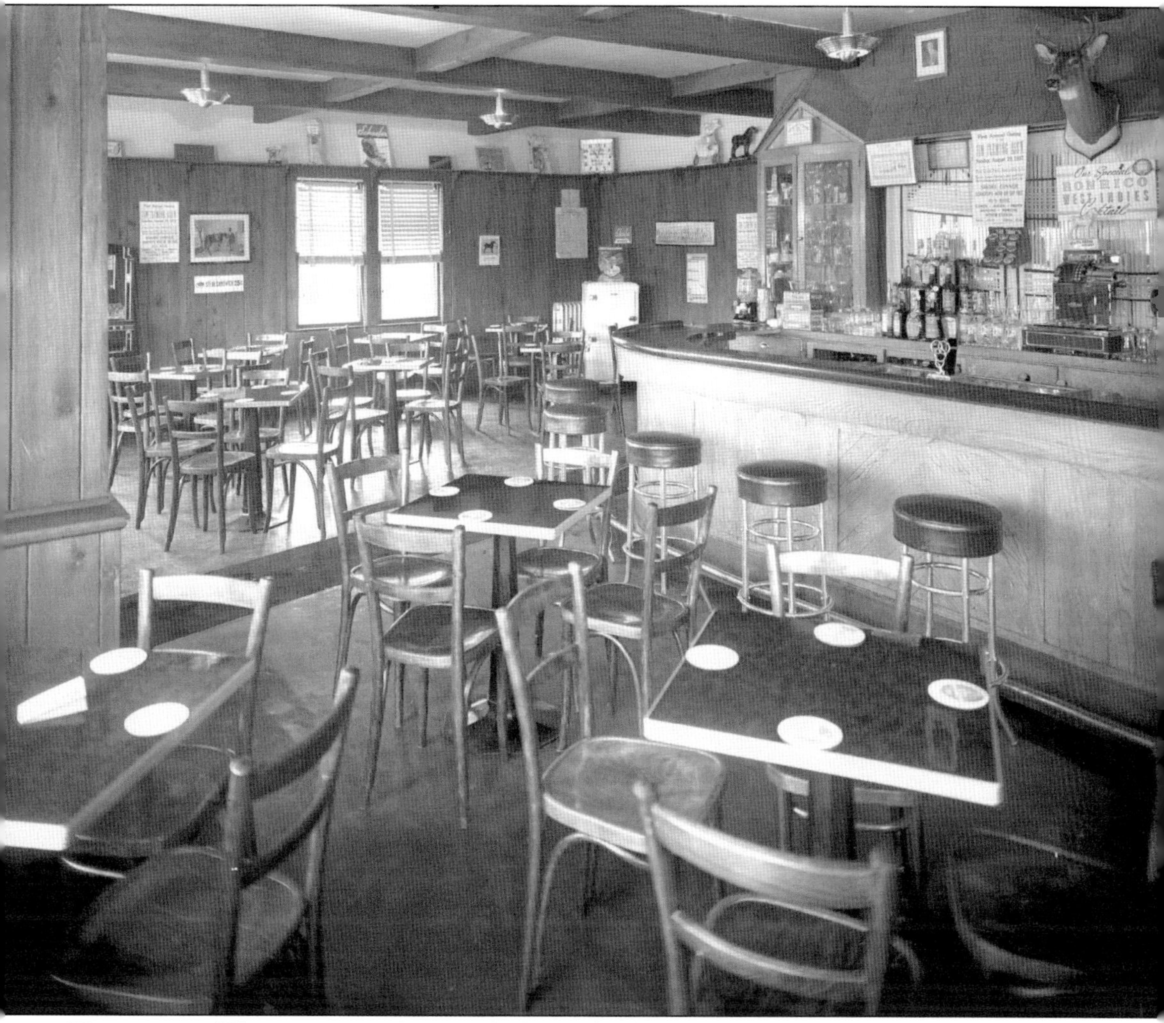

The interior of Flemmings, another popular bar and grill, is seen above. This photograph is dated 1935. (Courtesy of Queens Borough Public Library, Long Island Division.)

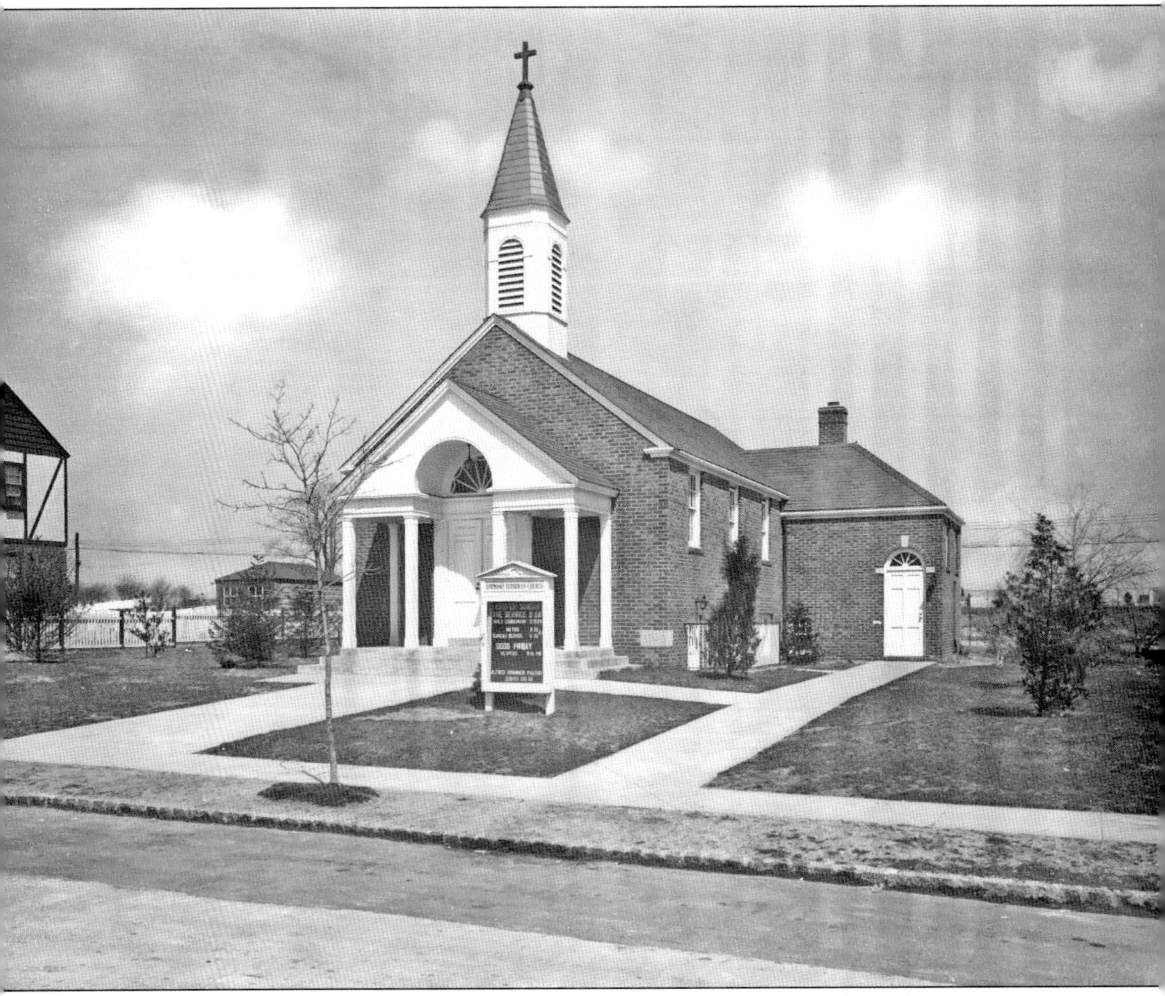

This is the refurbished Epiphany Lutheran Church on 228th Street and 130th Avenue in 1941. It is still classically beautiful, standing in the same place it has always been. (Courtesy of Queens Borough Public Library, Long Island Division.)

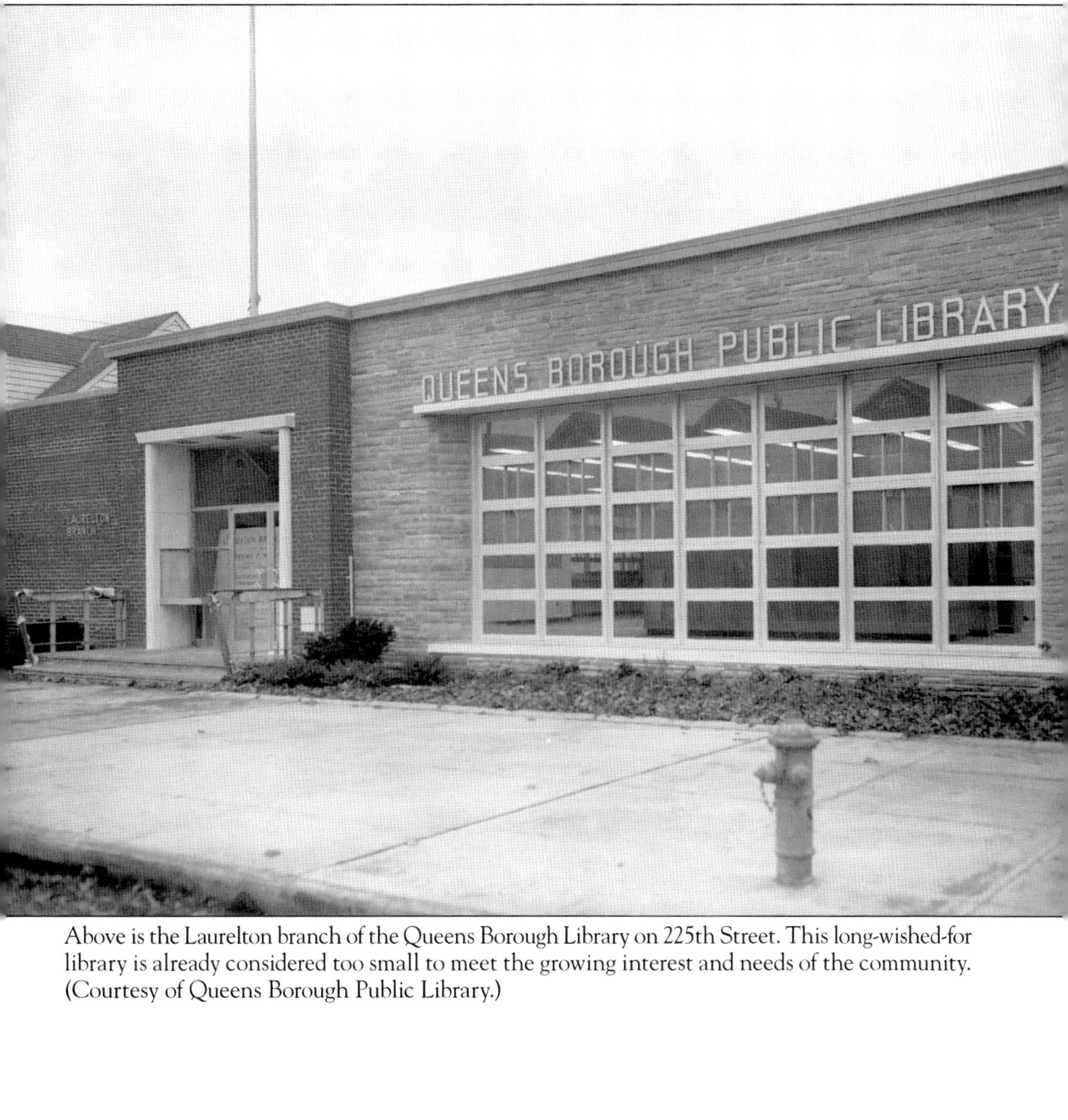

Above is the Laurelton branch of the Queens Borough Library on 225th Street. This long-wished-for library is already considered too small to meet the growing interest and needs of the community. (Courtesy of Queens Borough Public Library.)

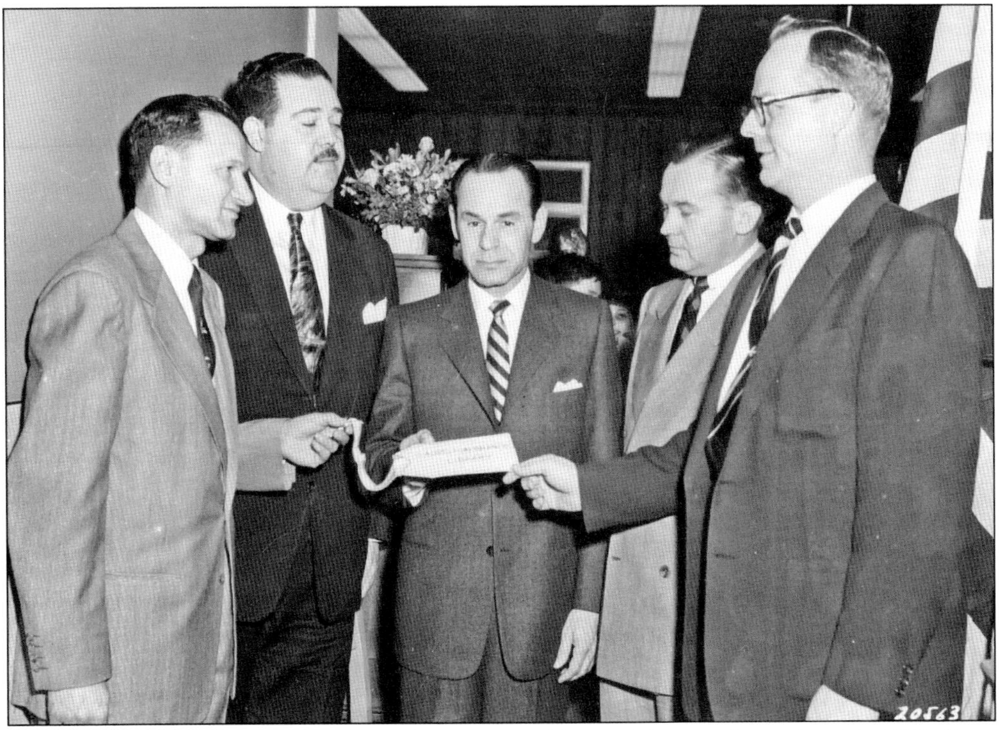

At long last, Laurelton acquired the library it had longed for on November 11, 1955. Seen here on its opening day, the town dignitaries make it official. (Courtesy of Queens Borough Public Library.)

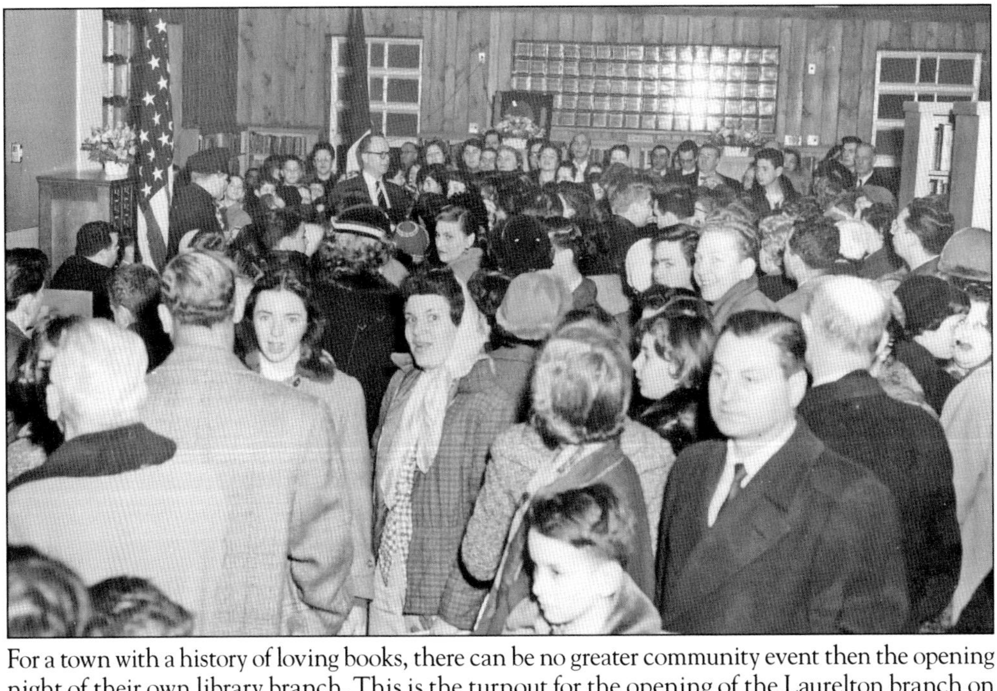

For a town with a history of loving books, there can be no greater community event then the opening night of their own library branch. This is the turnout for the opening of the Laurelton branch on November 11, 1955. (Courtesy of Queens Borough Public Library, Long Island Division.)

Two

Growing up Enchanted

There is a pervasive feeling among people who grew up in Laurelton in the decades from the 1930s to the 1960s that not only was Laurelton a special place, but that their own age group was a special generation, luckier and more gifted than that of any other. This is as true of the generation that experienced the Depression as it is of the one that experienced the Second World War. The experiences of young Laureltonians were, for the most part, different from their parents, many of whom had grown up in countries where life was harsh. Many of the newly immigrated residents were experiencing true freedom for the first time and the luxury of having a whole house and their own room to live in. When these parents' own children were growing up, they were quick to point out that their children's problems were not quite as difficult as the ones they had in their youth.

The children who grew up there experienced a true utopian society. Life seemed to revolve around a number of beloved areas: schools, sports, playing with other children on the block, houses of worship, the stores on Merrick, and the movie theater. Therein lied perhaps the greatest American childhood ever experienced. The expression "it takes a village" had no better example than in Laurelton where scores of adults, many of whom worked and lived within the Laurelton borders, kept a watchful but distant eye. Children led independent lives without the constant hovering of today's helicopter parents.

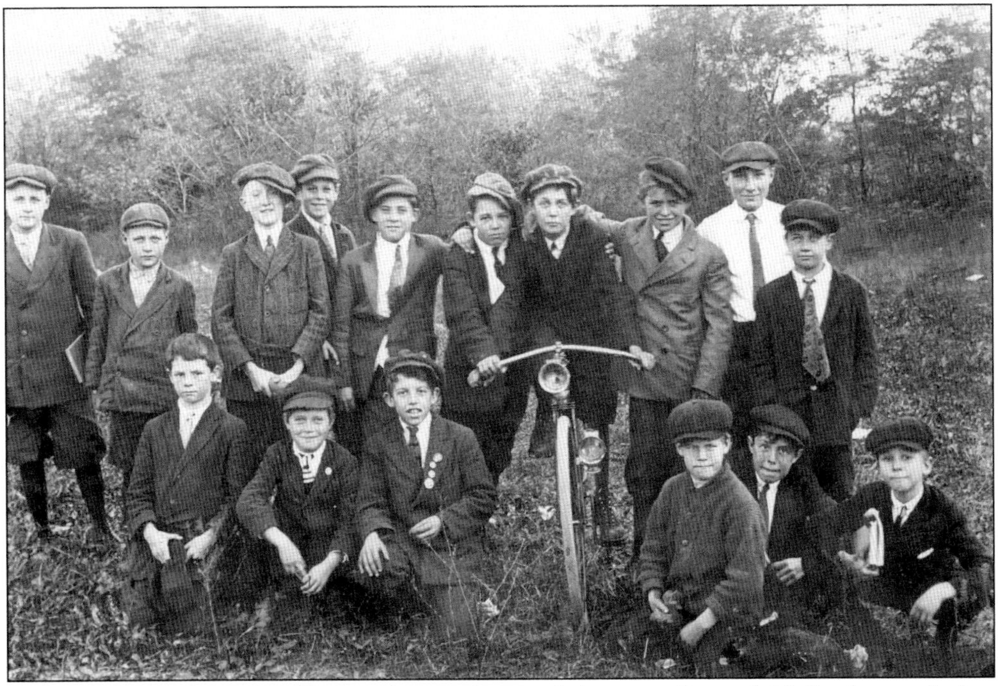

A group of Laurelton schoolboys gather in the woods between Springfield Gardens and what eventually came to be known as Laurelton, either going to or coming from the only public school in the vicinity at that time, P.S. 37. Also known as the Higbie Avenue School, P.S. 37 was located in Springfield Gardens. (Courtesy of Queens Borough Public Library, Long Island Division.)

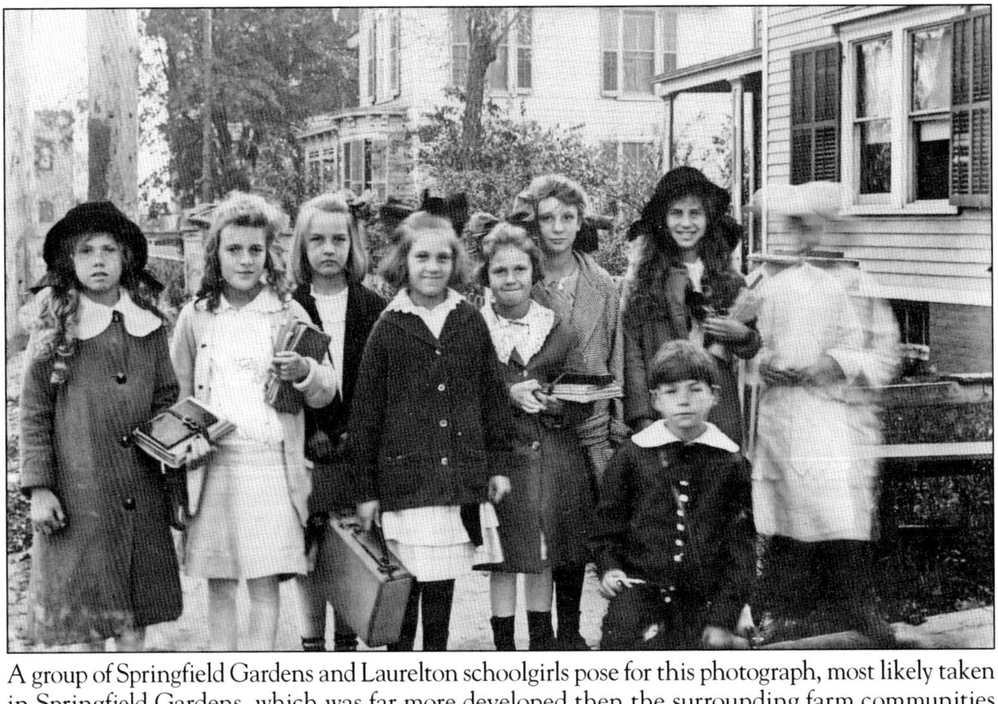

A group of Springfield Gardens and Laurelton schoolgirls pose for this photograph, most likely taken in Springfield Gardens, which was far more developed then the surrounding farm communities at that time. (Courtesy of Queens Borough Public Library, Long Island Division.)

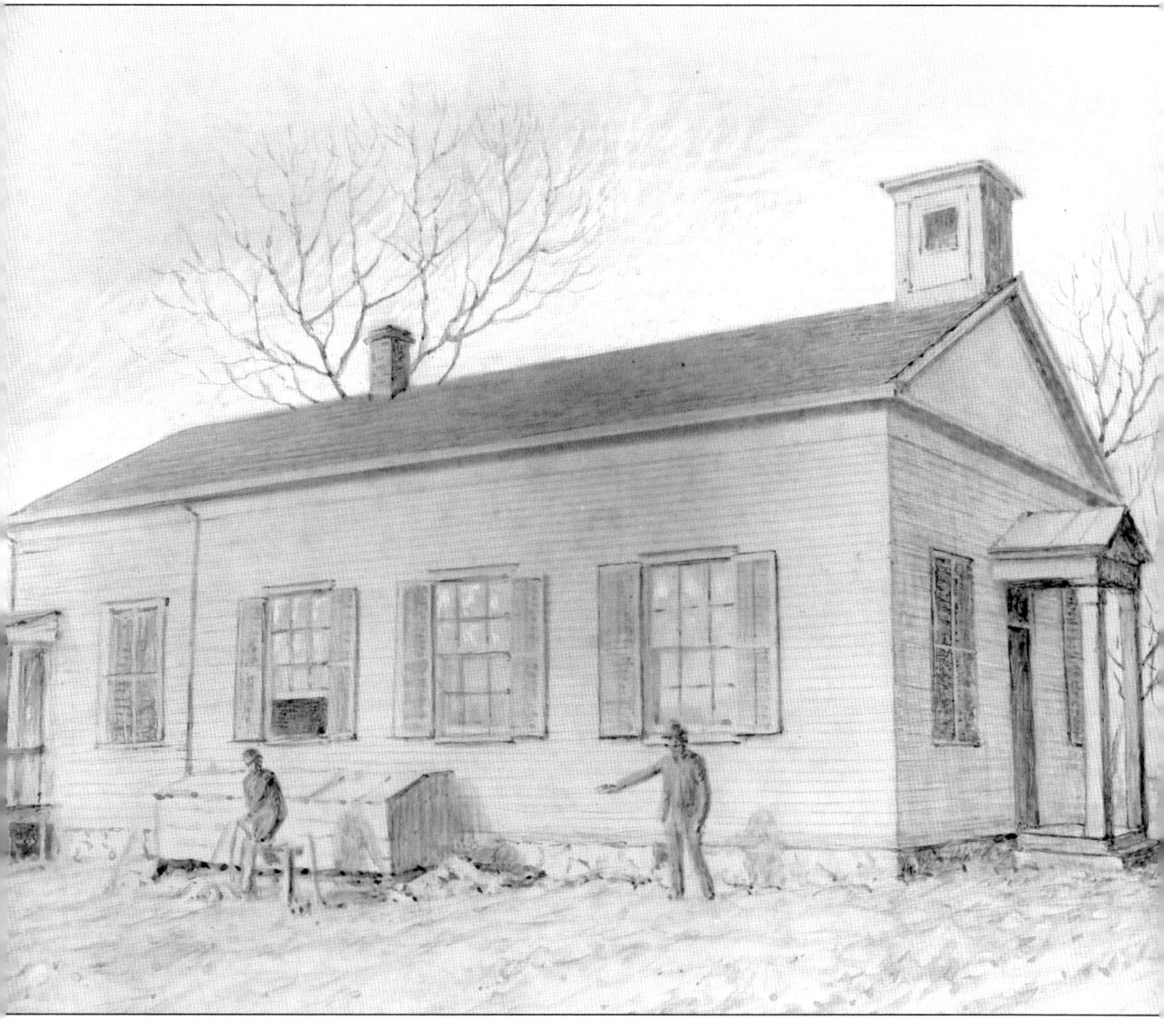

The early residents of Laurelton, or Rosedale as it was known then, had only one single-room schoolhouse for all of its student population. Pictured here is an original etching of such a building. The school was a wooden structure, long held to be a fire trap, and was demolished in the early 1940s. P.S. 156 opened in 1930 as a kindergarten-through-eighth-grade elementary school serving Laurelton. (Courtesy of Queens Borough Public Library, Long Island Division.)

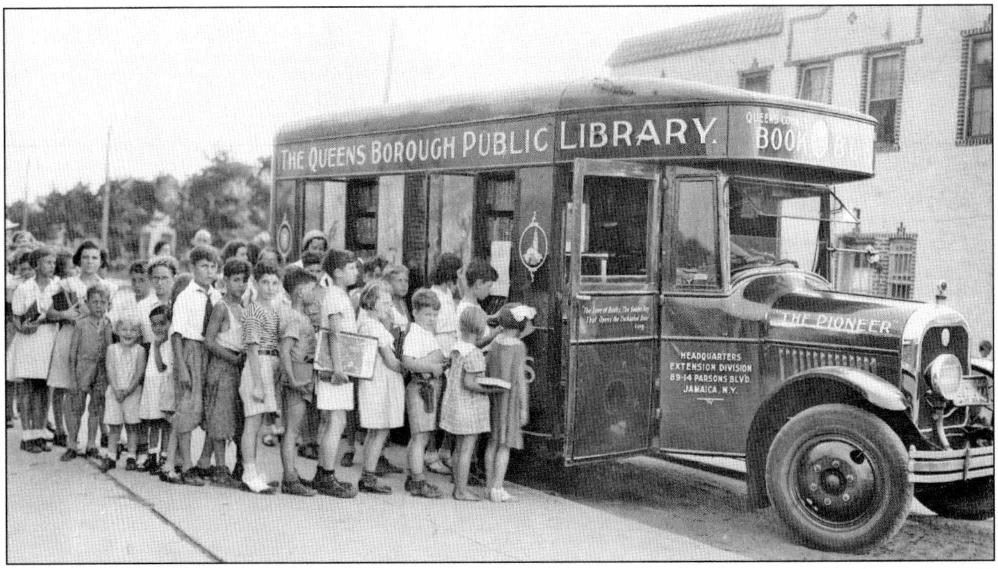

The library bus with the apropos name of "The Pioneer" served Laurelton's book-loving youth in the early 1930s. The Library Headquarters Extension Division, at the time located on Parsons Boulevard and Eighty-ninth Street, operated the library bus. Note that the third boy in line has his revolver and holster at the ready, and the fifth child in line is returning his oversized *Boy's Life* magazine. Lang's quotation on the bus door, "The Love of Books, The Golden Key, That Opens the Enchanted Door," pays homage to the love of books that Laureltonians will be celebrating years later when an actual branch opens on 225th Street. (Courtesy of Queens Borough Public Library, Long Island Division.)

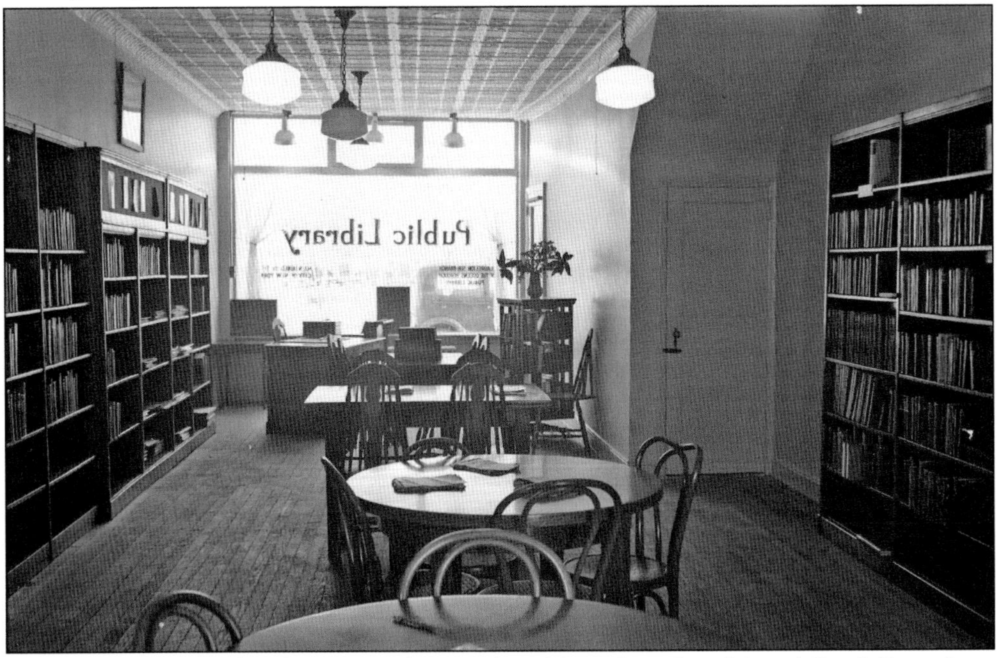

The library bus was replaced in 1936 with a storefront library branch on Merrick Road. Seen above is the interior of this sub-branch of the library, which was open only three days a week: Monday, Wednesday, and Friday. (Courtesy of Queens Borough Public Library, Long Island Division.)

Before the storefront library branch on Merrick Road, as seen here, Laurelton residents used a storefront library in Rosedale that could be reached by using the overpass or walking through the woods. (Courtesy of Queens Borough Public Library, Long Island Division.)

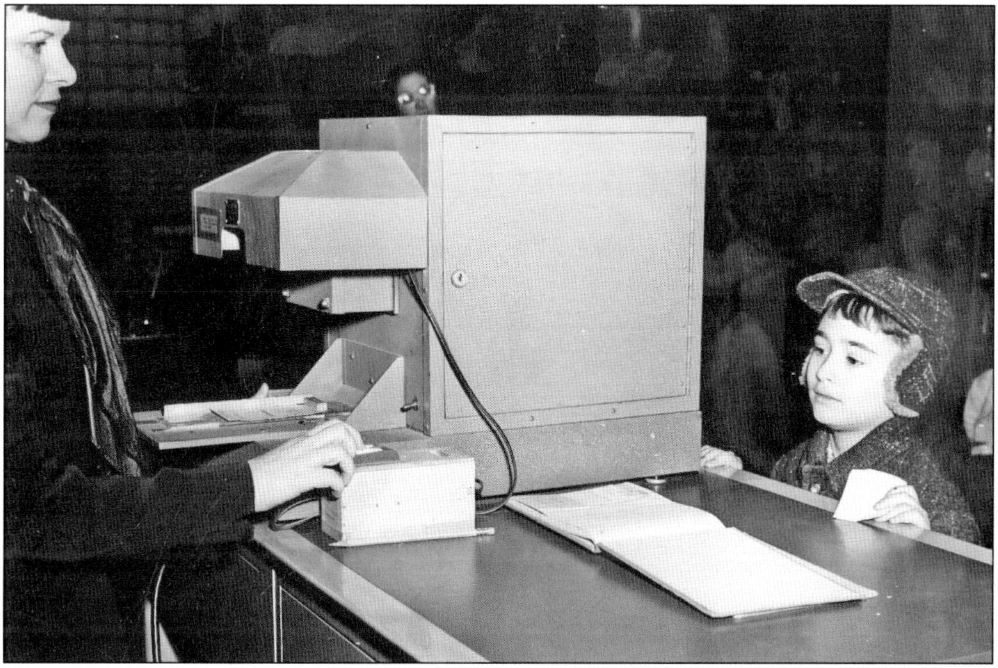

In this photograph, a child checks out a book at the recently opened Laurelton library branch in 1955. (Courtesy of Queens Borough Public Library, Long Island Division.)

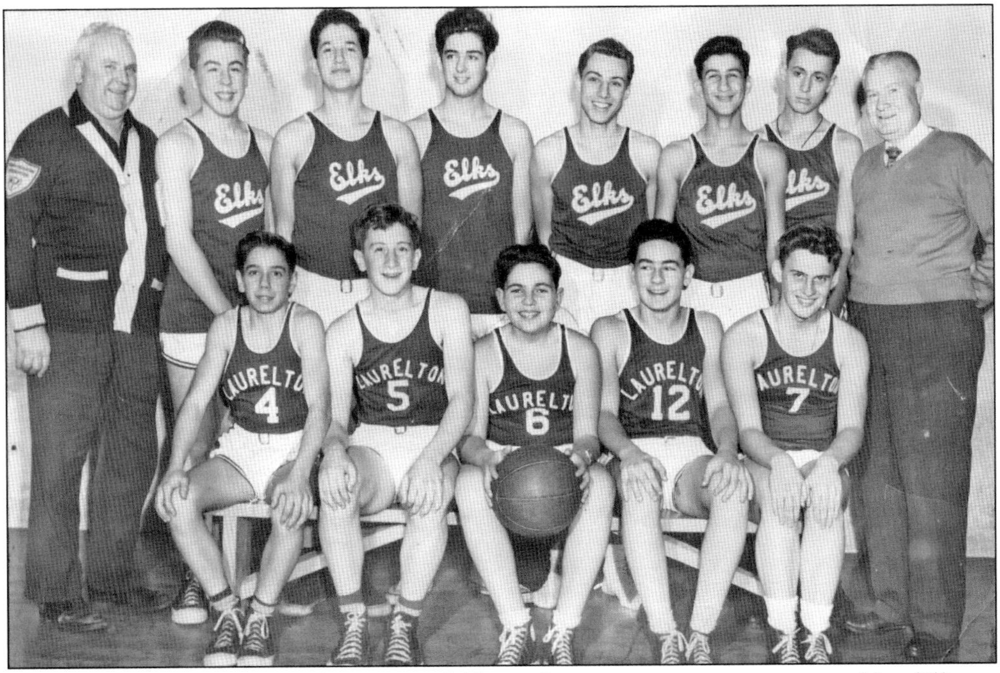

Laurelton had many organized sports available, and various teams were sponsored by different civic organizations, such as the 1950–1951 Laurelton Elks Lodge No. 878's basketball team. They came in second place in their division. Joel Karpay, No. 6, is holding the ball. (Courtesy of Joel Karpay.)

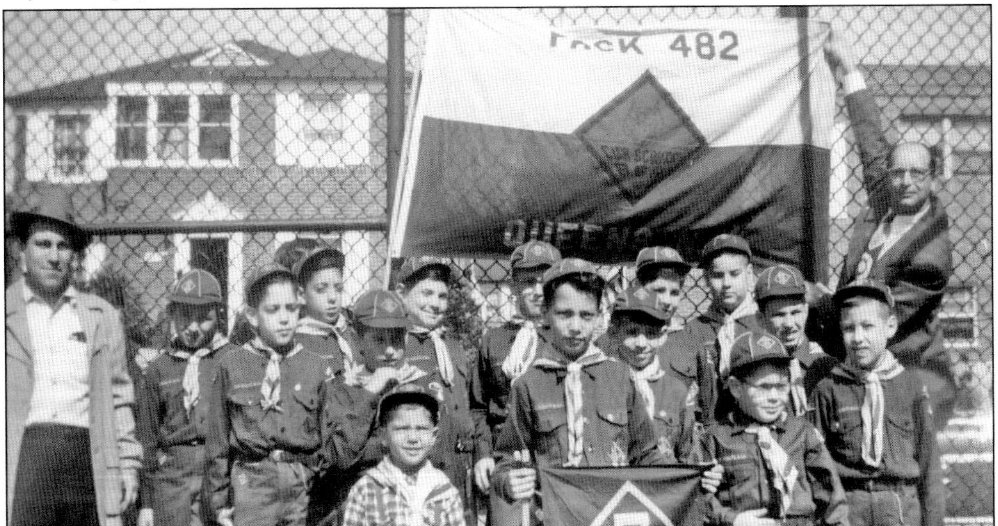

This is Cub Scout Troop 482 in June 1958, assembling for the Memorial Day parade down Merrick Road. The troop was organized by Jack Harris (in hat on left). Harris was also responsible for organizing Shomer Shabbat Little League Baseball. Pictured from left to right are (first row) Jay Harris (mascot), Danny Goldschmiedt (holding banner), and unidentified; (second row) Jerome Schwartz, Eddie Parver, Michael Kreisler, and two unidentified; (third row) Harris, Marc Zipstein, Barry Schwartz, Barry Berger, Steven Schneider, and three unidentified. (Courtesy of Reba Harris Solomon.)

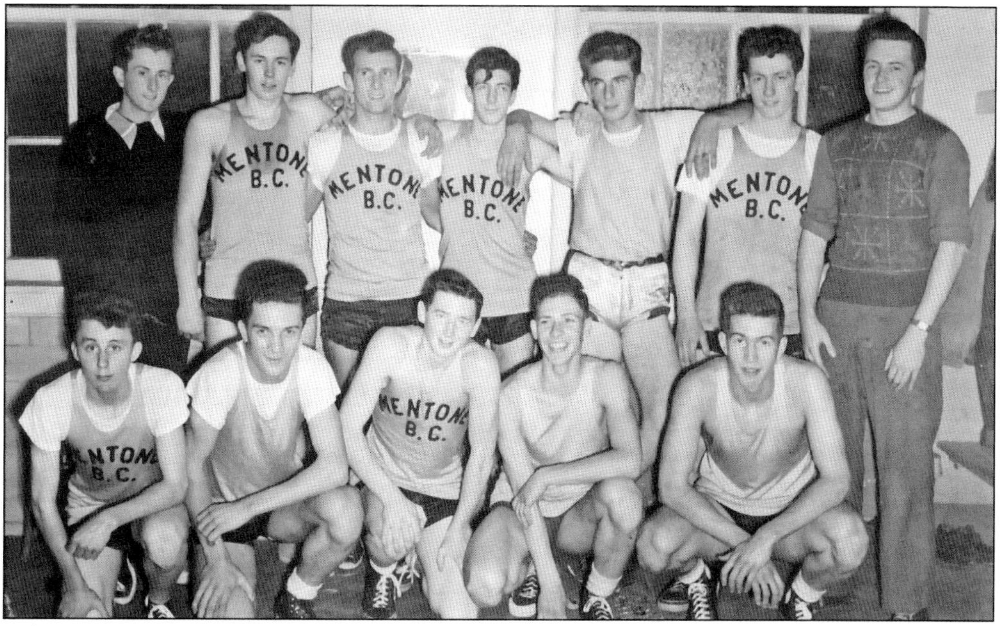

Taken in 1956 in the gymnasium at P.S. 156, the Mentone Boys Club basketball team of Laurelton practiced during the day at the Mentone Playground on North Conduit Avenue. The Mentones was an informal social club for youth residing in the area for eight years. Their home games were played on the court in the P.S. 156 gym. From left to right are (kneeling) Marty Keane, Mario Musso, Dick Lahey, Morty Goldstein, and Jim Pike; (standing) George "Jet" Little, Bill Brennan, Frank Sangiorgio, Franny Mandel, Frank O'Lear, Harvey Teichert, and Denis Leary. (Courtesy of Tom Smith.)

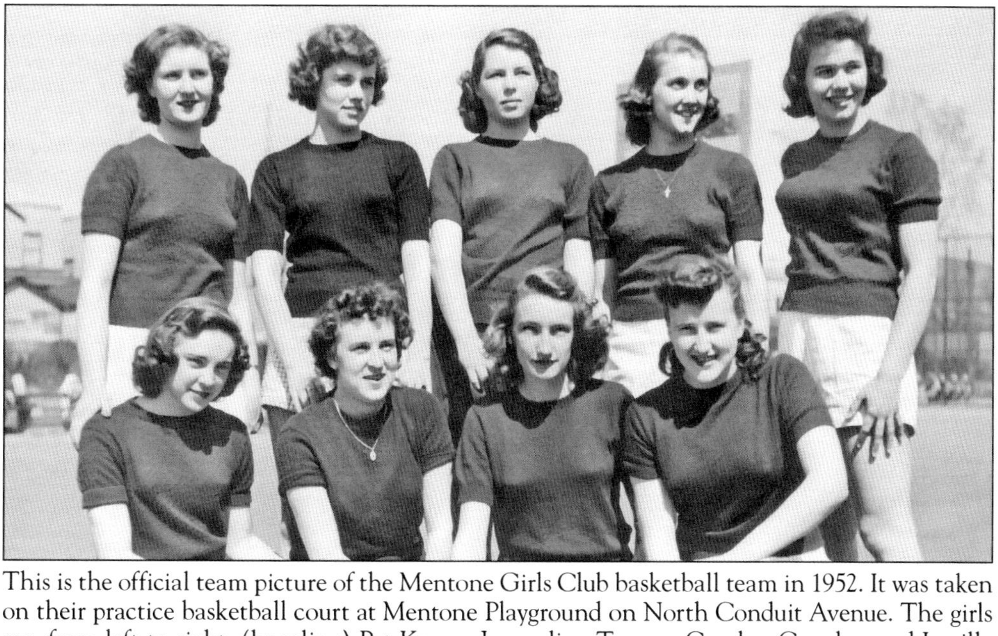

This is the official team picture of the Mentone Girls Club basketball team in 1952. It was taken on their practice basketball court at Mentone Playground on North Conduit Avenue. The girls are, from left to right, (kneeling) Pat Keane, Jacqueline Tressay, Carolyn Crossley, and Lucille Tressay; (standing) Trudy Byrnes, Valerie English, Dorothy Leonard, Barbara Smith, and Pat Baumgardner. Coach Ralph Killmeyer is not pictured. (Courtesy of Tom Smith.)

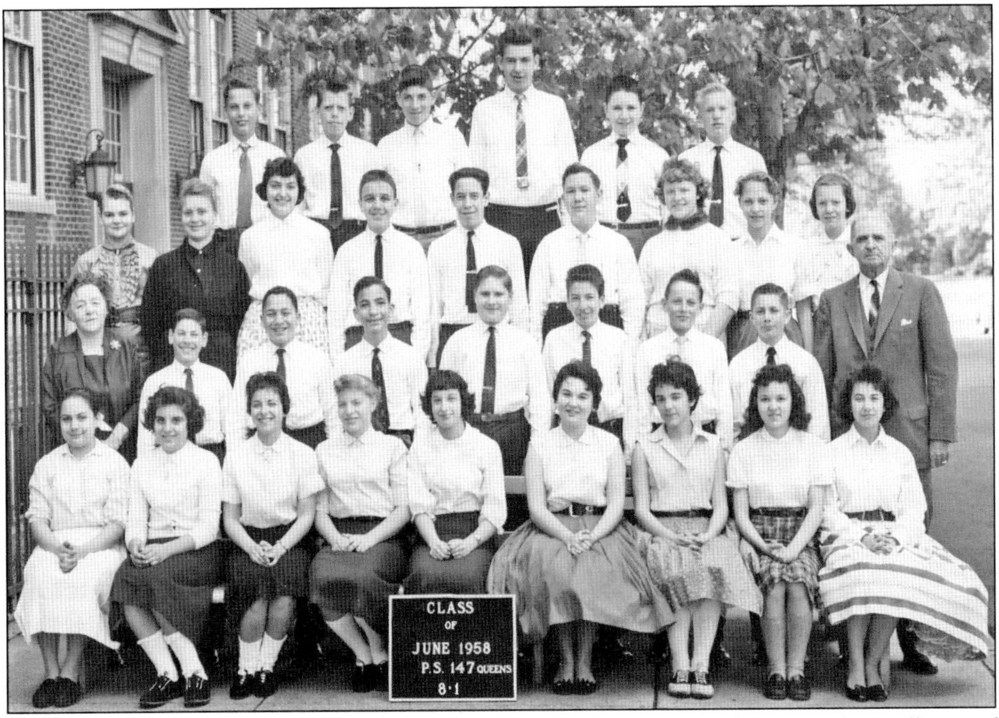

This is just one of the many school graduation pictures that are tucked away in photo albums of Laurelton alumni. Ron Miller, who was affectionately known as "Moose," provided this image. He is pictured second from the right in the back row of this 1958 graduation picture from P.S. 147. (Courtesy of Ron Miller.)

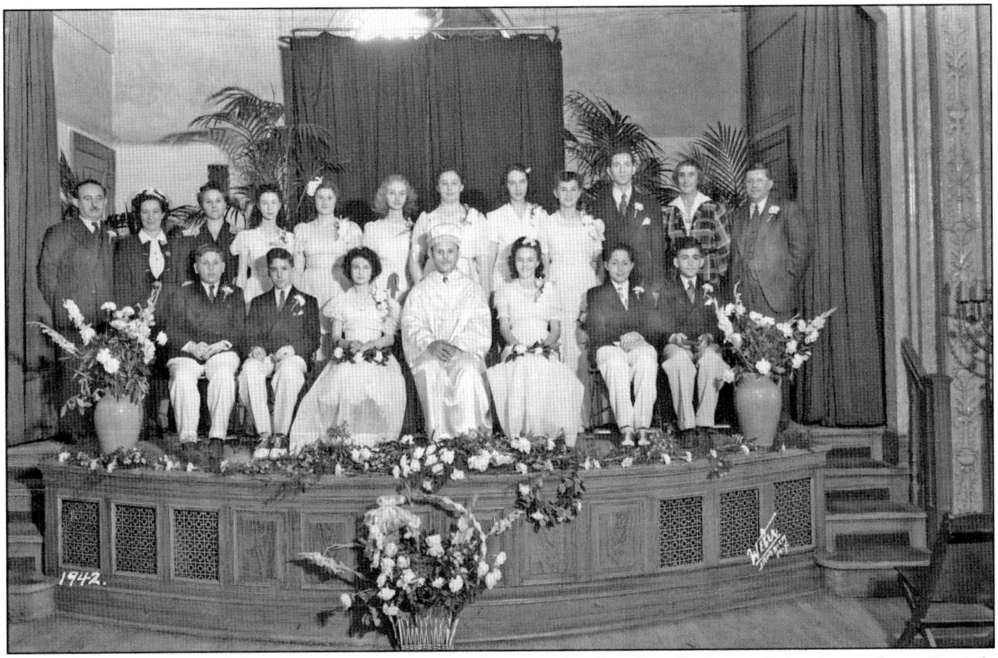

Seen here are Rabbi Teplitz and the 1942 graduating high school class of the Laurelton Jewish Center. (Courtesy of Queens Borough Public Library, Long Island Division.)

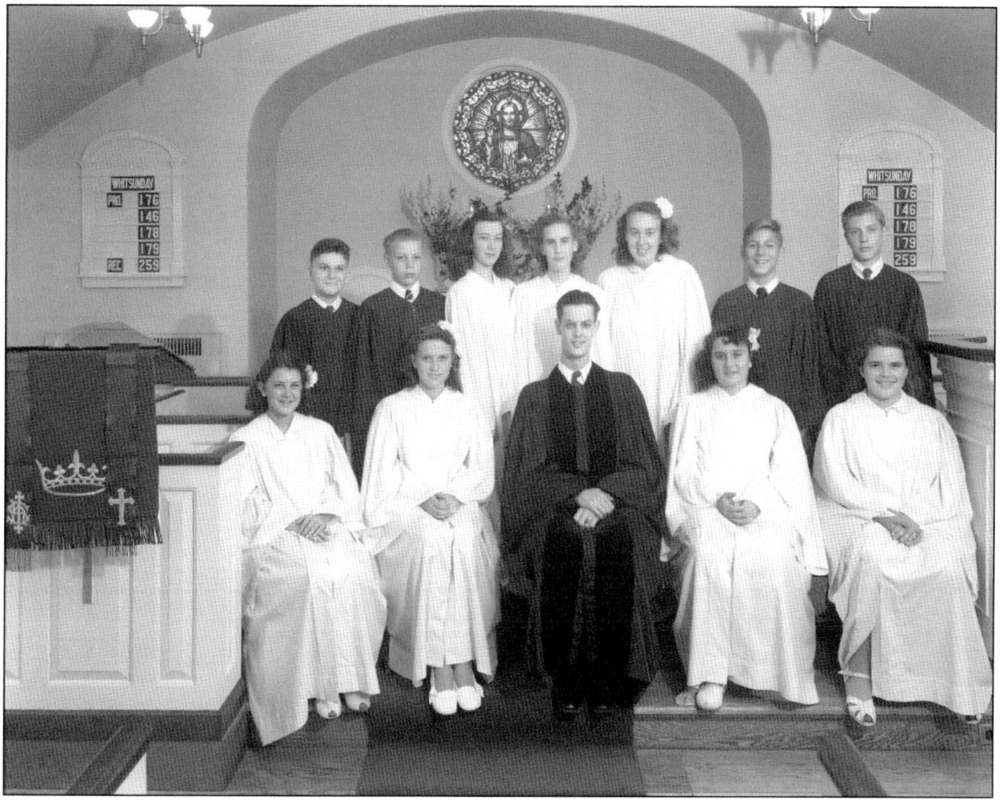

The Epiphany Lutheran Church confirmation class of 1935 is pictured above with Rev. Wilbur Cowen Jr. The church is still serving the Laurelton community at its original location on 130th Avenue. (Courtesy of Queens Borough Public Library, Long Island Division.)

The 1937 Laurelton Stagers, the dramatic club of the Laurelton Jewish Center, is shown here. The gentleman to the left, Douglas Krantzer, was an equity actor of some note who was provided to the Laurelton Jewish Center by the Federal Theater Project, a branch of the Works Progress Administration. Coauthor Annette Henkin is seated in the first row, second from left. (Courtesy of Annette Henkin Landau.)

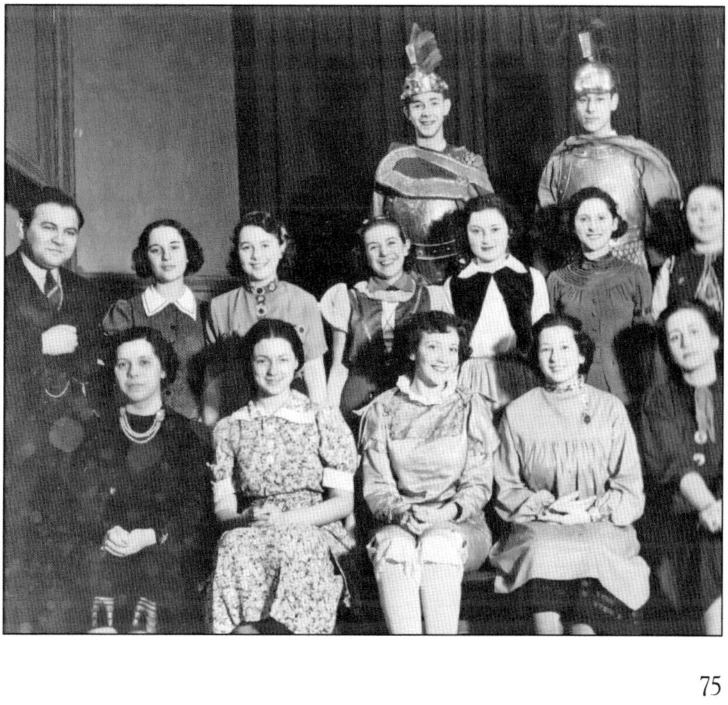

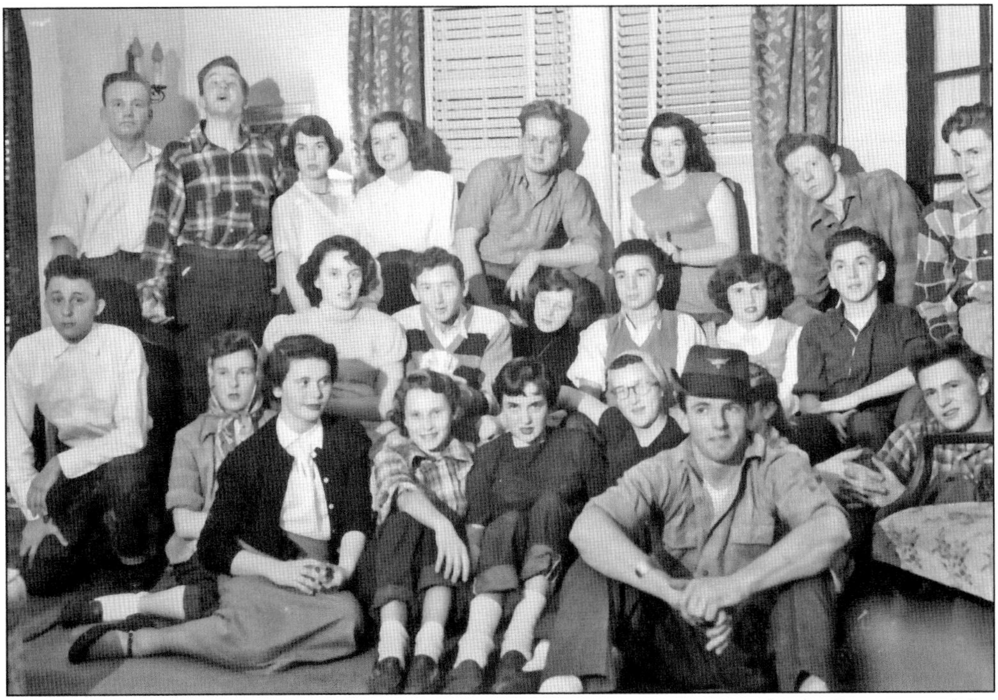

In this photograph, the Mentones enjoy a seasonal house party. Tom Smith, the historian of the Mentones, has written about the "Mentones Mystique." (Courtesy of Tom Smith.)

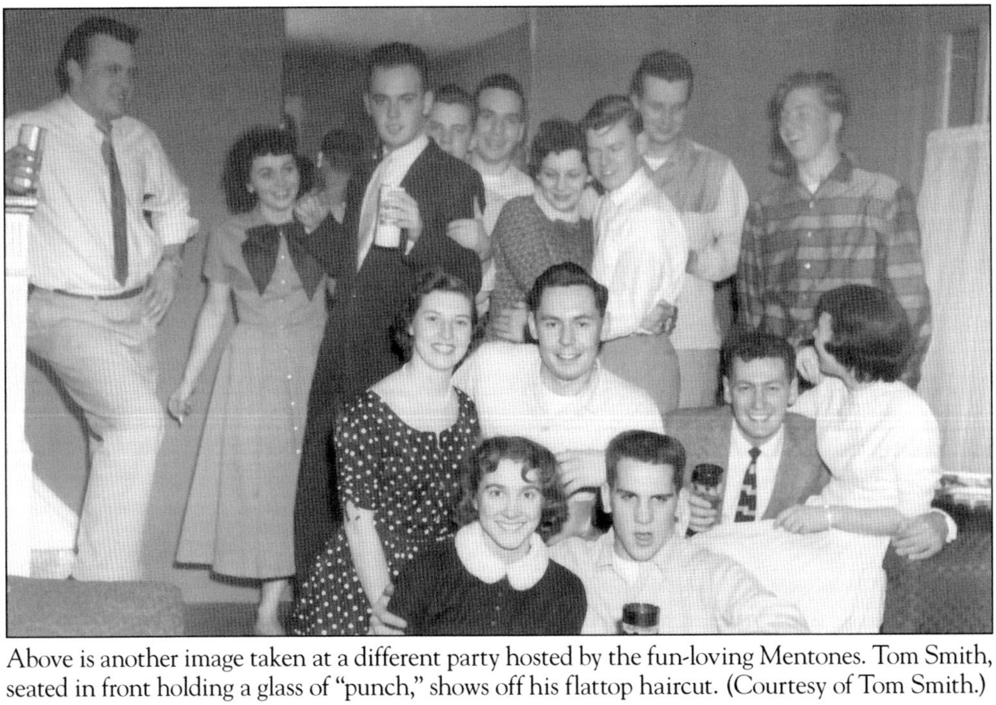

Above is another image taken at a different party hosted by the fun-loving Mentones. Tom Smith, seated in front holding a glass of "punch," shows off his flattop haircut. (Courtesy of Tom Smith.)

Alvin Kavaler is seen here in the mid-1930s with his bike. Bicycles were a crucial part of the childhood experience in Laurelton, as it was the only method of transportation besides walking or public transportation available to children. Notice, however, that the appropriate attire for boys at that time was still short pants. Alvin's father, Dr. David Kavaler, was one of the first full-time dentists in Laurelton. (Courtesy of Bernard Kavaler.)

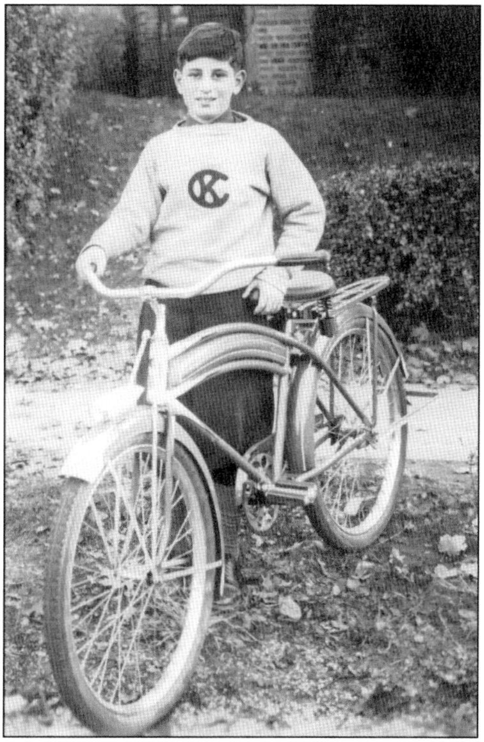

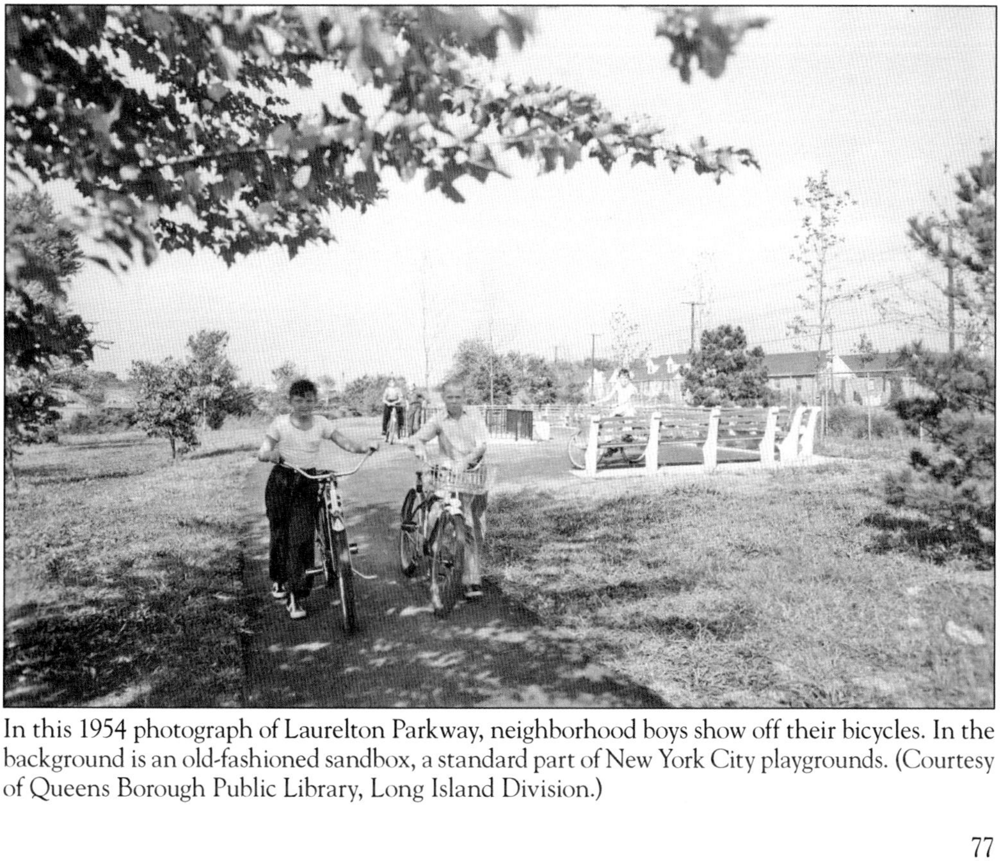

In this 1954 photograph of Laurelton Parkway, neighborhood boys show off their bicycles. In the background is an old-fashioned sandbox, a standard part of New York City playgrounds. (Courtesy of Queens Borough Public Library, Long Island Division.)

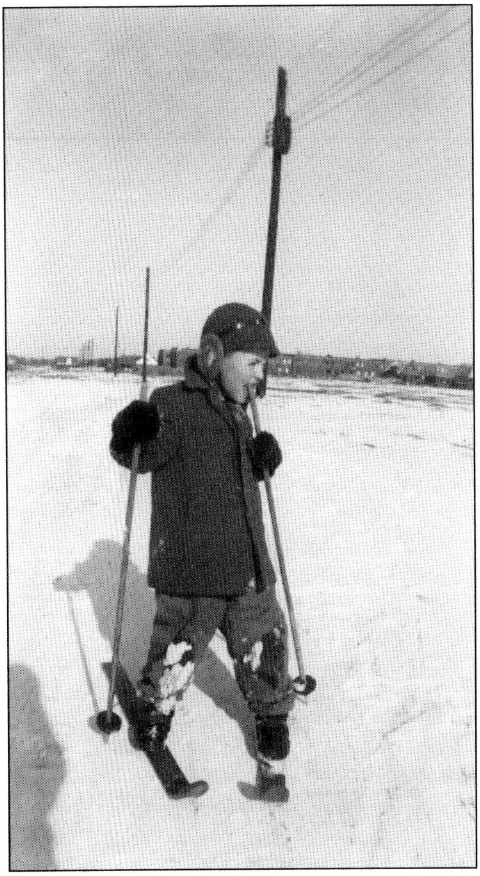

Billy Lederer, age six, plays on his skis in the 1948 snowstorm. Since Billy's grandfather, Peter Gannon, had purchased the property before most of the major development in Laurelton, it was never graded and therefore, it was several feet higher than the surrounding properties, which were all leveled. This provided the Lederers with their own bunny hill. (Courtesy of Bill and Larry Lederer.)

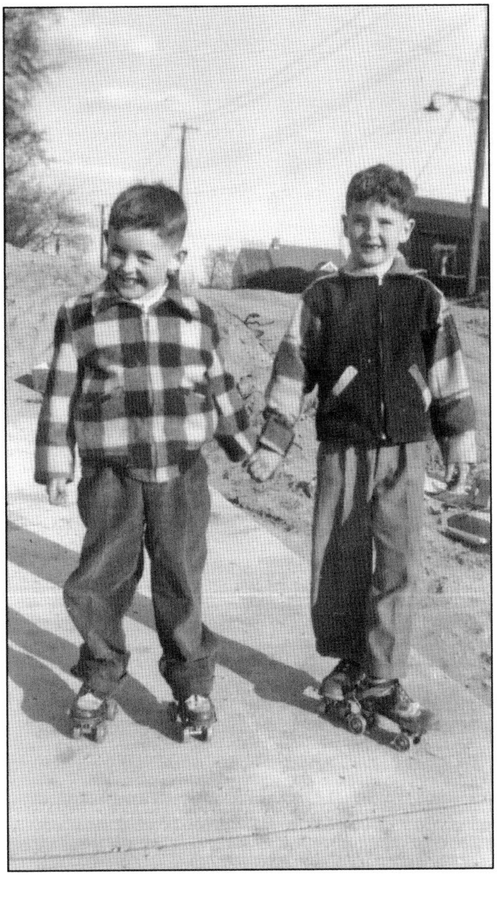

Billy Lederer (left) and brother Larry Lederer skate down the incline on their grandfather's property on 129th Avenue. From this photograph, the elevation of the family's property over the surrounding area can be seen. (Courtesy of Bill and Larry Lederer.)

Jay Harris (left) and Mark Weinblatt discuss strategy for their punchball game in 1962 on 227th Street. Games such as this were regularly impromptu and organized by the players themselves, often entering into protracted negotiations about what was considered out of bounds and the placement of bases. Much of this activity took place in the street, with players keeping a vigilant eye out for oncoming cars. (Courtesy of Reba Harris Solomon.)

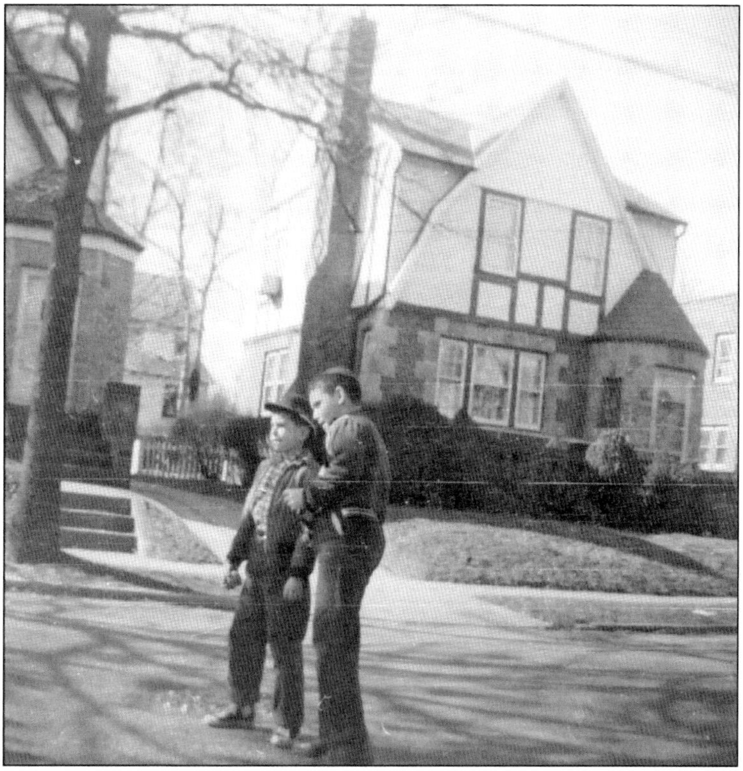

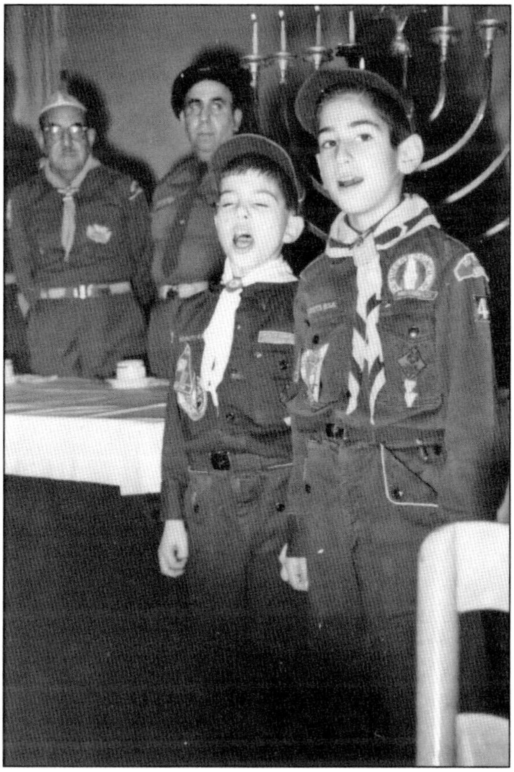

Jay Harris (left) and Gary Katz belt out their rendition of "I Had A Little Dreidel" at the Young Israel of Laurelton's Hanukkah celebration in 1961. (Courtesy of Reba Harris Solomon.)

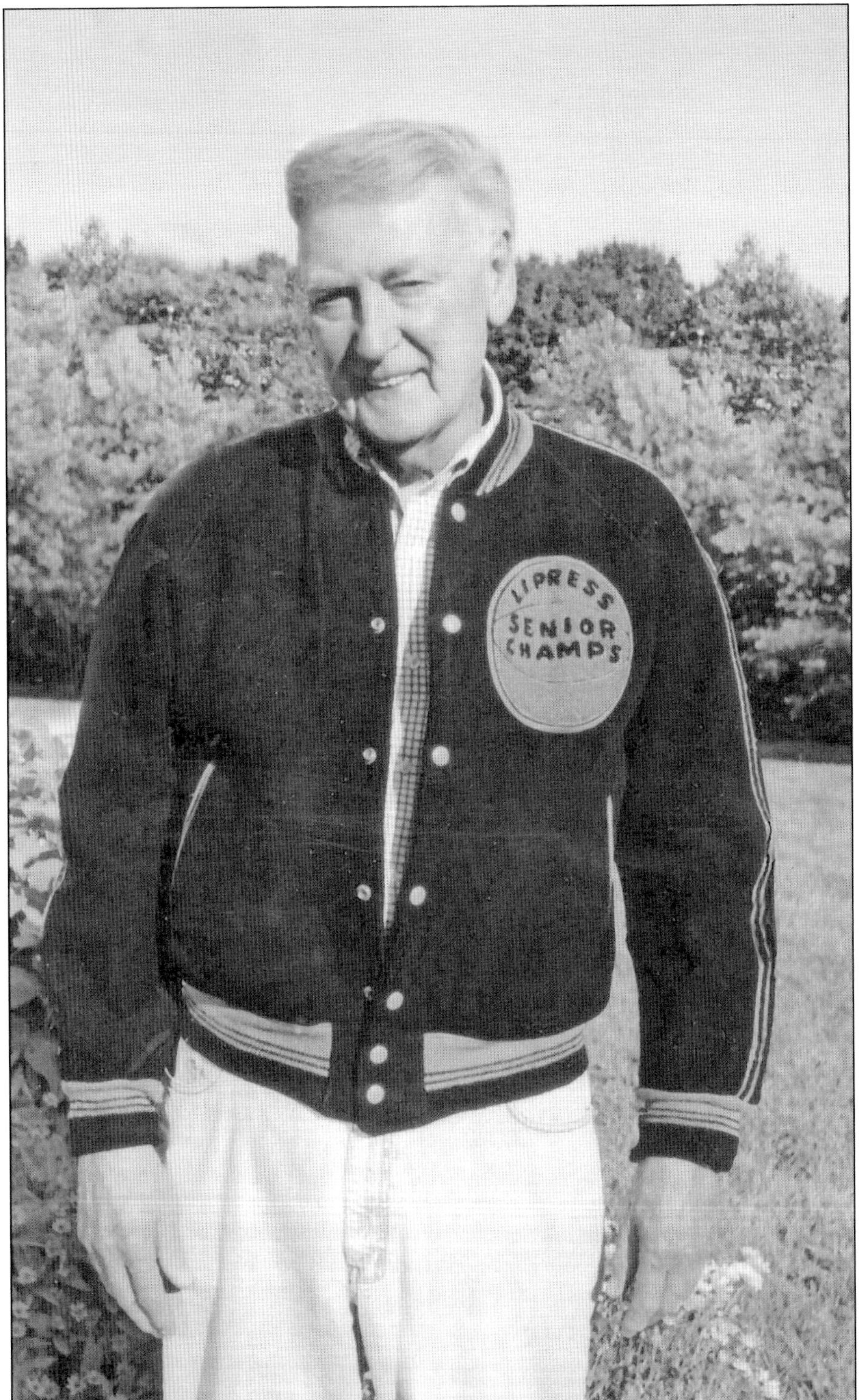

Harvey Teichert sports his Long Island Press championship jacket, which still fits after 40-plus years. (Courtesy of Tom Smith.)

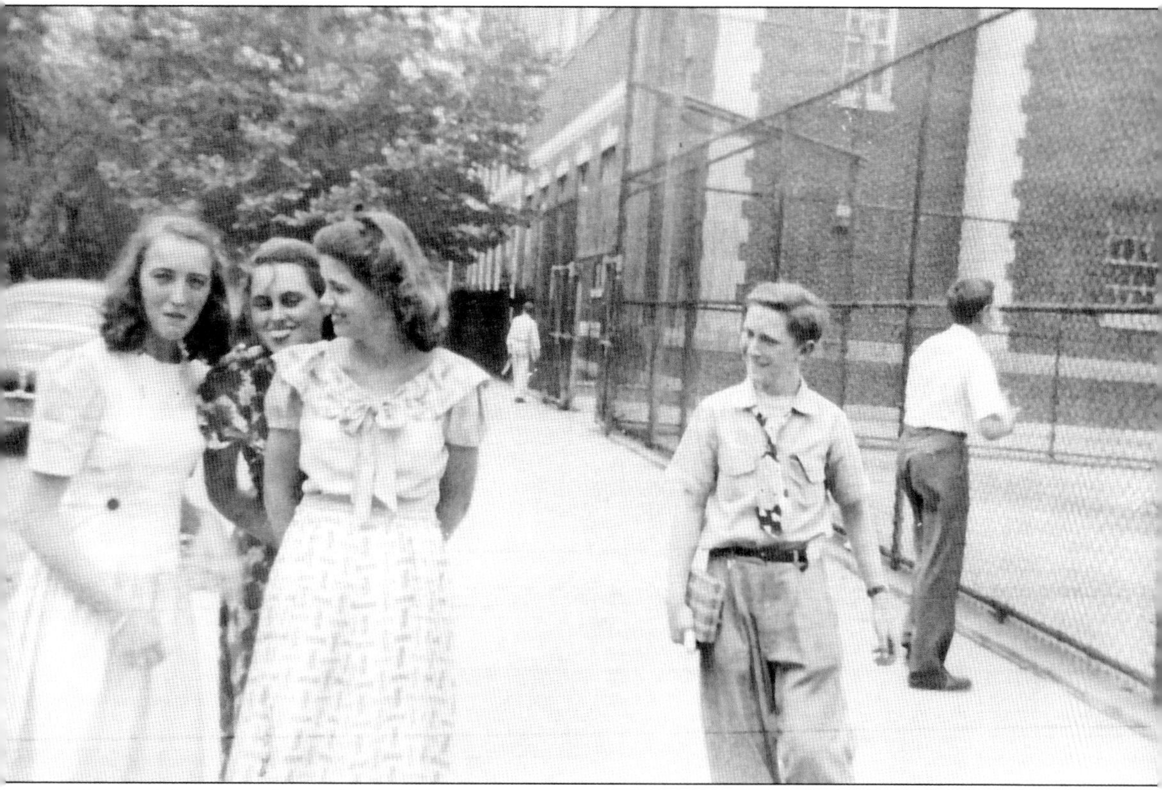

This is 228th Street behind P.S. 156, next to its playground, on graduation day in 1948. The girls to the left are Pat Baldwin, Florence Keller, and Valerie English. To the right is an unidentified student carrying the telltale sign of a senior—his plaid autograph book. (Courtesy of Tom Smith.)

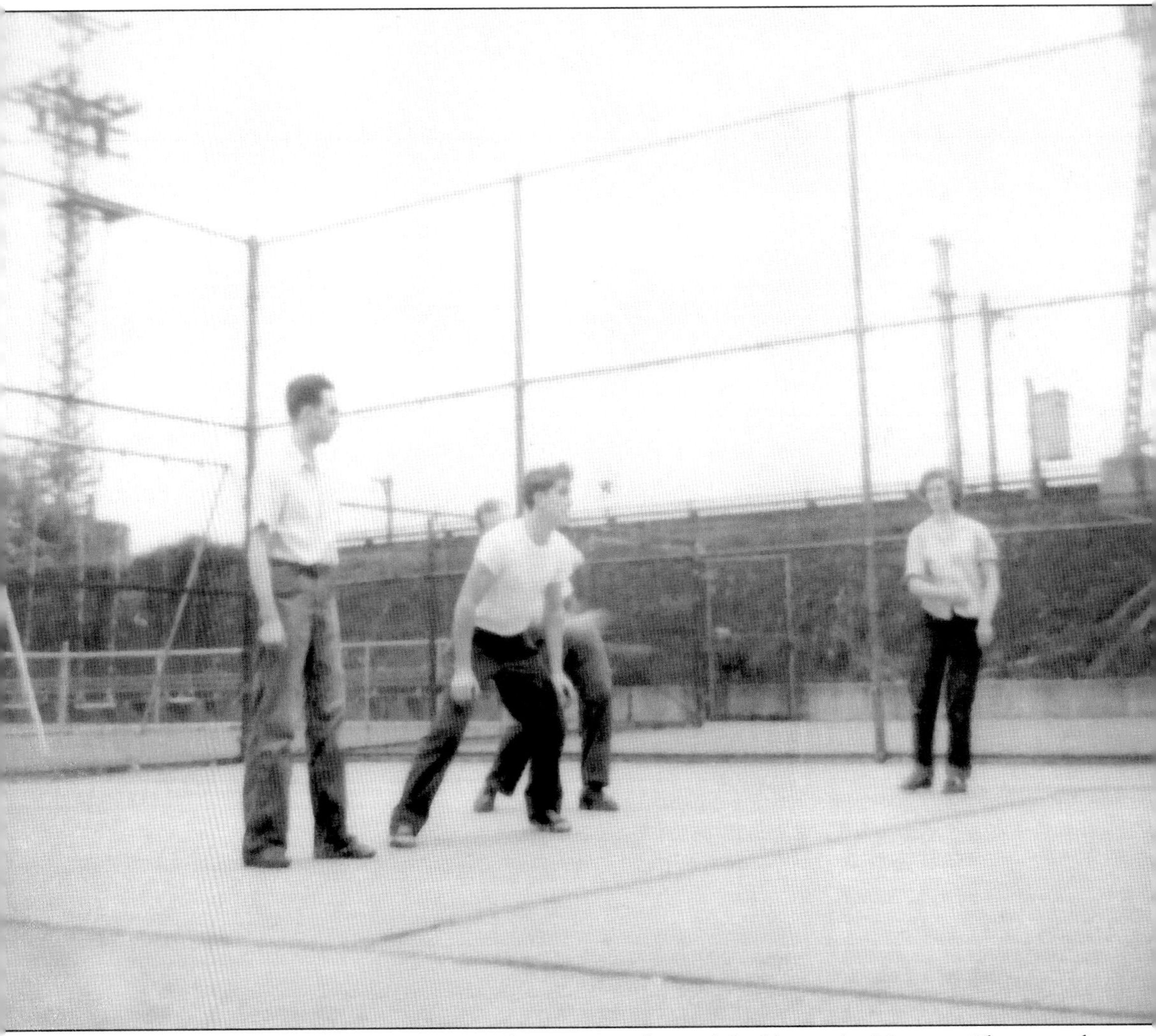

Taken in 1953, this group of teenagers plays a game of mixed doubles at the Mentone Playground handball courts. Pictured from left to right are "Slick" Charlie, Tom Smith, Larry Ross, and Trudy Byrnes. In the background, the adult swings of the playground and the beam for the recently elevated Long Island Rail Road tracks can be seen. (Courtesy of Tom Smith.)

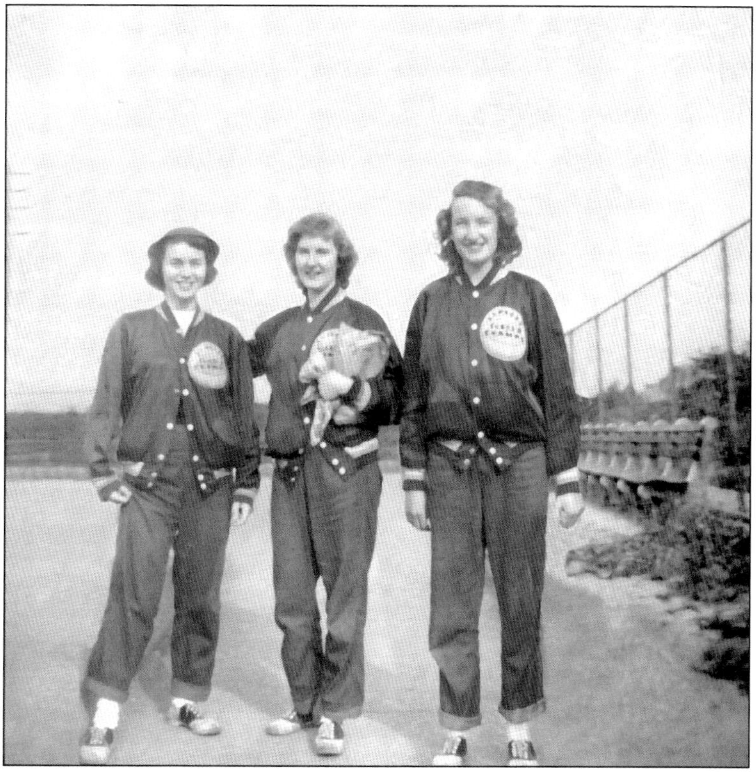

This picture was taken in 1952 at Mentone Playground on North Conduit Avenue. Three members of the Mentone girls' basketball team are sporting championship jackets they obtained by winning the Class B Division of the Long Island Press basketball league. Pictured from left to right are Pat Baumgardner, Trudy Byrnes, and Carolyn Crossley. (Courtesy of Tom Smith.)

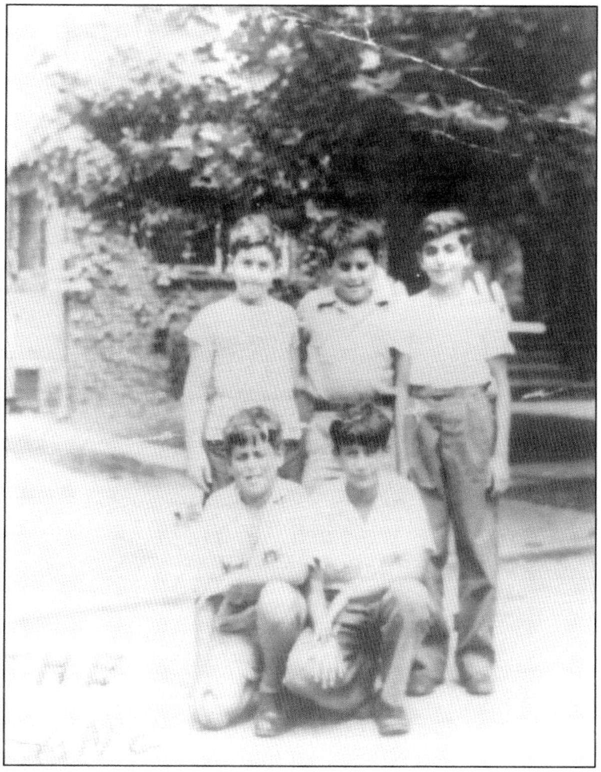

The Laurelton children in the 1945 photograph at left are, from left to right, (first row) Alan Frommer, age nine, and David Lippner; (second row) Alan "Drippy" Waters (also seen in the Elks basketball team photograph), Alan's twin brother Paul, and Bob Yaffe. (Courtesy of Paul Frommer.)

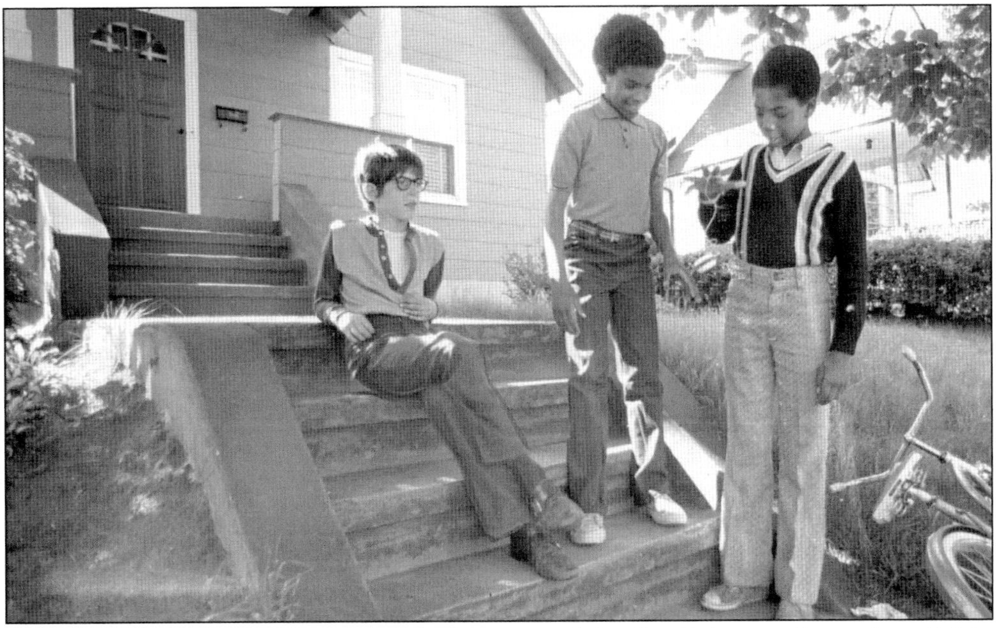

Above is Alan Goldman, age 12, sitting on the steps, with Lindley Farley, age 11, watching Calvin Shedrick, age 11, work his yo-yo magic in 1971. This photograph was published by the *Long Island Press* in a series of articles that portrayed Laurelton as a successfully integrated community. (Courtesy of Condé Nast Publications.)

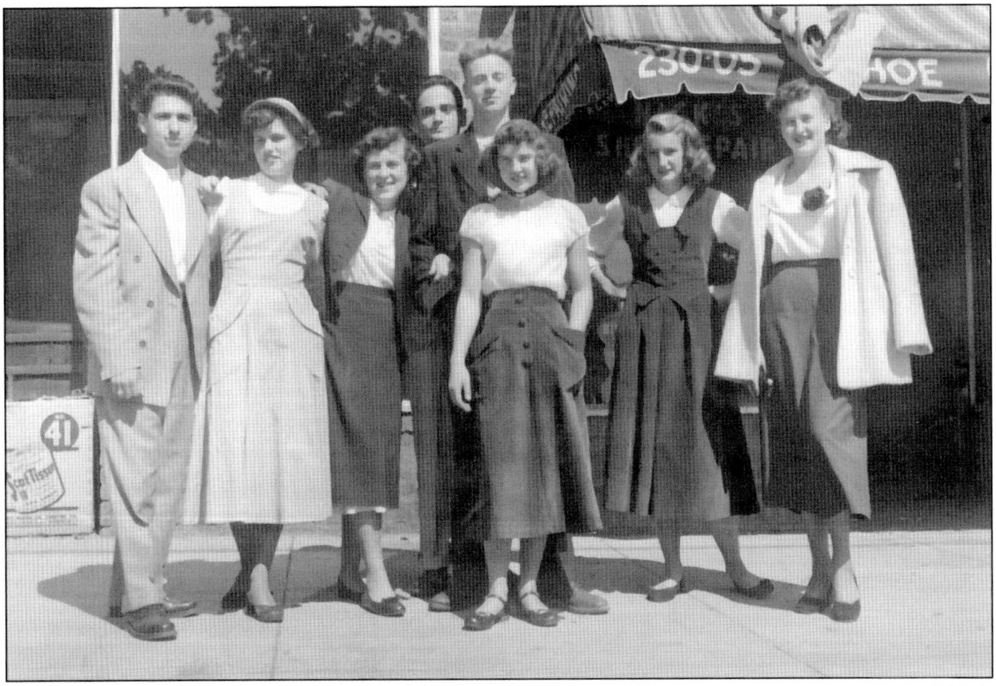

This scene of Easter Sunday morning after church was taken in 1955 on 141st Avenue near 230th Street. A group of Mentones gather in front of Nick Cavuoto's Shoe Repair Shop. Pictured from left to right are Dom Danna, Valerie English, Jacqueline Tressay, John Pereyo, Charlie Eichhorn, Pat Keane, Carolyn Crossley, and Lucille Tressay. (Courtesy of Tom Smith.)

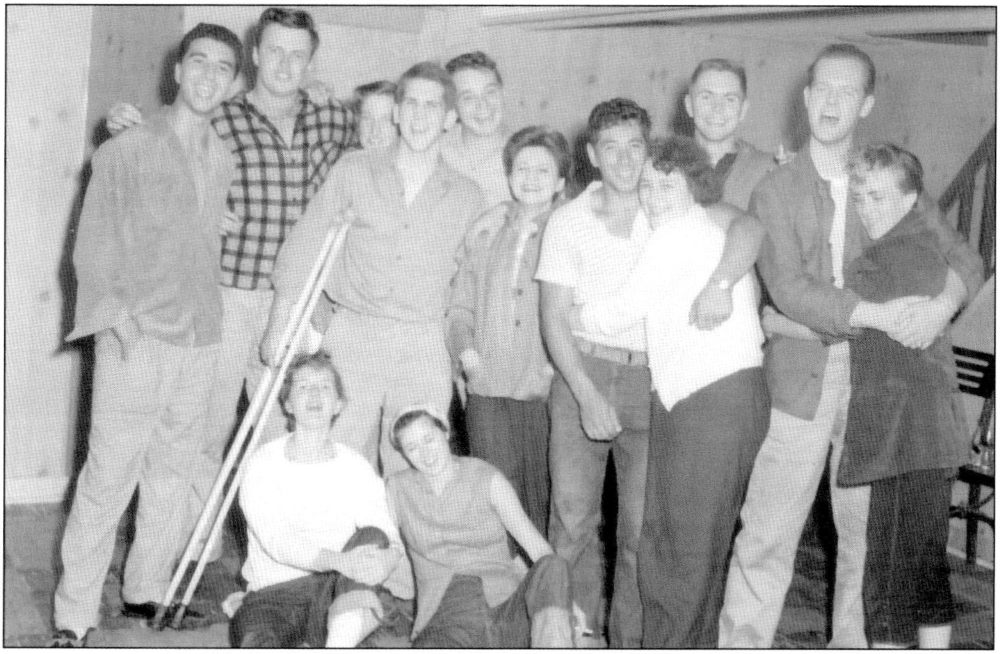

Taken in 1954, this photograph shows a typical seasonal Mentone party. This party was held in the finished basement of the Grasso residence on 231st Street between 141st Avenue and 139th Avenue. Maurice "Junior" Grasso, on the left with his hand in his pocket, is the host. Tom Smith is leaning on crutches due to a broken leg. (Courtesy of Tom Smith.)

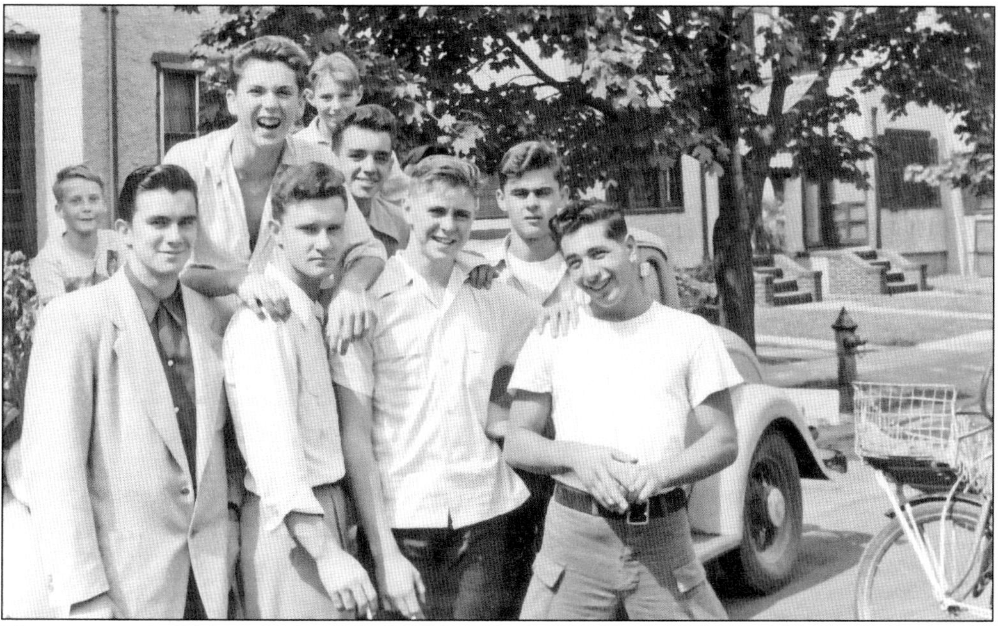

This image was taken outside of the Smith and Giordano residences at 232nd Street and 141st Avenue. Standing in front of a 1934 White Plymouth Coupe Rumble Seat are (first row) Frank Thomas, John Byrnes, Jack Austin, and John Giordano; (second row) Bruce Bleeck, Eddie Carroll, and Jack Marr; (third row) Bobby Peterson and Kenny Oliver. Note the bike with the wide basket and balloon tires, typical of those used by delivery boys. (Courtesy of Tom Smith.)

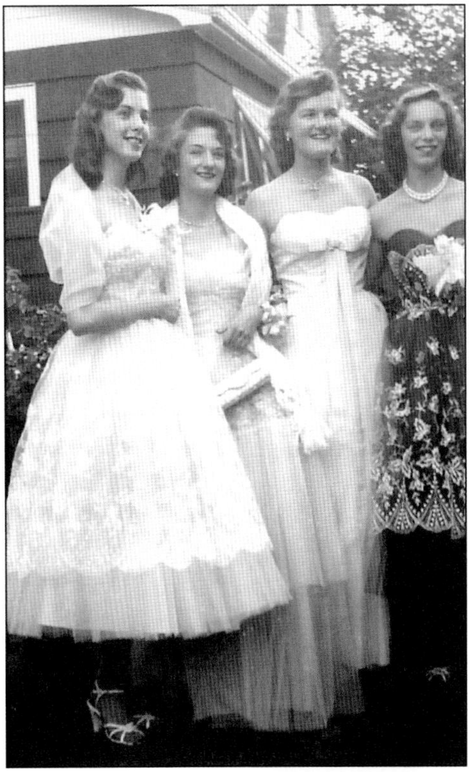

This was taken in front of the Crossley residence at 229th Street and 141st Avenue during the night of the Andrew Jackson High School prom in 1954. Pictured from left to right are Anita Voss, Phyllis Crossley, Catherine Brede, and Peggy Voll. (Courtesy of Tom Smith.)

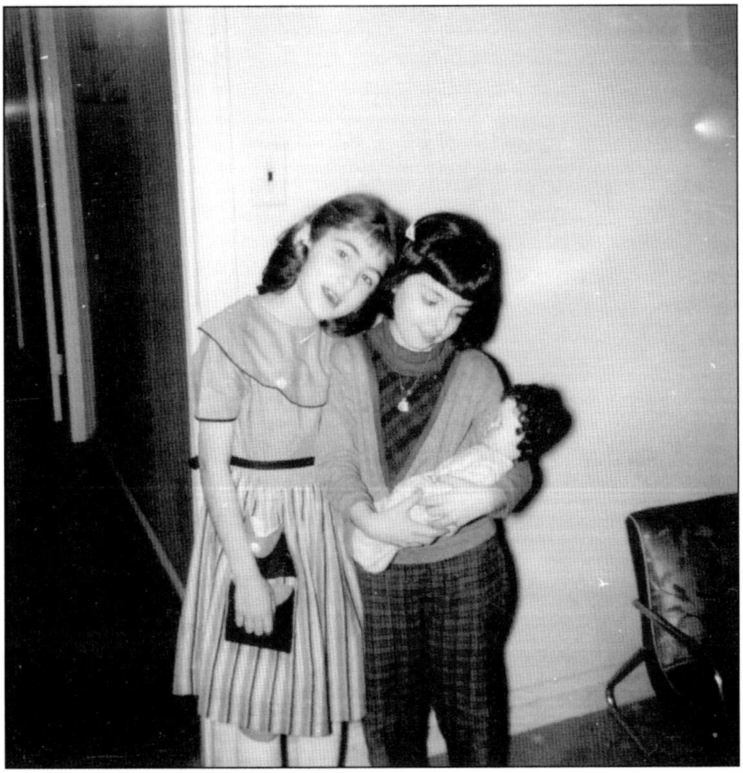

Reba Harris (right) cradles her Betsy Wetsy doll while her friend snuggles close in 1953. Although the doll had been introduced in the 1930s, its popularity spiked in the 1950s. Its claims to fame were its ability to urinate after drinking fluid and its separated toes. (Courtesy of Reba Harris Solomon.)

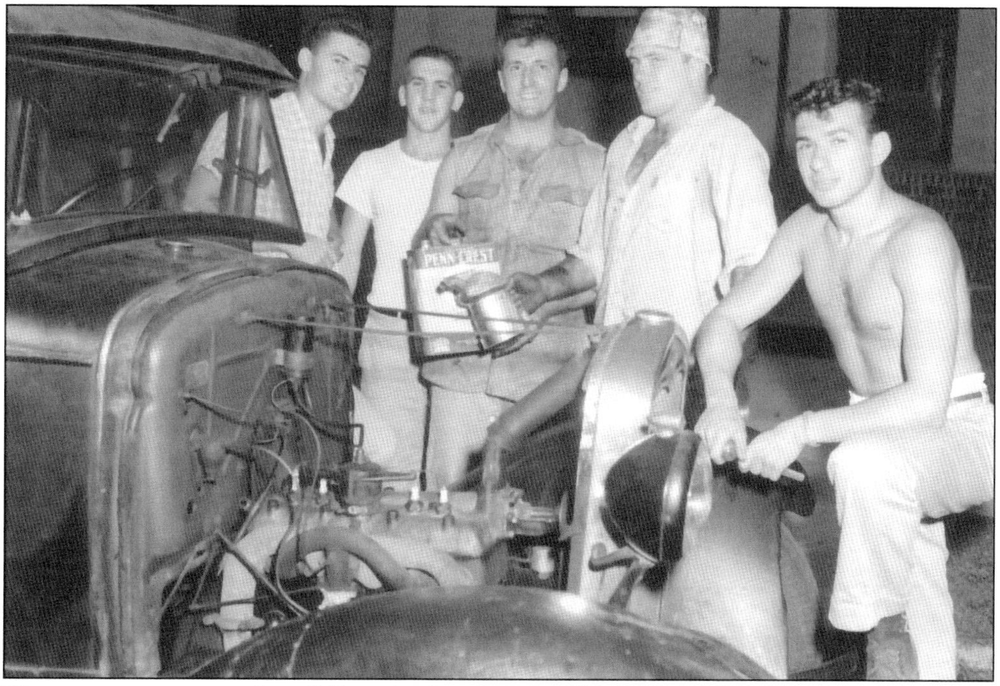

This scene was captured in 1952 at the Sangiorgio and Danna residences at 234th Street and Francis Lewis Boulevard. The vehicle is an early 1931 Standard Model A Ford Sedan. Pictured from left to right are Jack Marr, Tom Smith, Frank Sangiorgio, Denis Leary (car owner), and Dom Danna. (Courtesy of Tom Smith.)

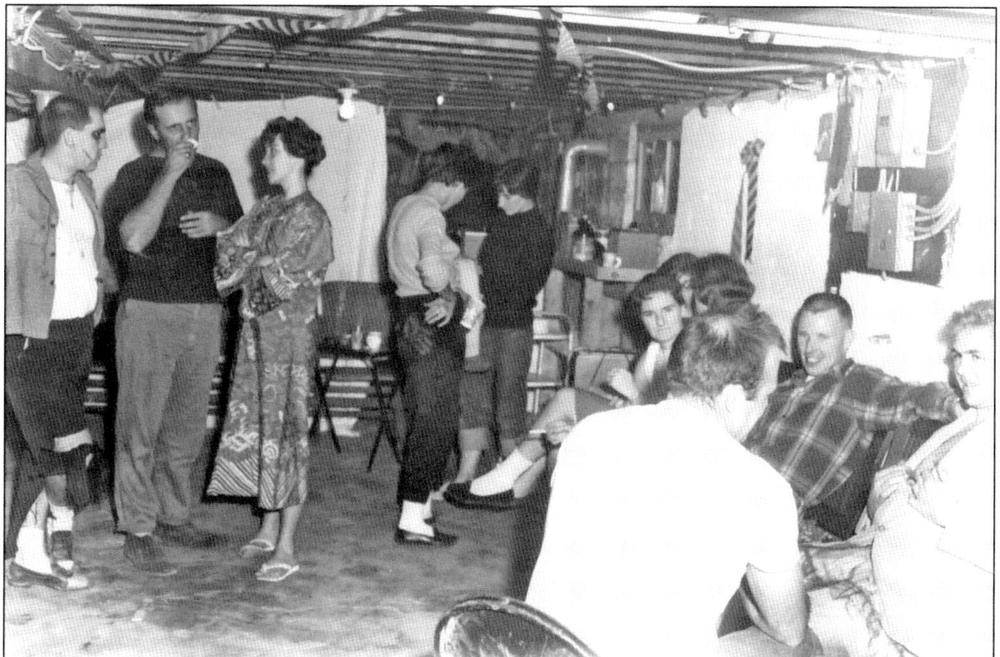

This was a 1955 Halloween costume party in the unfinished seven-foot-high basement of the Giordanos' Spanish-style house. (Courtesy of Tom Smith.)

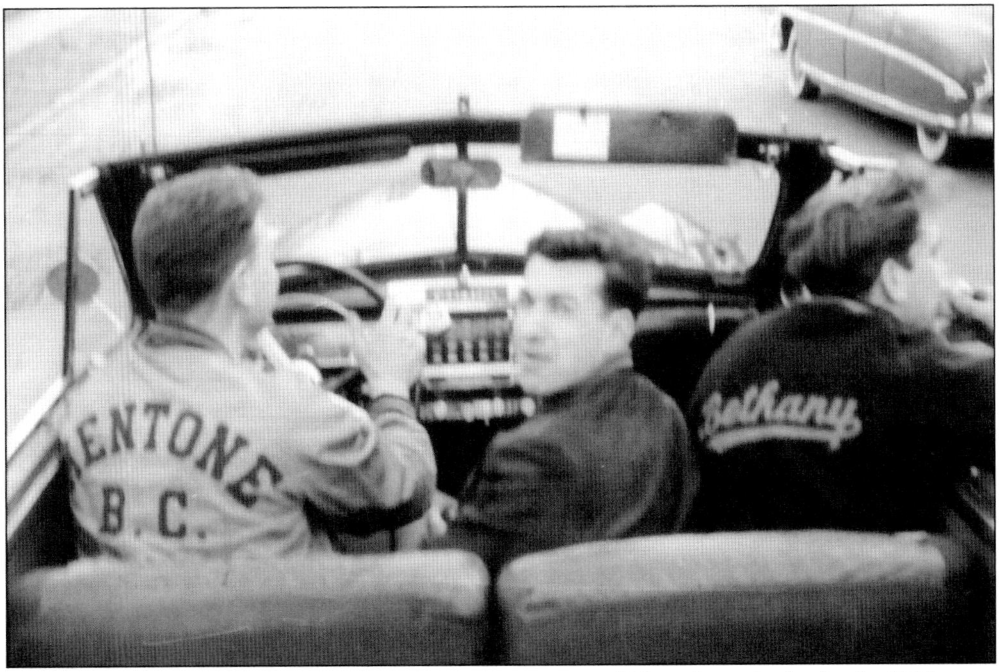

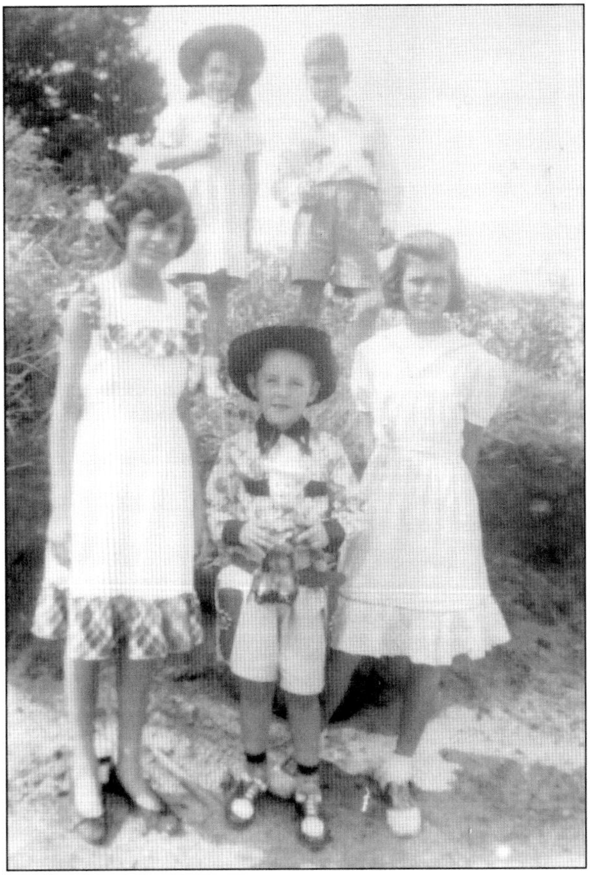

Taken from the back of a 1948 Chrysler Town and Country with fluid drive, owner and driver Harvey Teichert is wearing his Mentone Boys Club basketball jacket. Dom Danna is in the middle, and Tom Smith is on the right, wearing his Bethany Lutheran Church basketball jacket. (Courtesy of Tom Smith.)

Billy Lederer holds his Roy Rodgers doll while he poses with his friends on the Gannon property. Cowboys and sheriffs were considered cultural and romantic figures during the time.

Judy Rosenberg models a summer sunsuit in front of her new home at 229th Street in 1950. Her father, Artie, ran Hutt's Fish Market on Merrick Road, just up the block.

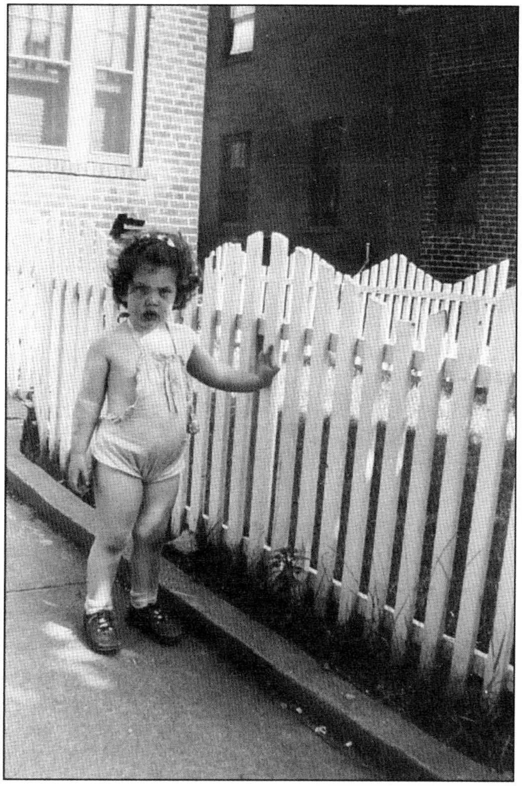

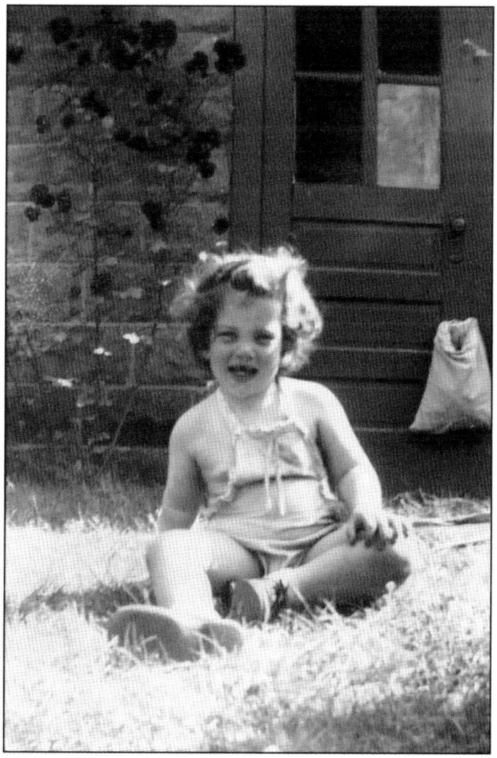

Judy Rosenberg is seen again in her sunsuit in the backyard. Behind her is the cloth bag that held the clothespins, sitting in front of the garage. Also visible are Artie Rosenberg's prized roses climbing up the garage wall.

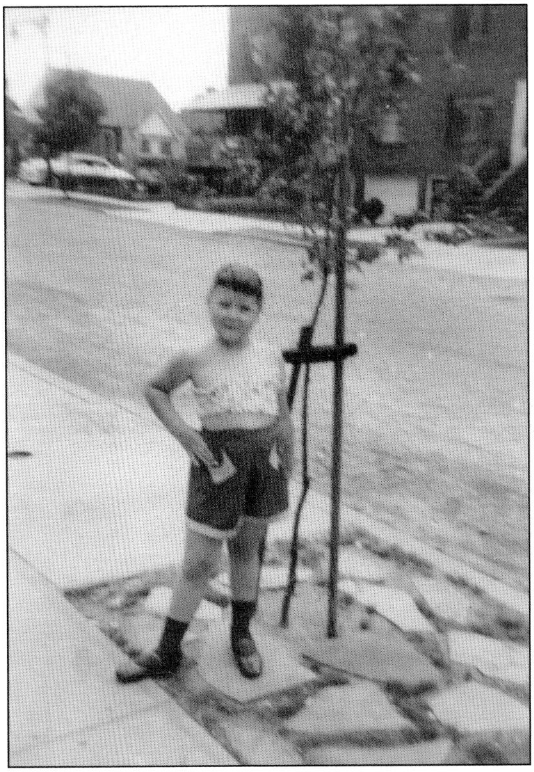

Barbara Miller is pictured in 1954 outside her house at 231-25 125th Avenue. This was the last block in Laurelton before Cambria Heights. She is nine years old. (Courtesy of Ron Miller.)

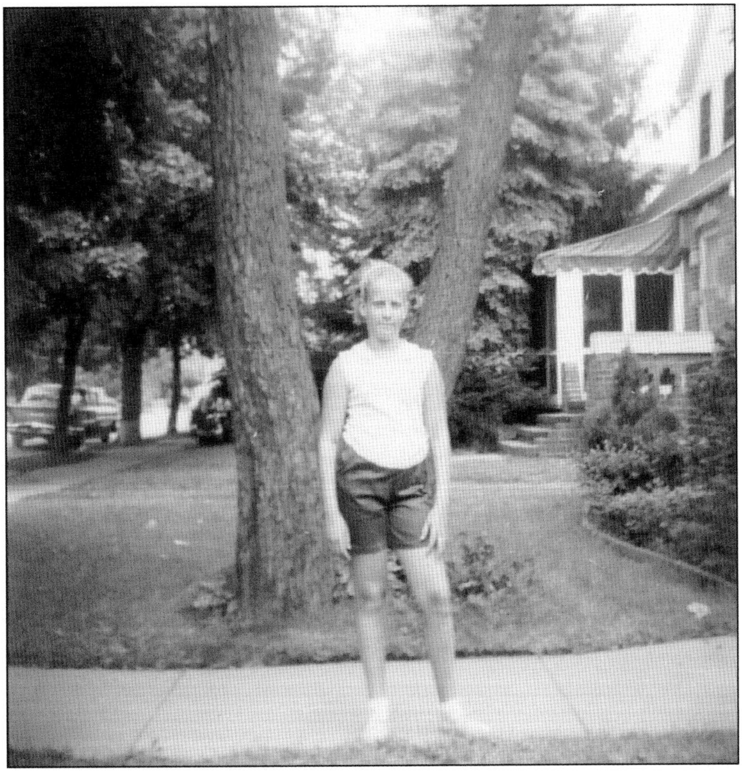

This is Marilyn Povodator in front of 135-25 227th Street, the home of her friend Reba Harris. This photograph was taken during the summer when many of Laurelton's children did not need day camps or much in the way of structured activity to stay busy all summer long. For example, Reba Harris and her friends spent long hours digging up the Harrises' backyard to make a miniature golf course. (Courtesy of Reba Harris Solomon.)

Sam Miller is pictured in his backyard while a neighbor's laundry dries on the line behind him. Laurelton home owners, most of whom had been city dwellers, loved their backyards, which were used for everything from laundry to barbecues to shooting baskets. (Courtesy of Ron Miller.)

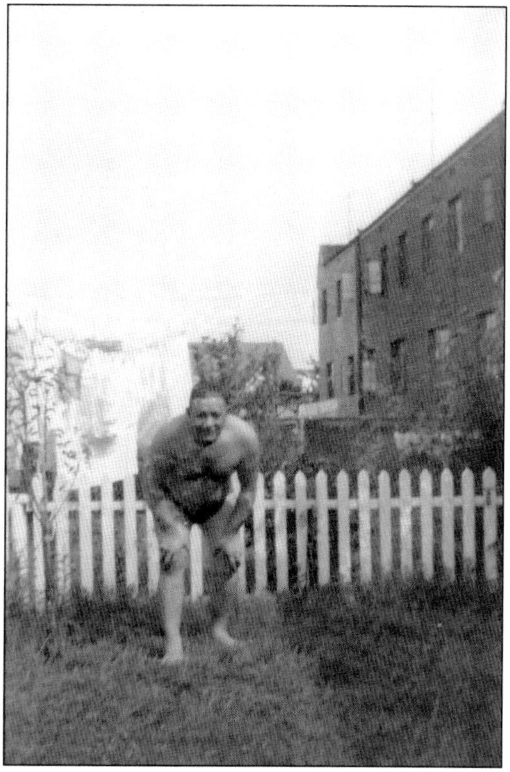

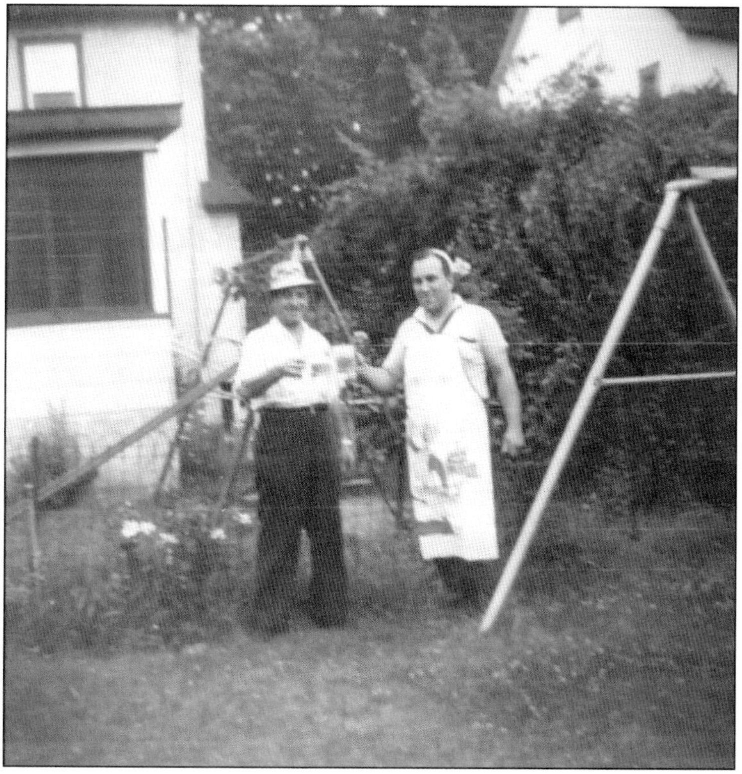

Jack Harris and his father-in-law, Sam Lesan hoist mugs of frosty cold beer during a backyard family barbecue in 1962. (Courtesy of Reba Harris Solomon.)

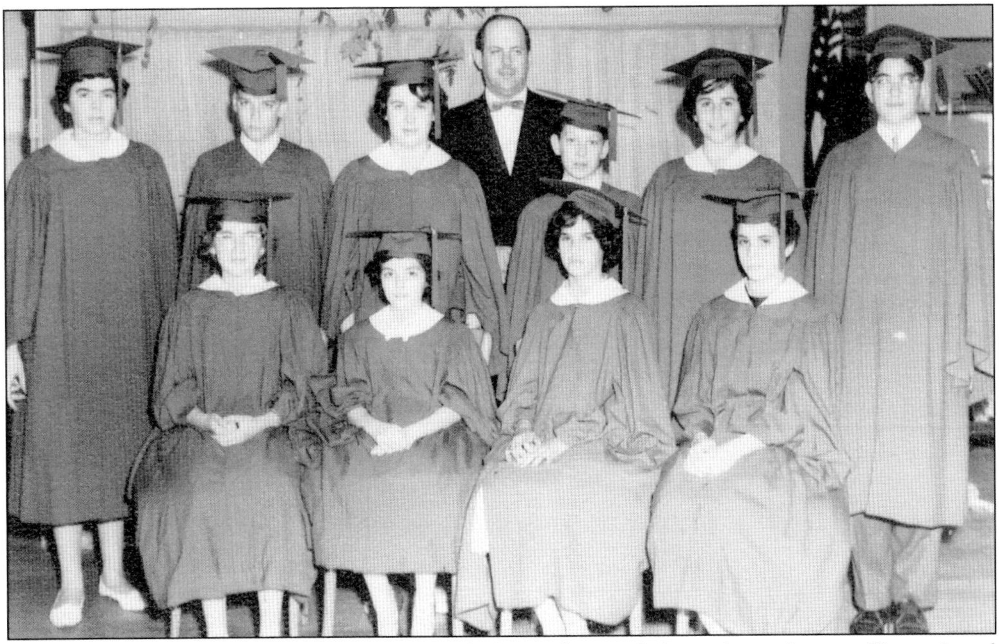

This is a photograph of the 1962 Young Israel of Laurelton eighth-grade graduation. Young Israel was an orthodox congregation and was one of four major synagogues in Laurelton. Pictured here from left to right are (first row) Merrill Silverstein, Reba Harris, Laurie Abraham, and Lynette Brown; (second row) Esther Fried, Kenny Povodator, Marianne Bayer, Larry Rutta, and two unidentified graduates; (third row) Rabbi Saul Romineck. The most well-attended synagogue in Laurelton was the conservative Laurelton Jewish Center, followed by Temple Beth-El and the Jewish Community House. (Courtesy of Reba Harris Solomon.)

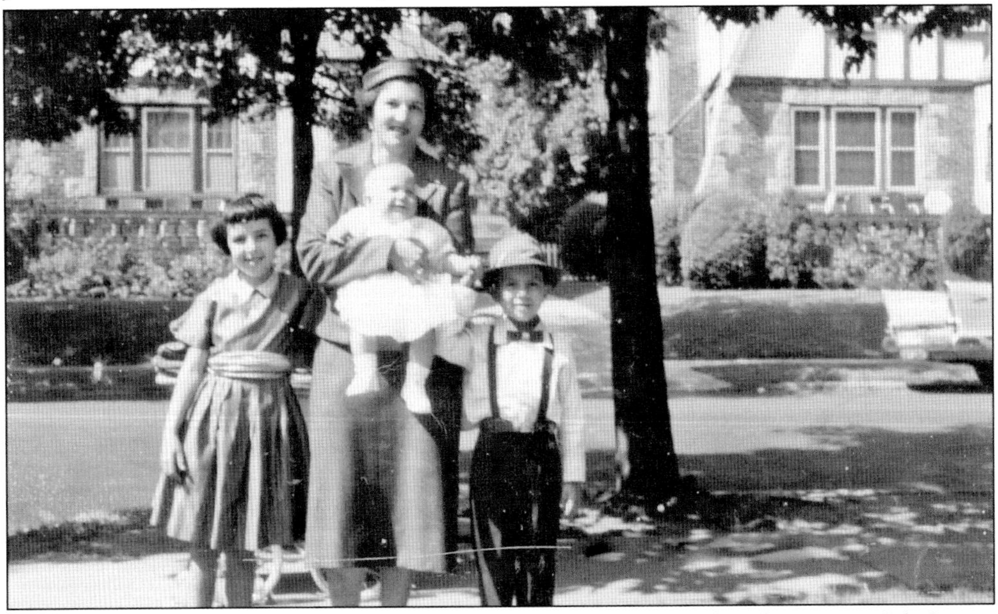

The Harris family, dressed for an occasion in 1957, poses outside their house at 227th Street. At left is Reba Harris, Sally Harris holds Hope Harris, and Jay Harris looks quite dapper in his Panamanian hat. (Courtesy of Reba Harris Solomon.)

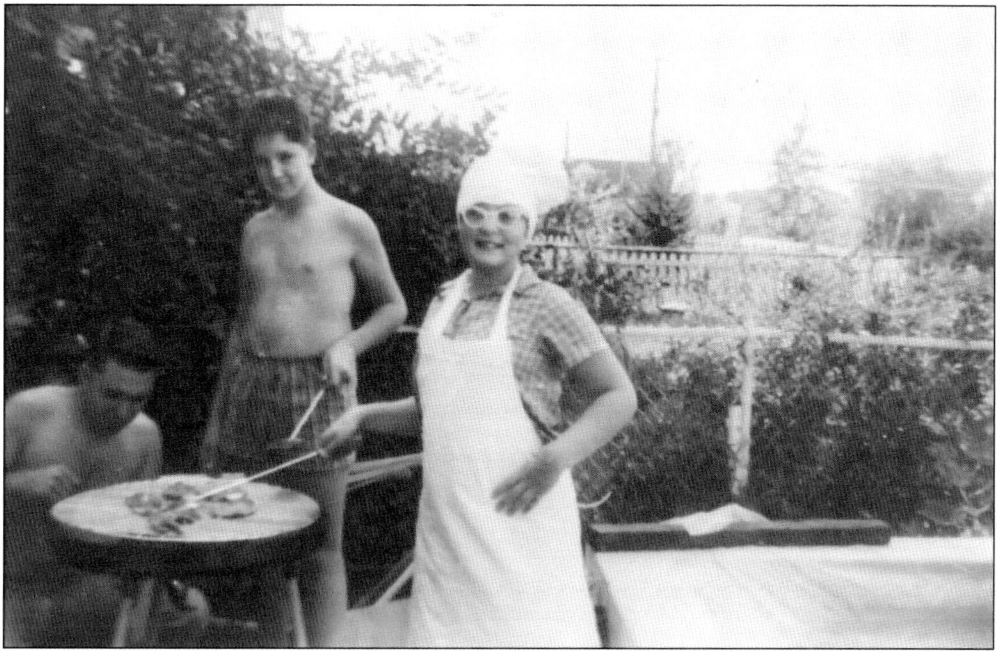

Barbara Miller grills up some chicken for her brother Ron and cousin Harvey Miller in 1959. Notice the cement-block pool built by her father and brother covered in the background. They were the only family on the block with their own pool. (Courtesy of Ron Miller.)

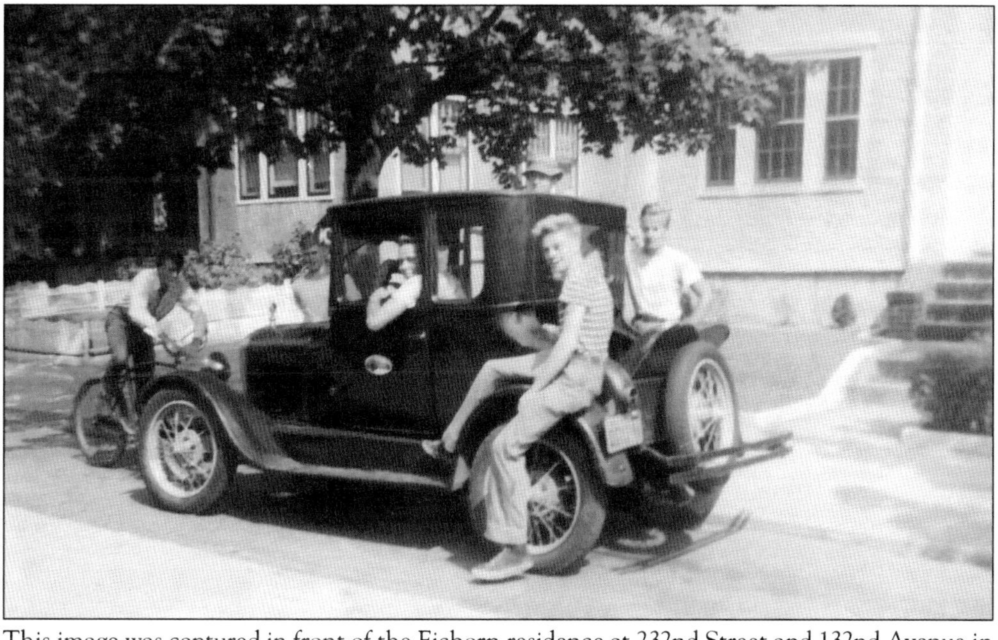

This image was captured in front of the Eichorn residence at 232nd Street and 132nd Avenue in 1950. Pictured from the left are Freddy Douglas (on bike), Jack Austin (standing by right front wheel), Billy Brennan (owner of the Model T Ford in the driver's seat), Denis Leary (peaking over the top of the car), Charlie Eichorn (sitting on the fender), and Larry Ross (standing by right rear wheel). This car had no starter; it had to be cranked to start and the choke and throttle were located on the steering wheel. (Courtesy of Tom Smith.)

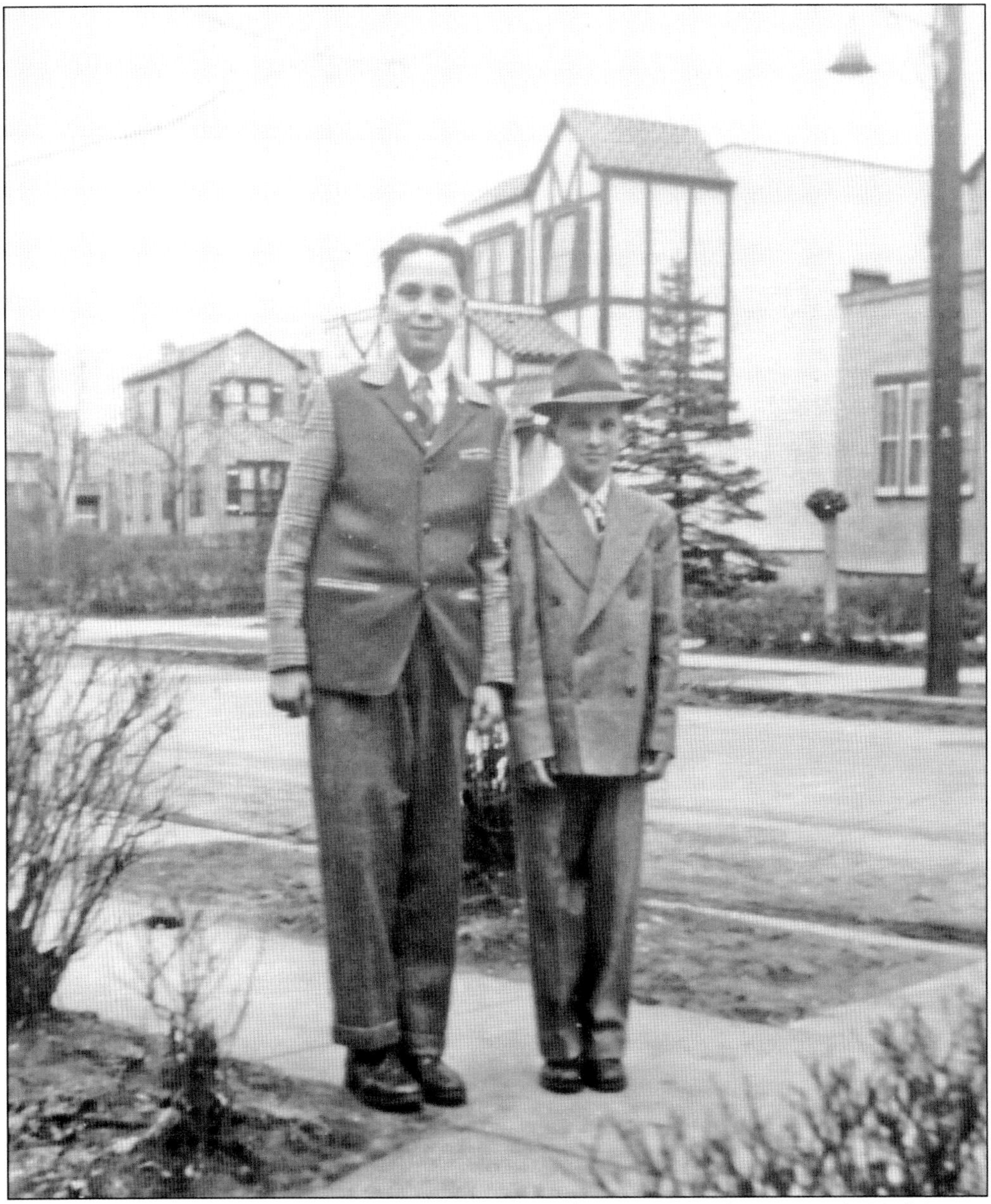

This 1955 photograph was taken on Mentone Avenue between 232nd Street and 233rd Street. Pictured from left to right are Wilfred Baisch and Jimmy Smith. (Courtesy of Tom Smith.)

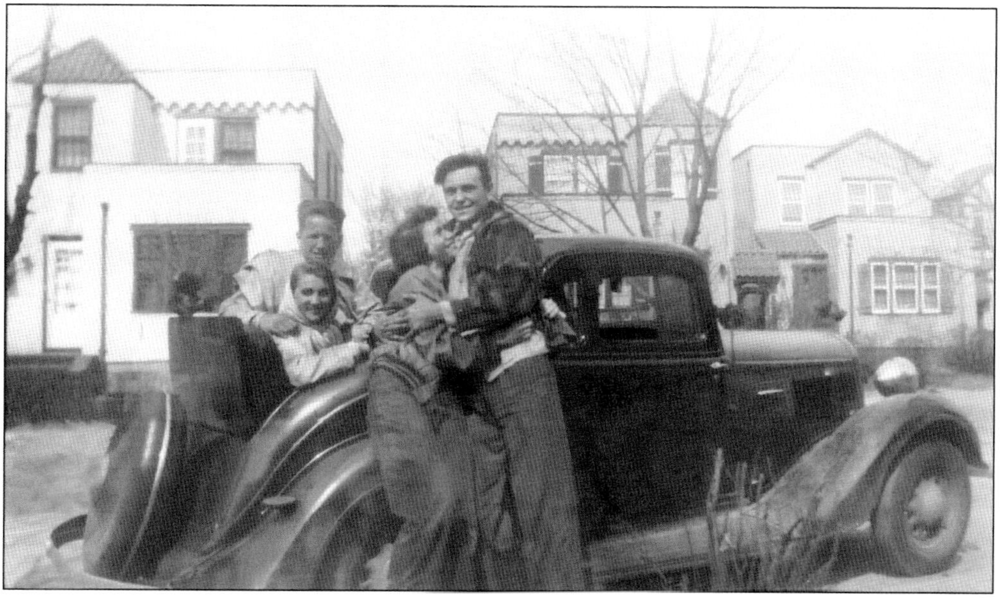

Pictured above in 1955 are Barbara Smith and Kermit Holmberg in the rumble seat, Pat Baumgardner, and Denis Leary, owner of the 1933 Plymouth Coupe They were photographed on Mentone Avenue between 232nd and 233rd Streets. (Courtesy of Tom Smith.)

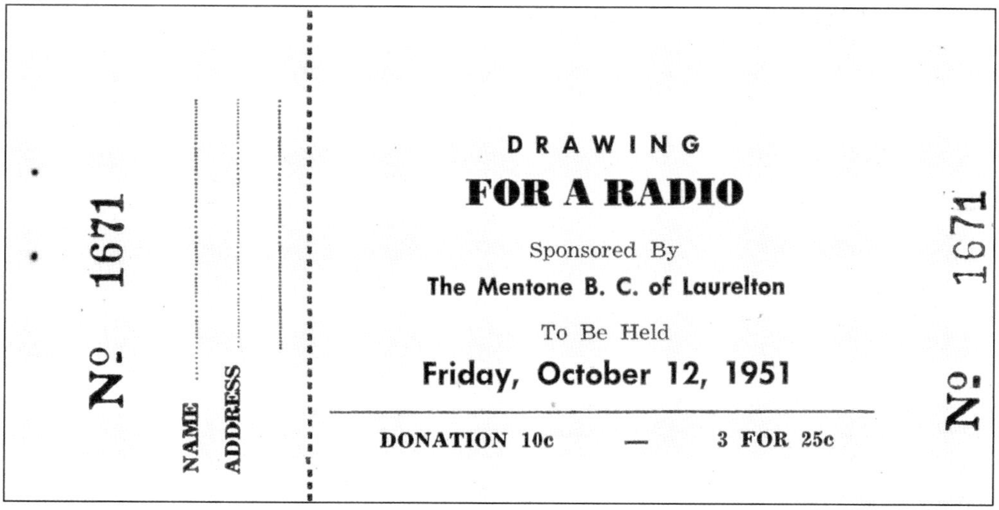

Nº 1671

NAME ....

ADDRESS ....

DRAWING

FOR A RADIO

Sponsored By

The Mentone B. C. of Laurelton

To Be Held

Friday, October 12, 1951

DONATION 10c — 3 FOR 25c

Nº 1671

The whole Mentone subculture had no adult supervision; it was all run by its teenage members. When it came to financing team uniforms for the basketball team, there were no commercial sponsors available to them. This is a copy of one of the raffle tickets sold by the boys on the Mentone basketball team to finance their team uniforms. (Courtesy of Tom Smith.)

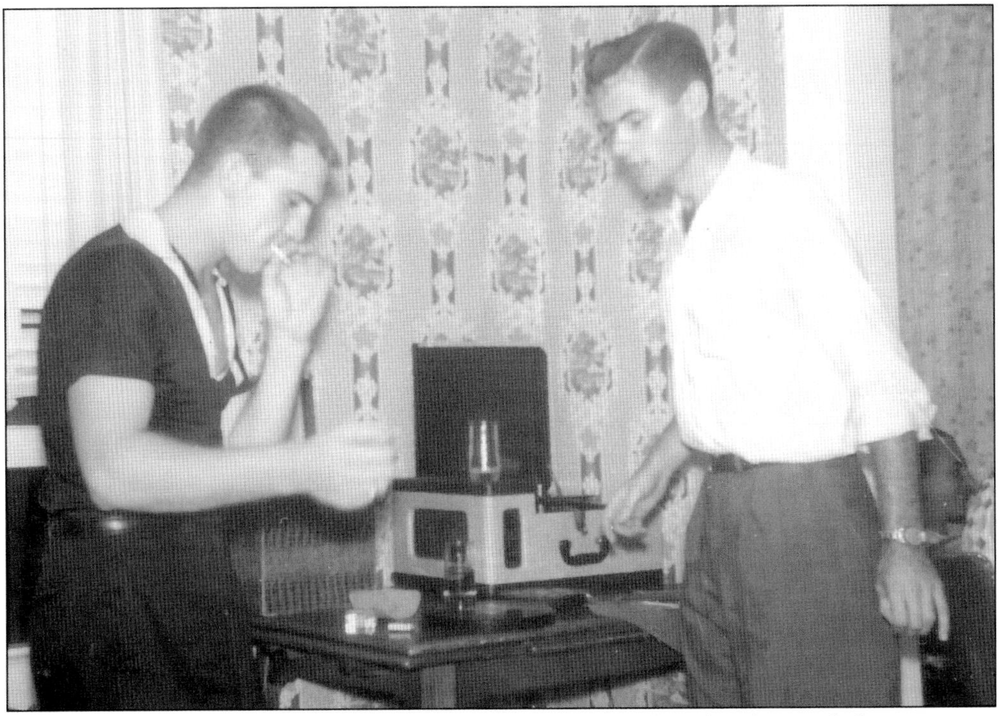

In this photograph, taken at a 1953 seasonal party, Tom Smith and Jack Marr light a cigarette and change the 33 rpm record, the high fidelity of its day. (Courtesy of Tom Smith.)

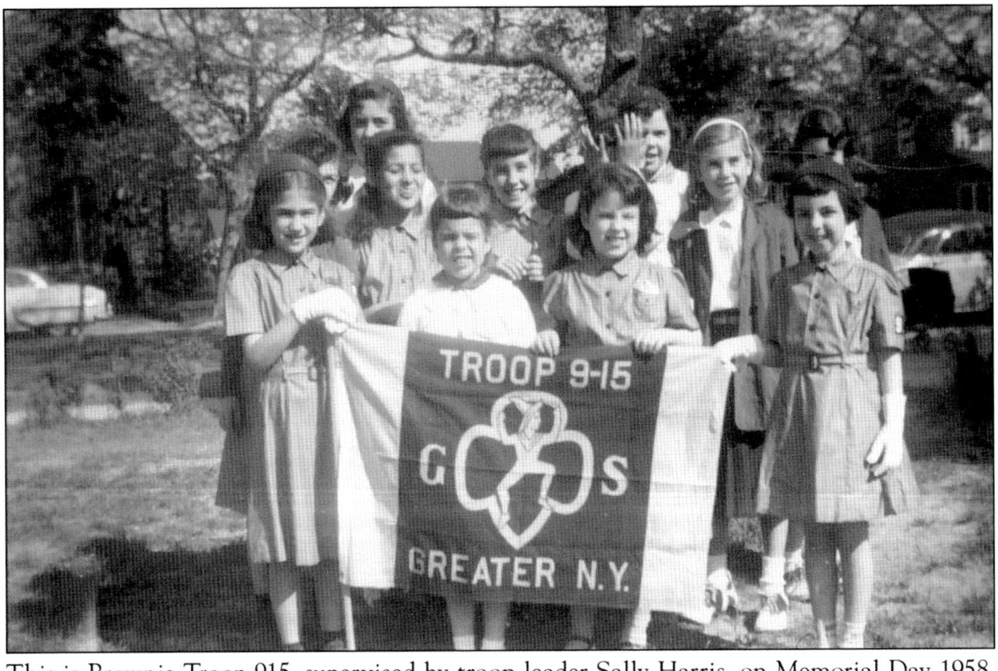

This is Brownie Troop 915, supervised by troop leader Sally Harris, on Memorial Day 1958. Pictured from left to right are (first row) Paula Katz, Phyllis Fried (the mascot), Dorris Kreisler, and Reba Harris; (second row) Ruth Gluckman, two unidentified Scouts, and Merrill Silverstein; (third row) Rena Perlman and Esther Fried. (Courtesy of Reba Harris Solomon.)

Three

Blockbusting and a Time of Change

Blockbusting is an objectionable scheme used by unethical real estate brokers to convince a stable neighborhood that is it about to undergo drastic change. The agents persuade the residents to sell their homes to them cheap before it is too late to salvage any of the home's accumulated equity. These brokers then resell the properties for outlandish profits to the new homeowners. White homeowners in Laurelton were susceptible to these tactics during the 1970s, and many left for points east on Long Island or elsewhere in the tristate area. As a result of blockbusting in Laurelton, legislation was passed that made such activities illegal in New York. However, a federal court later reversed the decision on the grounds that it infringed on the free speech rights of the agents. Immediately, blockbusting began in New Hyde Park, but the residents, remembering Laurelton, stood firmly against it and the attempt failed.

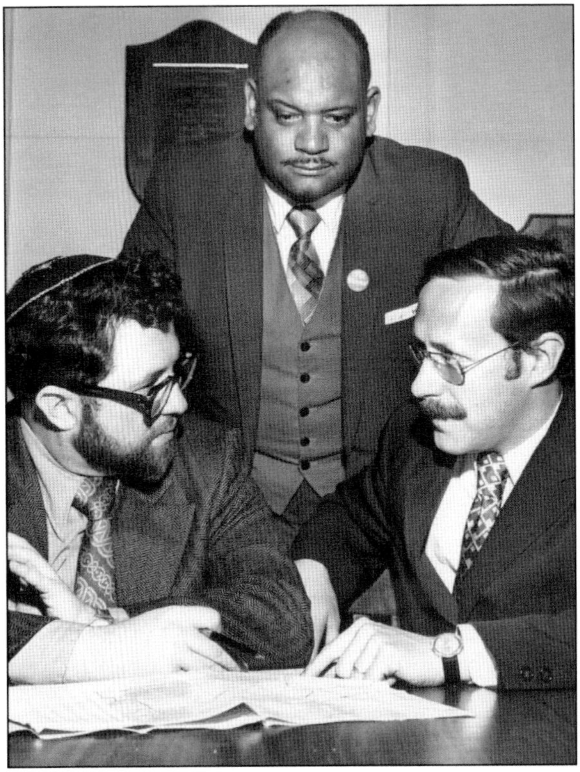

Pictured here seated on the left is Rabbi Sam Schrage, the director of the Neighborhood Action Program, meeting with Alan Hessel, also seated, the director of the Laurelton Branch of the Neighborhood Action Program, and assistant director Russell Washington, standing. (Courtesy Queens Borough Public Library Long Island Division.)

Russell Washington and Alan Hessel (below) stand outside the Neighborhood Action Program office on Merrick Road in Laurelton. Hessel was from Laurelton and took a leave of absence from his job as a pharmaceutical salesman in order to run this branch. There were other Neighborhood Action Programs in places that were also undergoing transition like Washington Heights and the South Bronx. (Courtesy of Queens Borough Public Library, Long Island Division.)

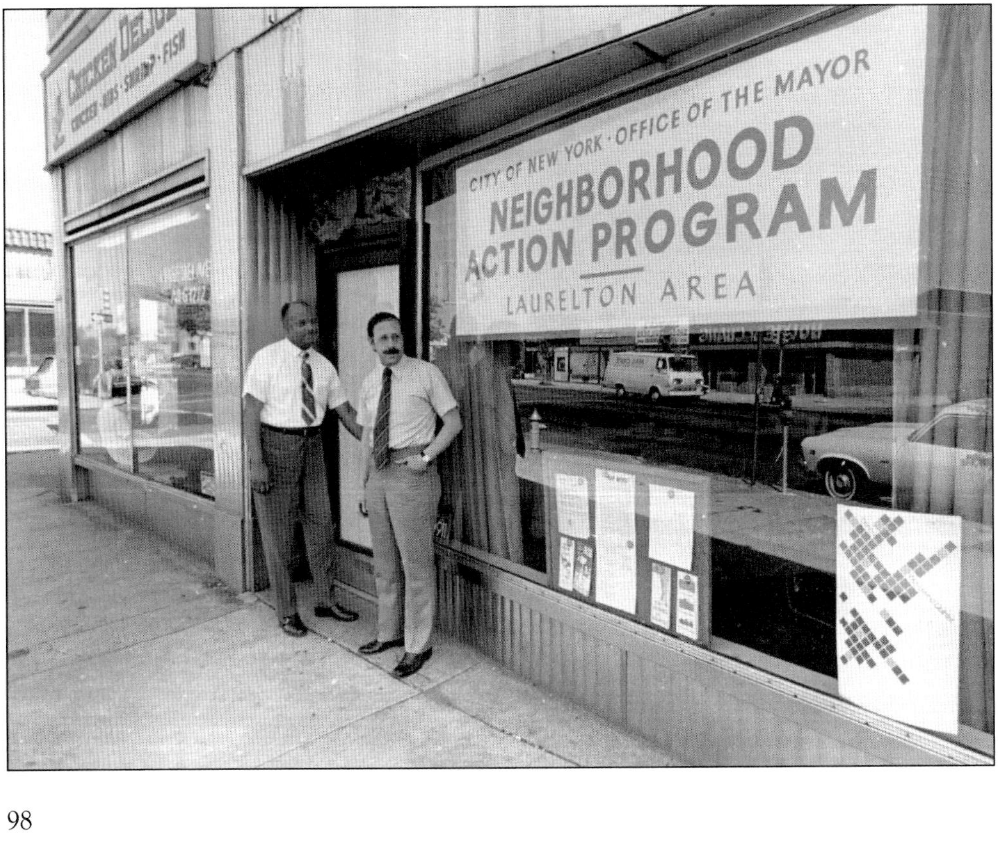

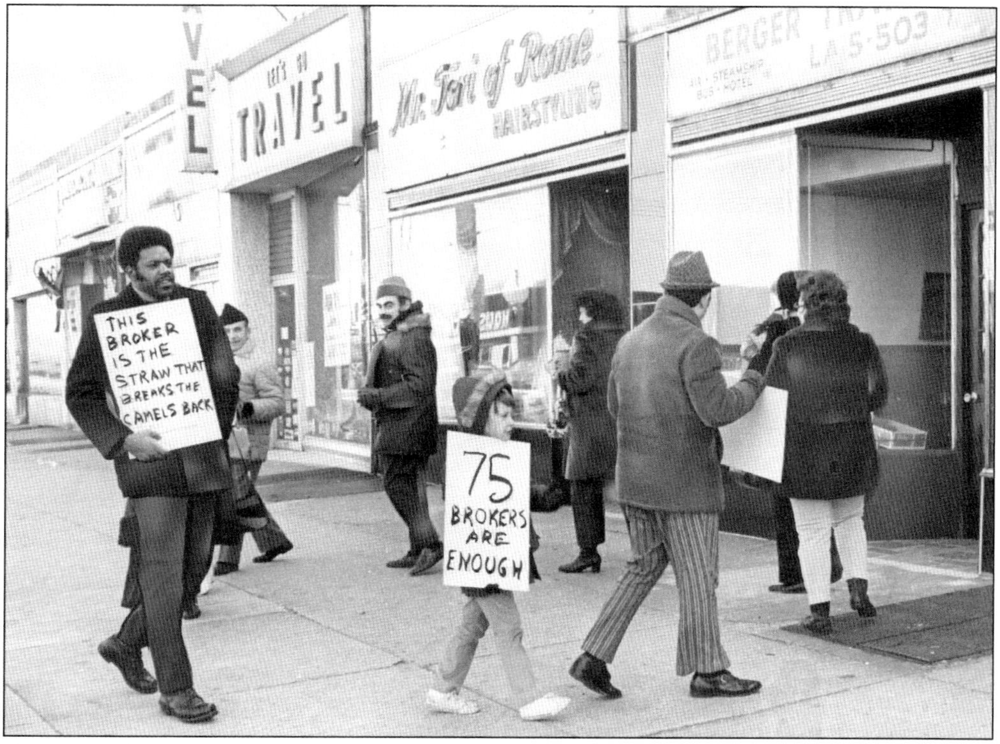

Here, Laurelton residents are protesting outside of Berger Real Estate office on Merrick Road in objection to the office's alleged involvement with blockbusting activities. (Courtesy of Queens Borough Public Library, Long Island Division.)

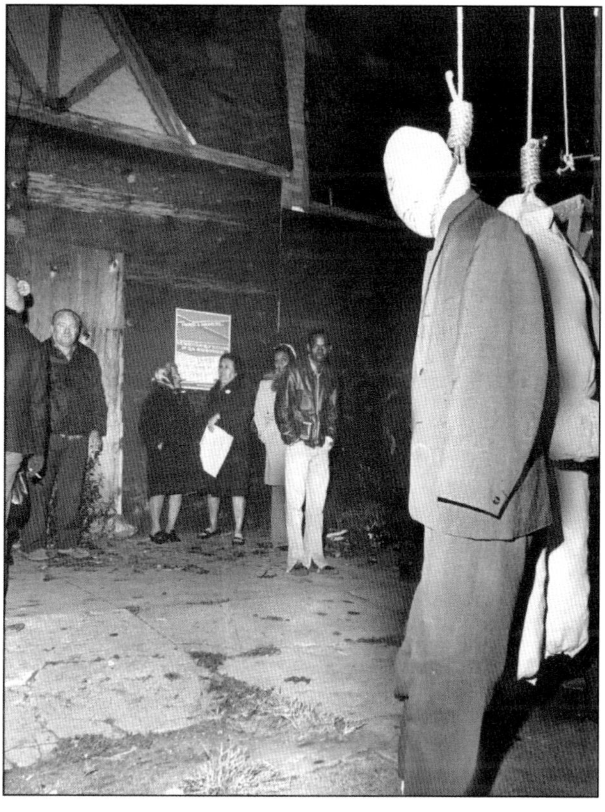

Seen at right in 1975, landlords of stores are being hung in effigy. These boarded-up stores are at 225th Street and 141st Avenue. The 80 residents who gathered were chanting, "We hung the four landlords on the sour apple tree." (Courtesy of Condé Nast Publications.)

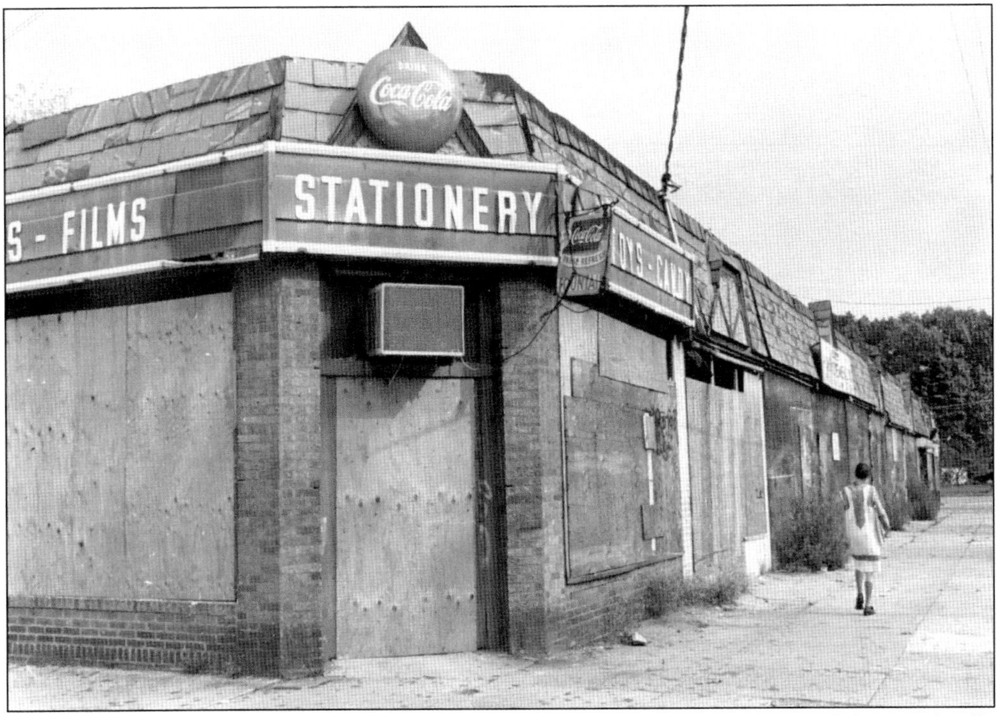

This is one of the stores near Mentone Avenue that eventually became part of the Cinderella Project, an urban renewal plan funded by Con Edison during the 1970s. Eventually, this strip was turned into townhouses that could be purchased for a reasonable $45,000. (Courtesy of Queens Borough Public Library, Long Island Division.)

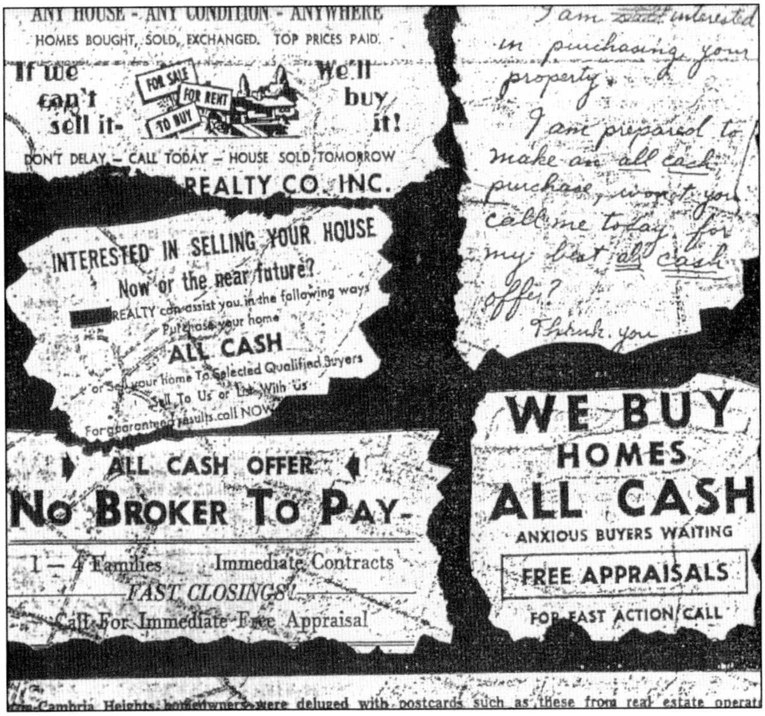

These are examples of the kind of tactics used by blockbusting real estate brokers, offering cash to homeowners who could be manipulated into selling at low prices. (Courtesy of Queens Borough Public Library, Long Island Division.)

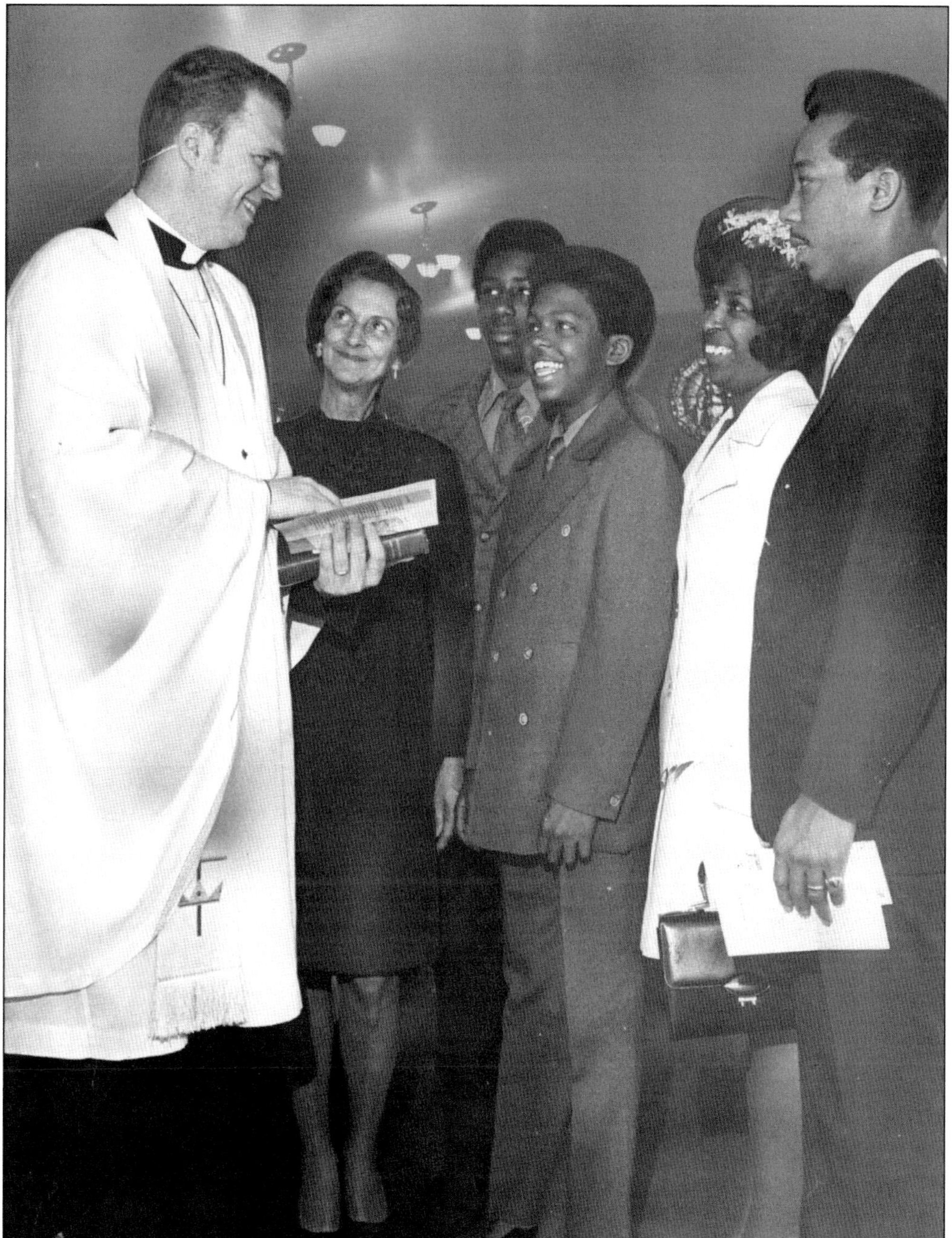

Pictured here are Rev. Wilbur Cowen Jr. and Julia Hludzinski welcoming Dennis and Robert Poe and their parents, Mr. and Mrs. Charles Poe, to Epiphany Lutheran Church in 1973. (Courtesy of Queens Borough Public Library, Long Island Division.)

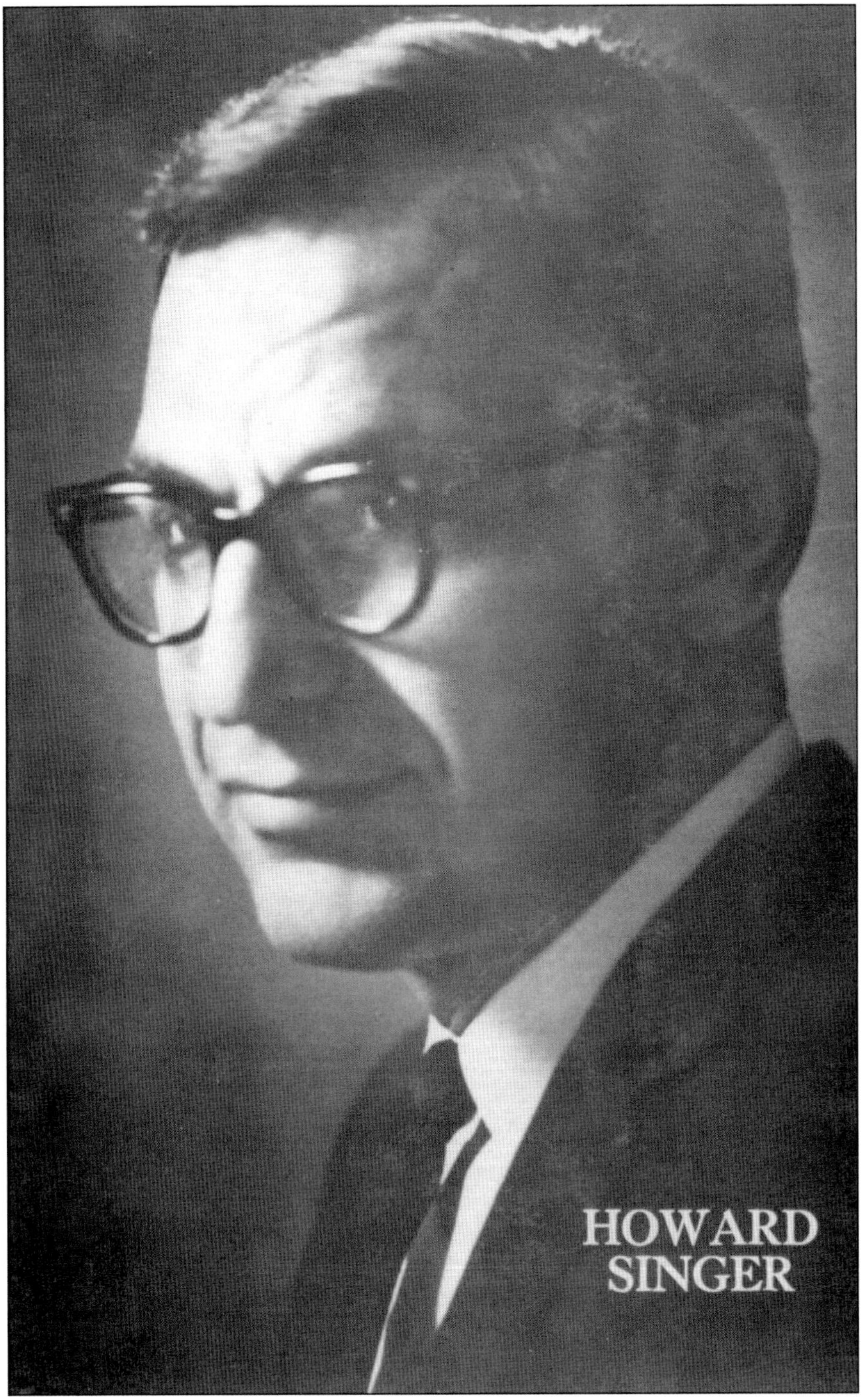

Rabbi Howard Singer, rabbi of Laurelton Jewish Center, is pictured during the tumultuous 1970s. He championed the idea of an integrated community and began a movement to integrate Laurelton that eventually led to statewide legislation banning the practice of blockbusting. He was also a well-known author. His book was adapted into a movie—*Wake Me When It's Over*, which starred Ernie Kovacs. (Courtesy of Bernard Kavaler.)

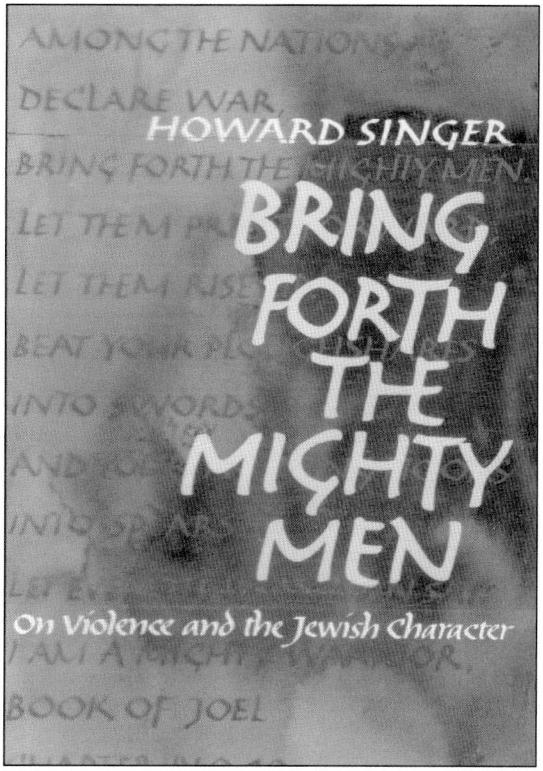

Rabbi Howard Singer of the Laurelton Jewish Center attended real estate courses so he could learn to run a free real estate agency with the purpose of achieving integration. He was also the author of a number of books on Jewish problems. The book jackets of two of his publications are shown here. (Courtesy of Bernard Kavaler.)

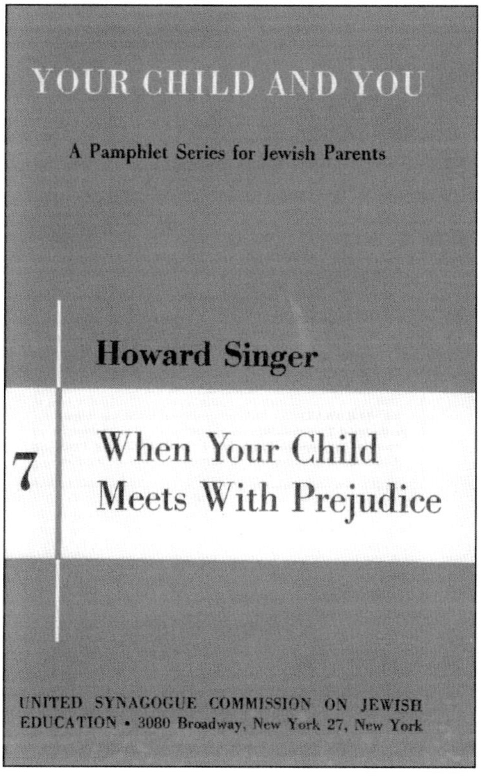

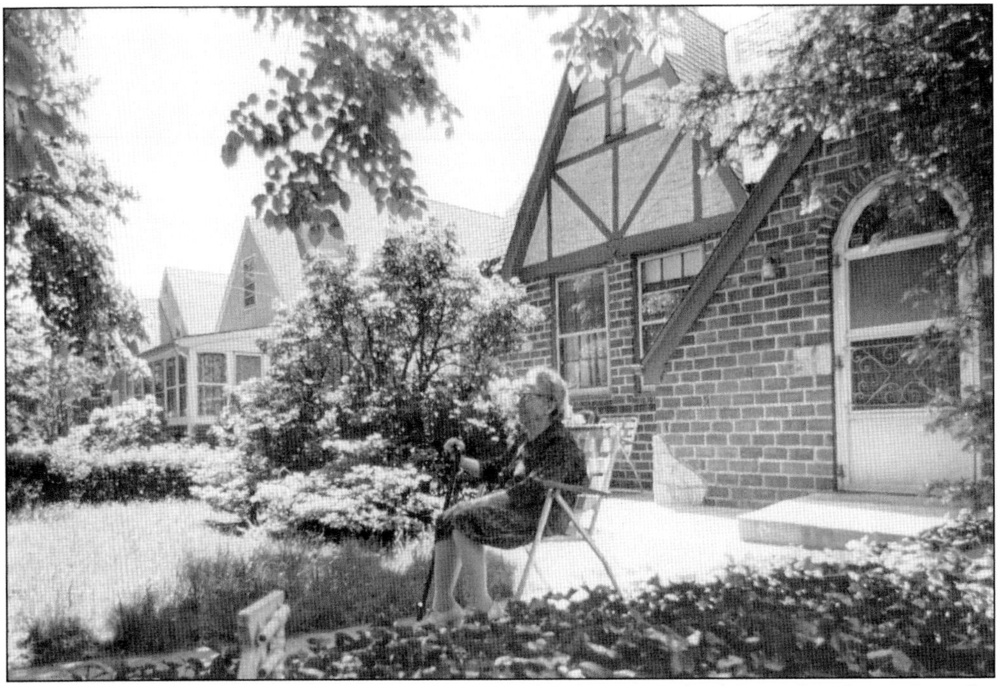

These photographs were taken for a series written by the *Long Island Press* that focused on the success of the efforts to integrate Laurelton. A picture of a young African American was next to an image of an elderly white resident. (Both, courtesy of Condé Nast Publications.)

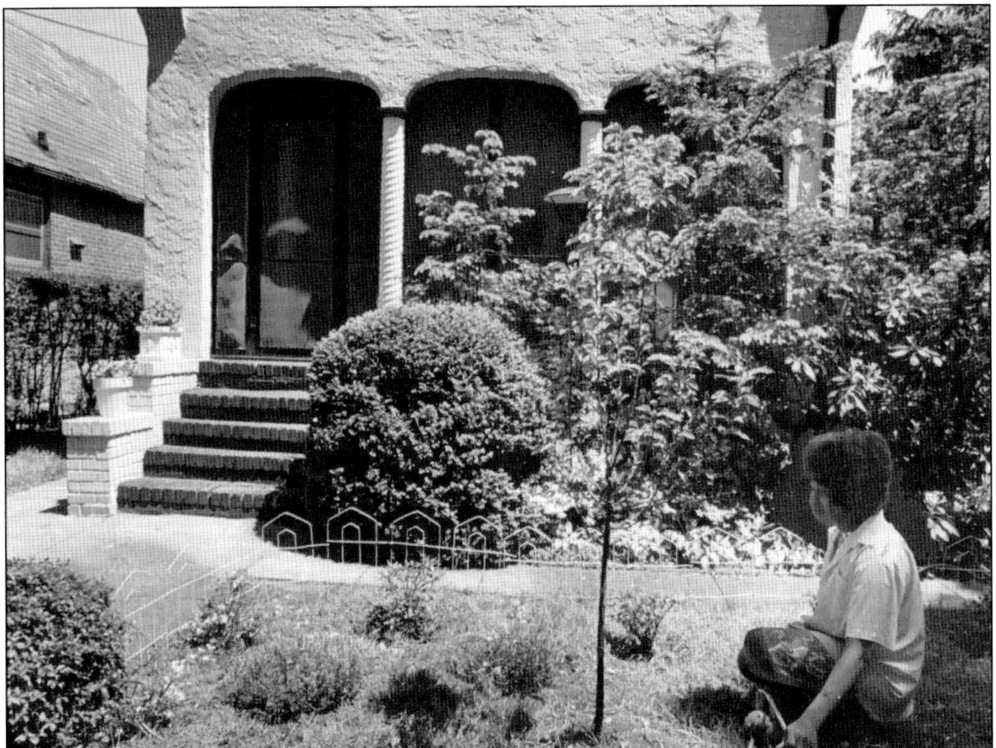

Four

Laurelton, A Love Story

Time goes on, and history has much to tell us. A people with a tragic history of annihilation comes to play a major role in a small town that once excluded their kind. Another race with a devastating history of enslavement takes its place by default, the unexpected result of unscrupulous practices by a local industry. Magically, the town seems little changed by its ordeal, except that it has grown more beautiful. The faces are slightly different, but the grown-ups worry about the same grown-up problems, such as how to pay the mortgage or make the schools better, while the children grow up enchanted.

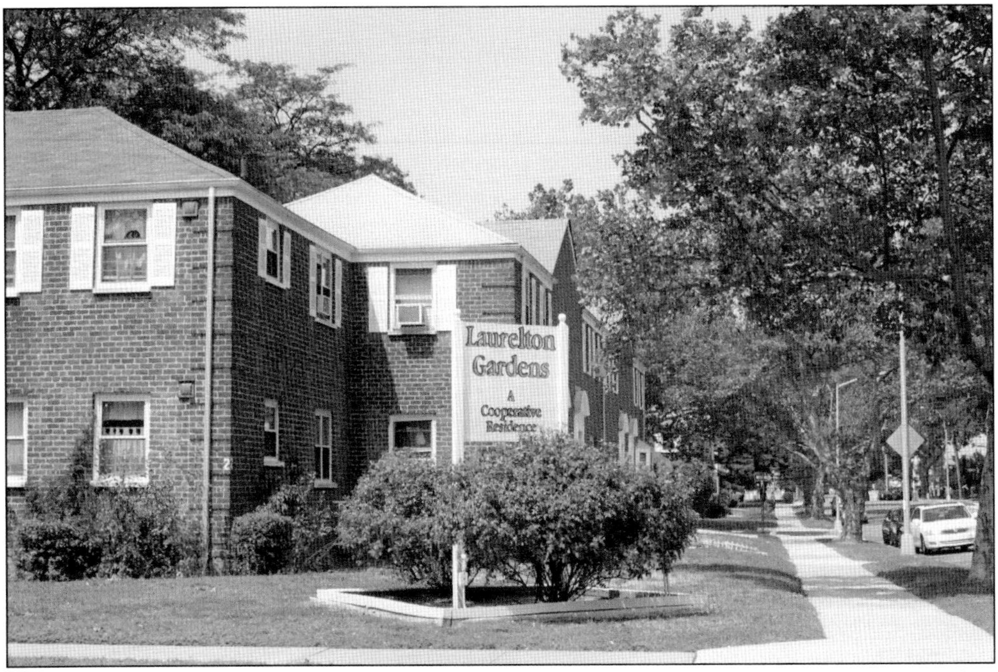

This is Laurelton Gardens, a cooperative development that was built on the property that had been the Schmitt Farm. There was tremendous opposition to multifamily development coming to Laurelton, which previously had no garden apartments. Three hundred residents showed up at the public hearing in 1950 to protest the building of this cooperative. (Courtesy of Dasha Weinstock.)

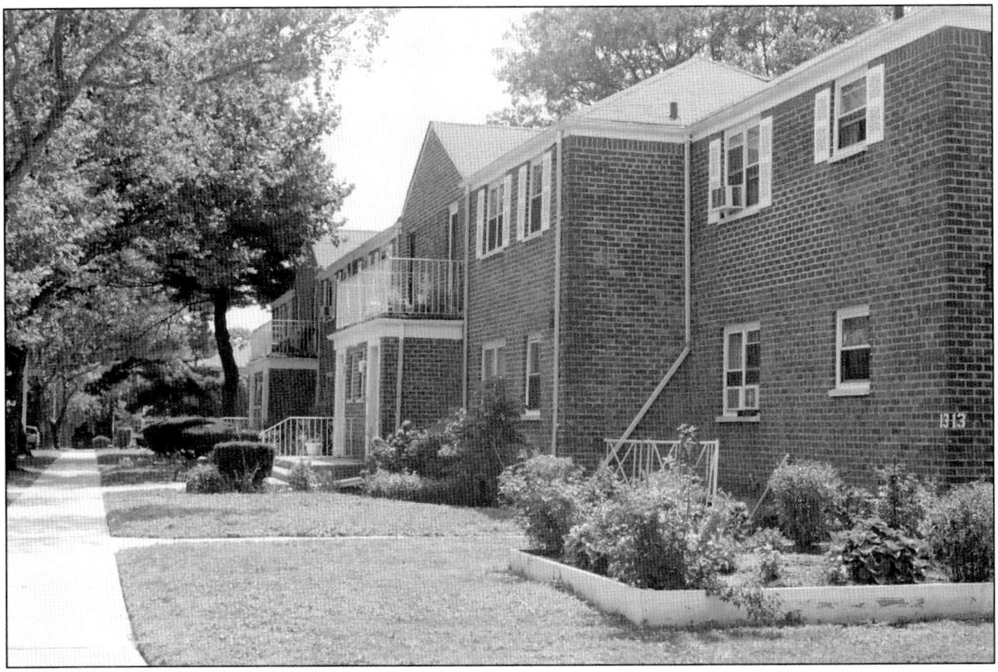

Laurelton Gardens, as it is seen from Laurelton Parkway, is beautifully landscaped and well maintained. (Courtesy of Dasha Weinstock.)

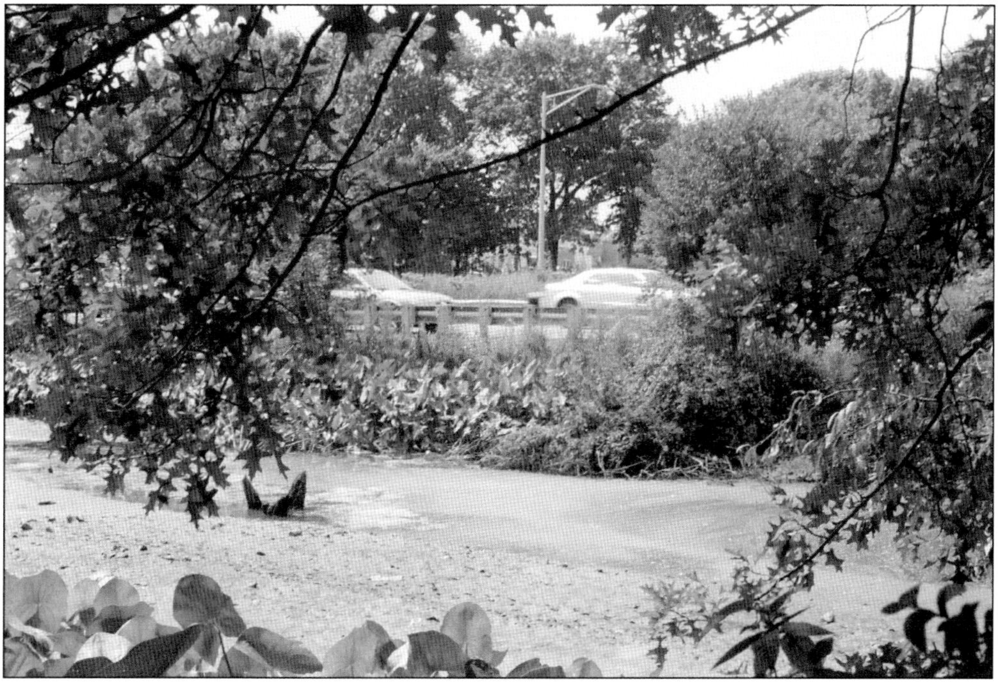

The Twin Ponds, as they appeared in 2010, are diminished from their previous glory, though one can occasionally catch a glimpse of egrets at the ponds. (Courtesy of Dasha Weinstock.)

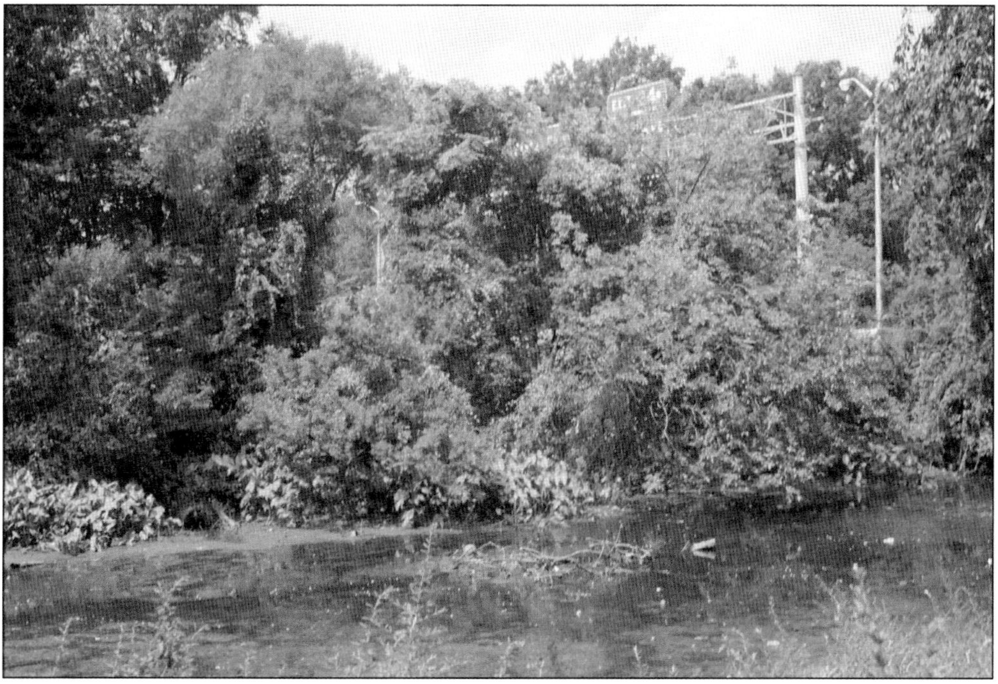

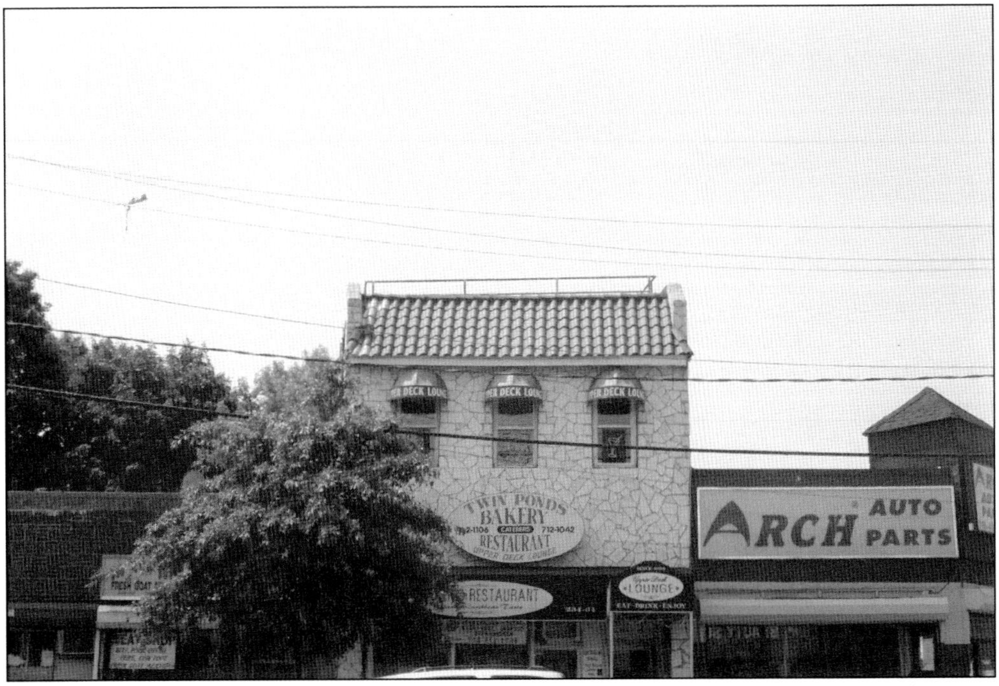

The Twin Ponds Bakery is seen here as it appeared in 2010. Although the name remains the same, this establishment now specializes in West Indian cuisine. (Courtesy of Dasha Weinstock.)

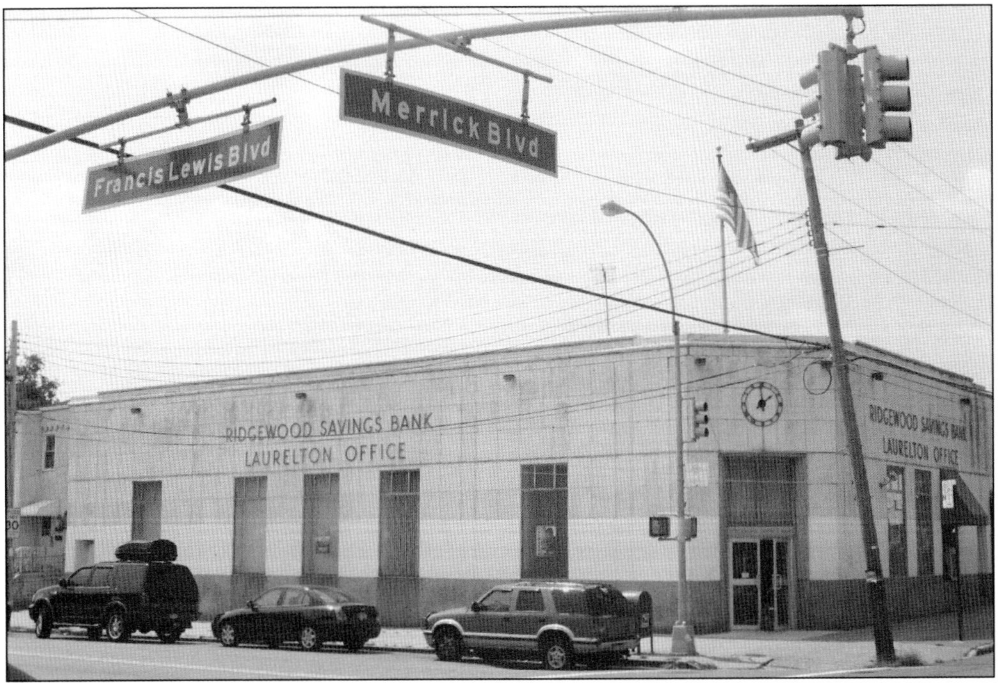

This is a photograph of the Ridgewood Savings Bank, which opened at this location in 1950. Many Laurelton alumni report having their first savings account in this bank, including Bernard Madoff. It was rumored that bank robber Willie Sutton considered a heist at this branch but ultimately dismissed the idea because the deposits were too low. (Courtesy of Dasha Weinstock.)

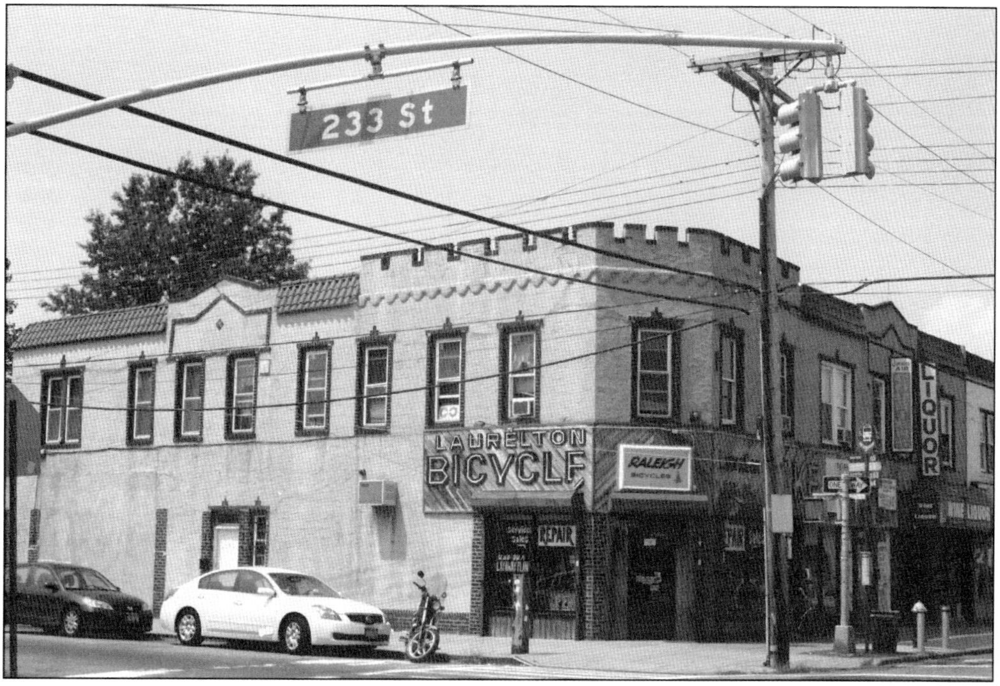

Here is the Laurelton Bicycle shop, formerly Kerns, on the corner of 233rd Street and Merrick Boulevard. Many former residents of Laurelton recall the owners of the shop, the Kern family. (Courtesy of Dasha Weinstock.)

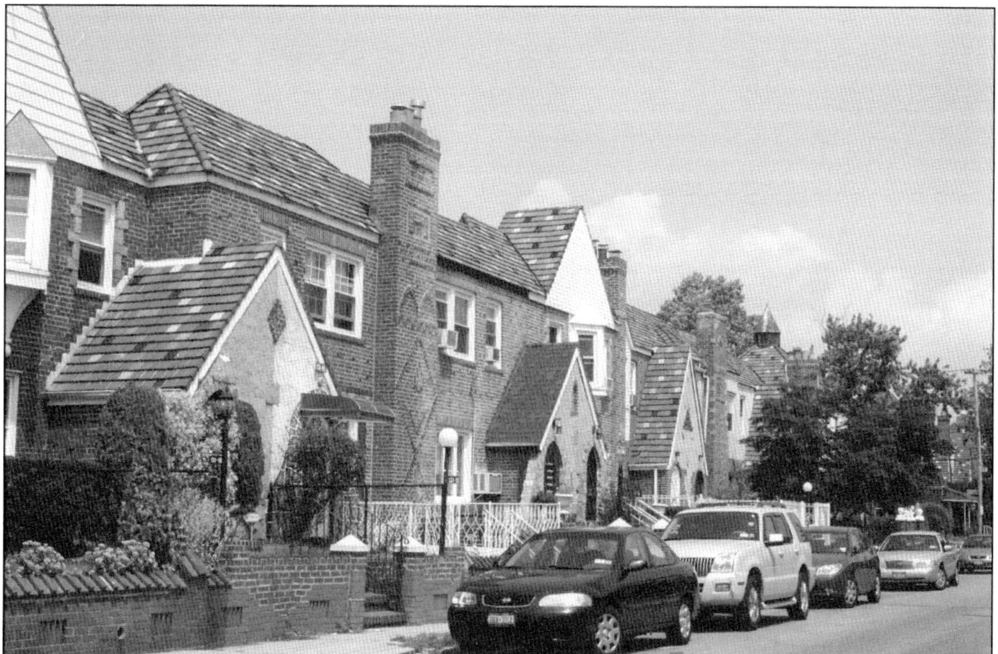

This is a typical streetscape in modern-day Laurelton. It is clear that these attached homes have grown graceful with age. (Courtesy of Dasha Weinstock.)

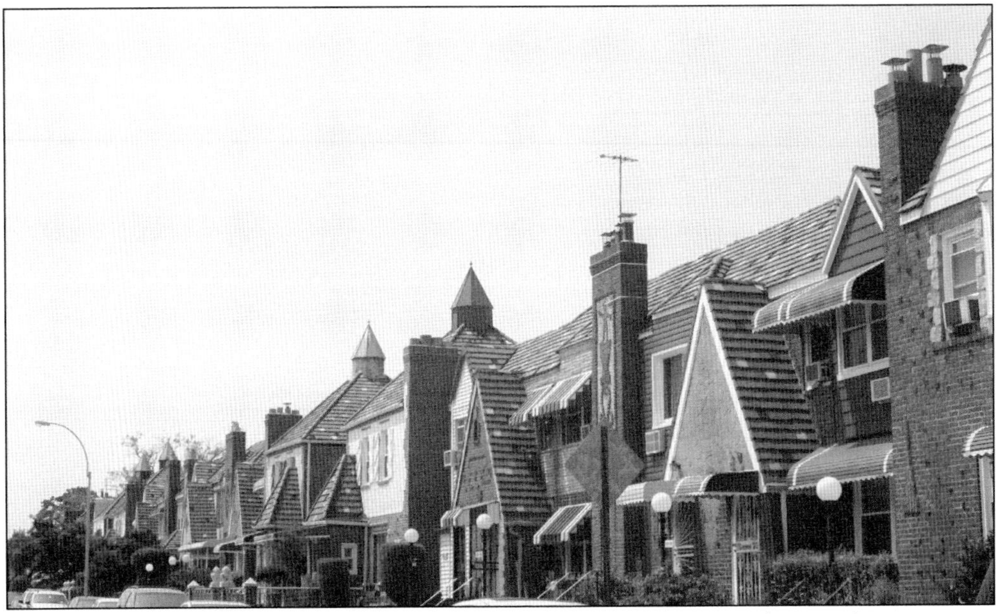

This is lovely 226th Street between 131st and 130th Avenues. Symmetry and painstaking attention to detail enliven these attached houses. (Courtesy of Dasha Weinstock.)

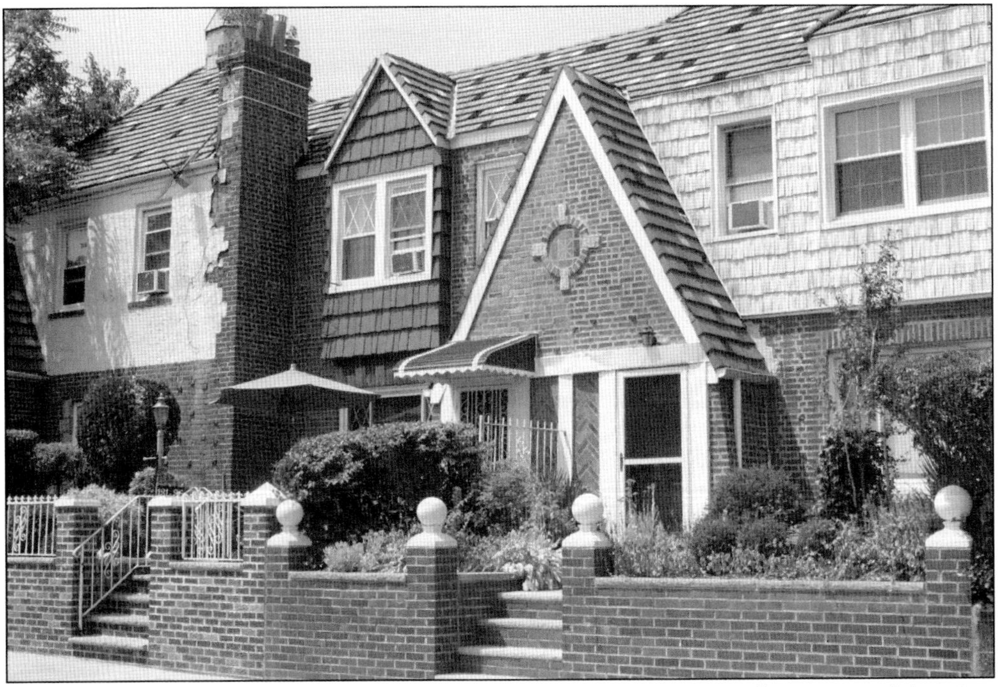

It is clear from the conditions of these homes that not only are they well maintained, but that the original materials chosen by the builders some 80 years ago could withstand the test of time. (Courtesy of Dasha Weinstock.)

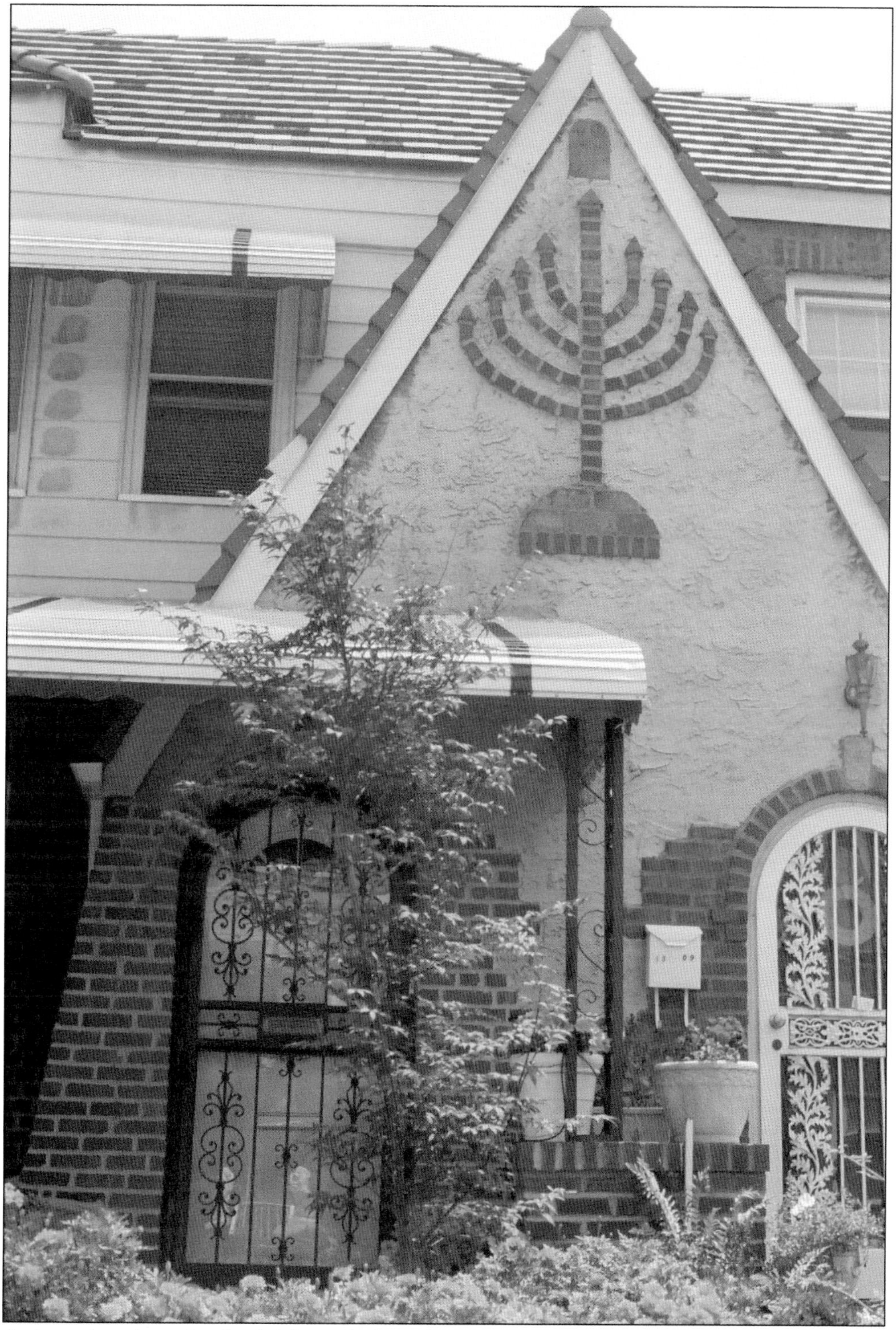

As is evident from this brick Menorah, Laurelton was once an area that was heavily populated by people of the Jewish faith. (Courtesy of Dasha Weinstock.)

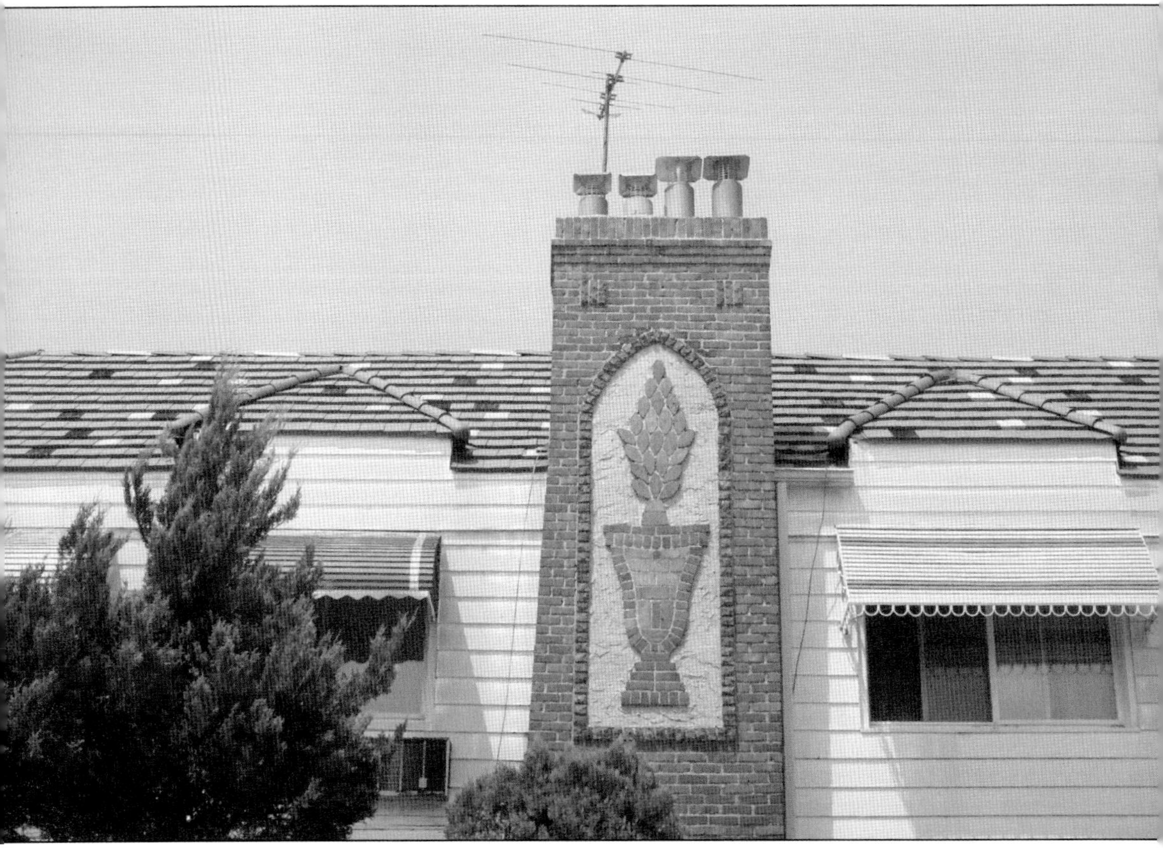

Here is a fine example of the fanciful brickwork that decorated chimneys on a row of attached homes located north of Merrick Road. (Courtesy of Dasha Weinstock.)

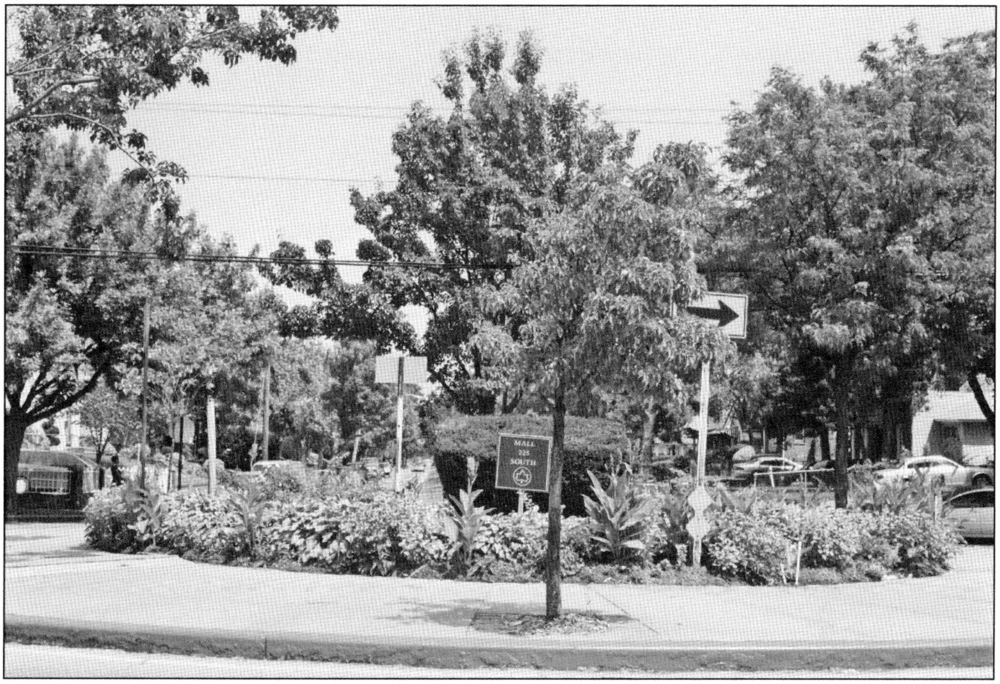

The roundabout on 225th Street boasts a beautiful garden. The green thumbs of Laurelton's residents have drawn the attention of many garden enthusiasts. (Courtesy of Dasha Weinstock.)

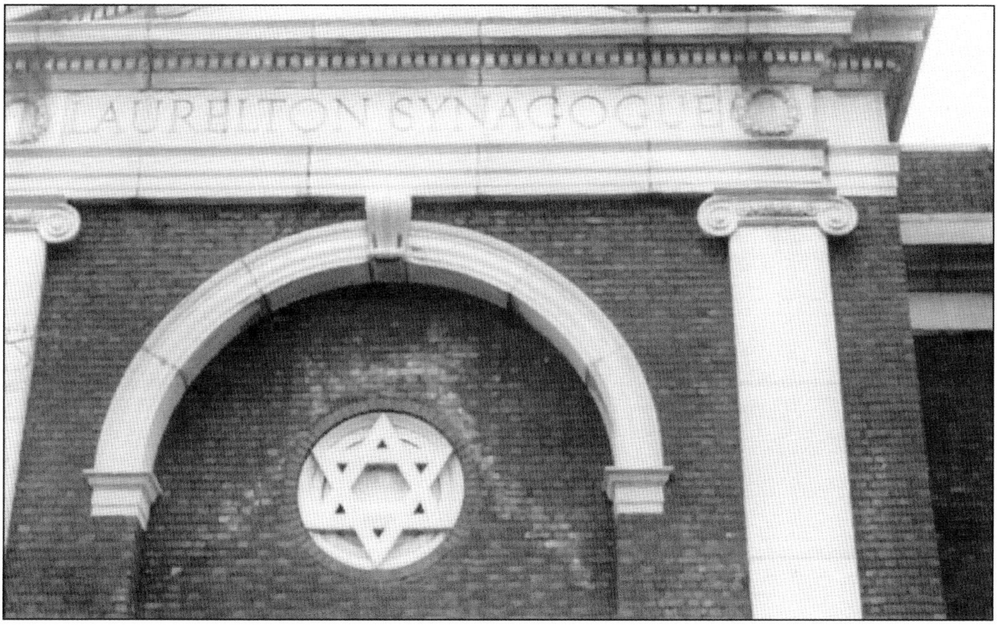

Above is the Laurelton Jewish Center or Laurelton Synagogue as it appeared in the 1950s. The Seventh-day Adventists have made few changes to the handsome exterior. (Courtesy of Marvin Merein.)

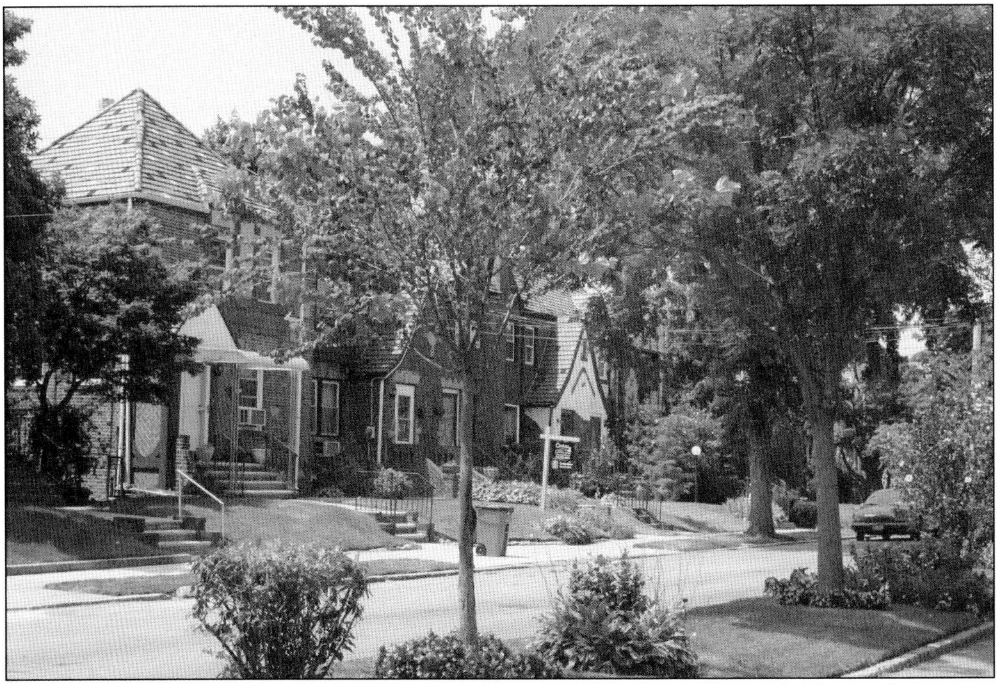
Pictured here is the Mall on 141st Avenue, one of the famous Garden Club of Laurelton street malls. The club holds its renowned contest on odd-numbered years with very substantial cash prizes awarded to the winners. (Courtesy of Dasha Weinstock.)

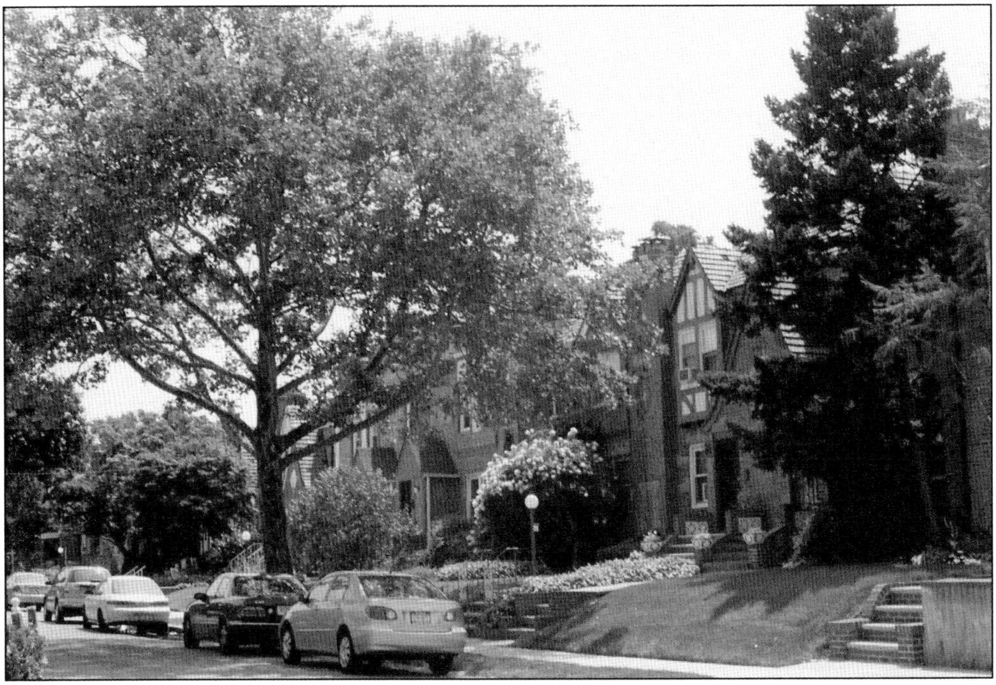
The above view is of another neighborhood where gardening talent grows in abundance. The community talents of the Laurelton gardeners keep growing. (Courtesy of Dasha Weinstock.)

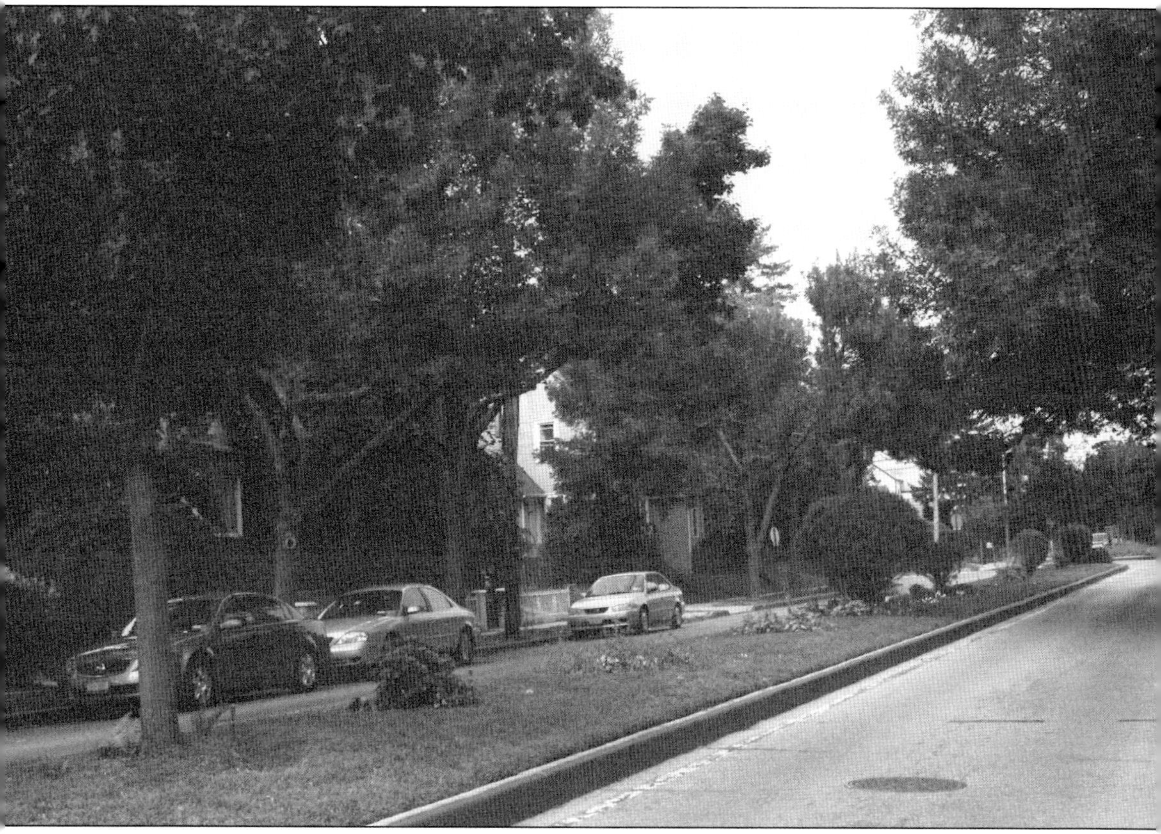

Pictured here is a view of the beautifully maintained 141st Avenue malls. (Courtesy of Dasha Weinstock.)

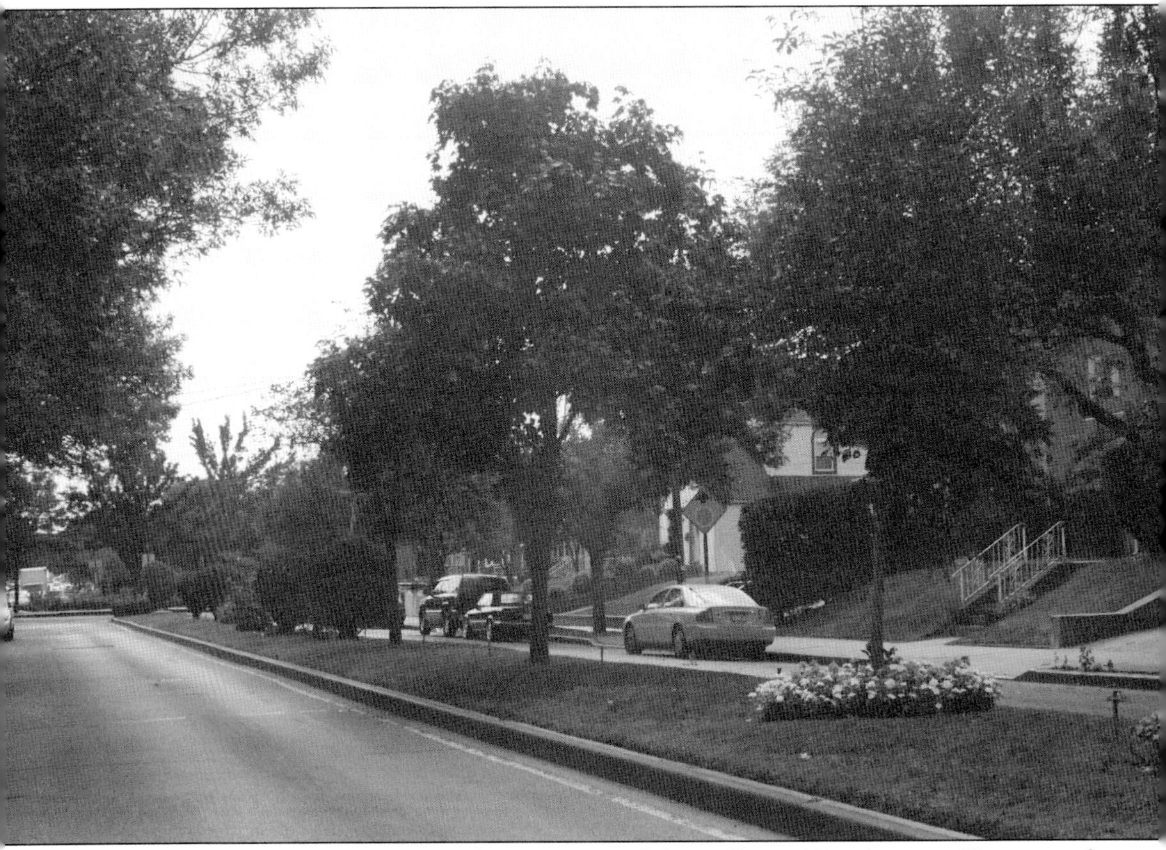

A Garden Club of Laurelton sign decorates one of the malls on 141st Avenue. (Courtesy of Dasha Weinstock.)

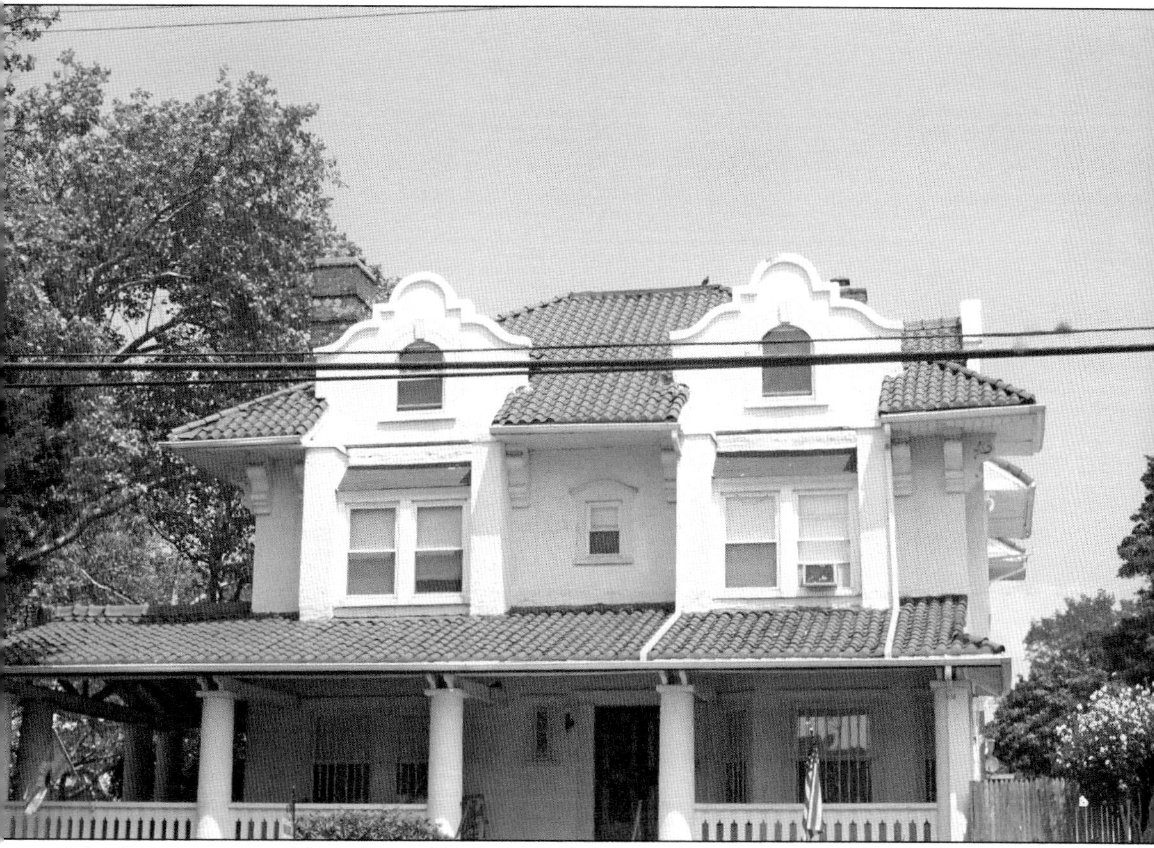

This house is a graceful example of the kinds of homes that were originally planned throughout Laurelton in Senator Reynolds's time. (Courtesy of Dasha Weinstock.)

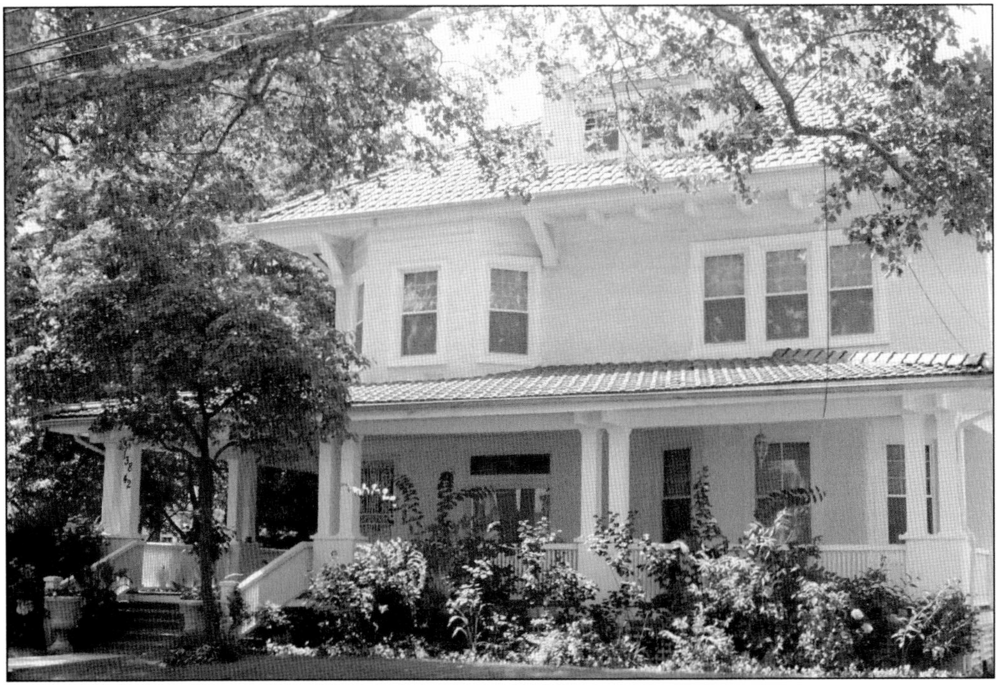

Here are two elegant examples of the homes first offered by Senator Reynolds in the early 1900s. They were obviously designed for people of means. (Courtesy of Dasha Weinstock.)

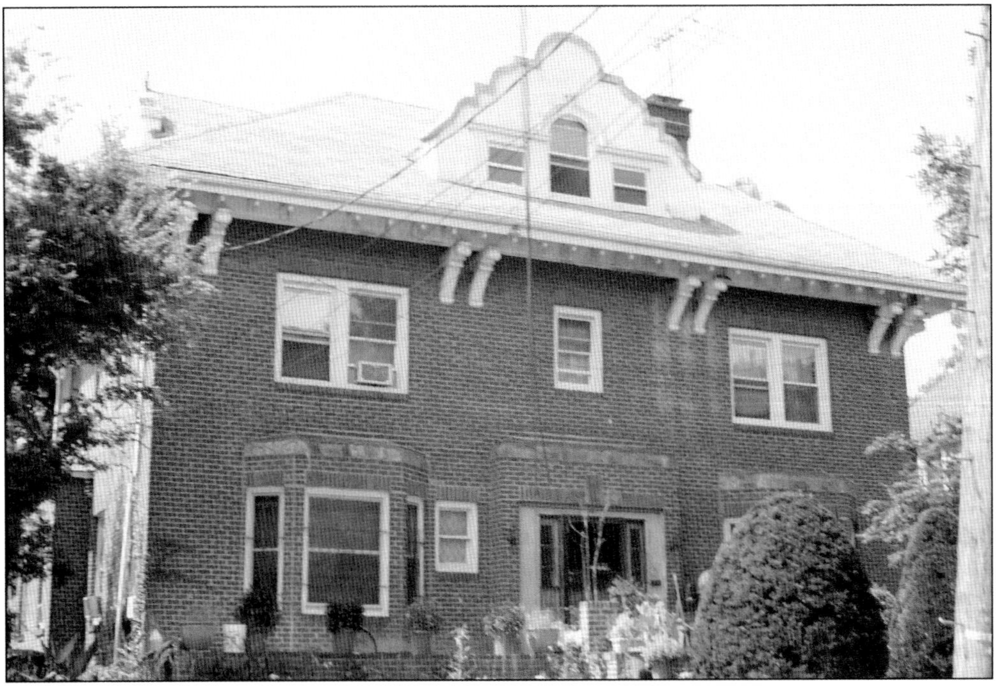

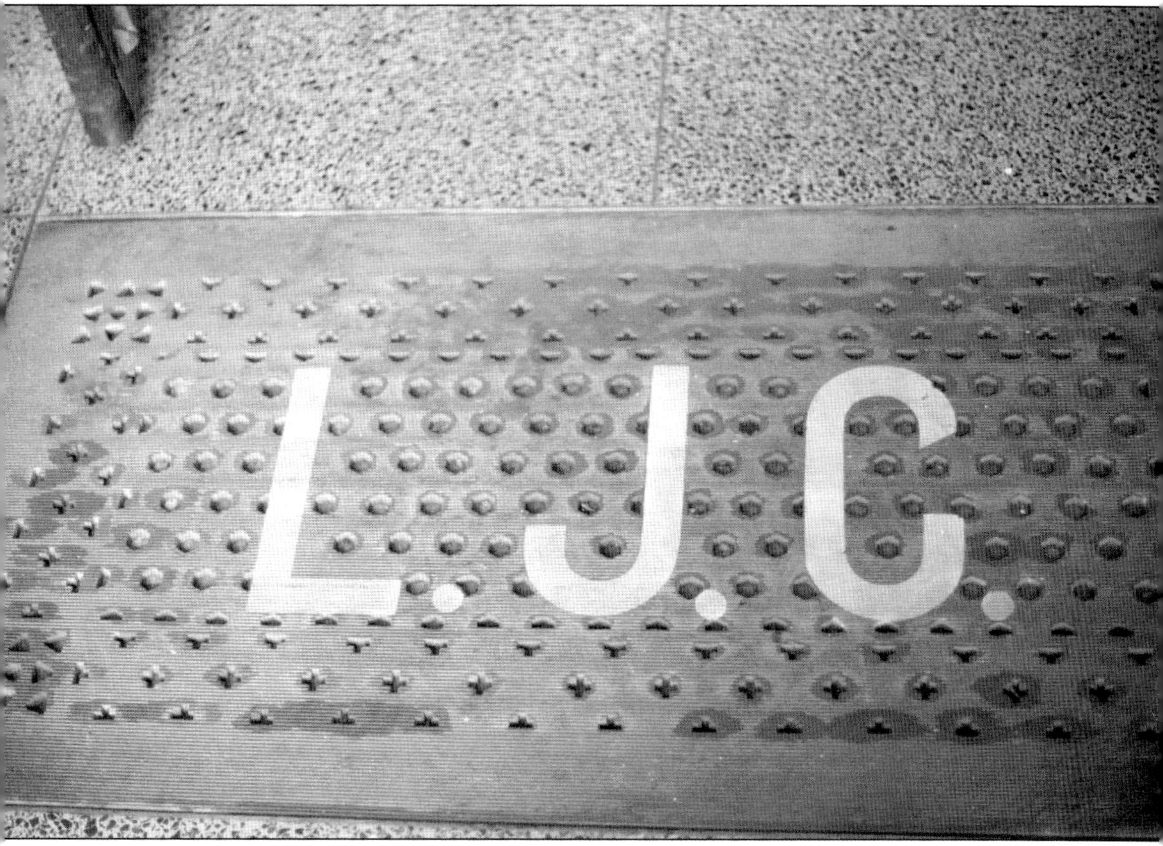

This is the floor mat still being used today by the Seventh-day Adventist Church, which bought the Laurelton Jewish Center in 1981. The initials "LJC" stand for the Laurelton Jewish Center. (Courtesy of Dasha Weinstock.)

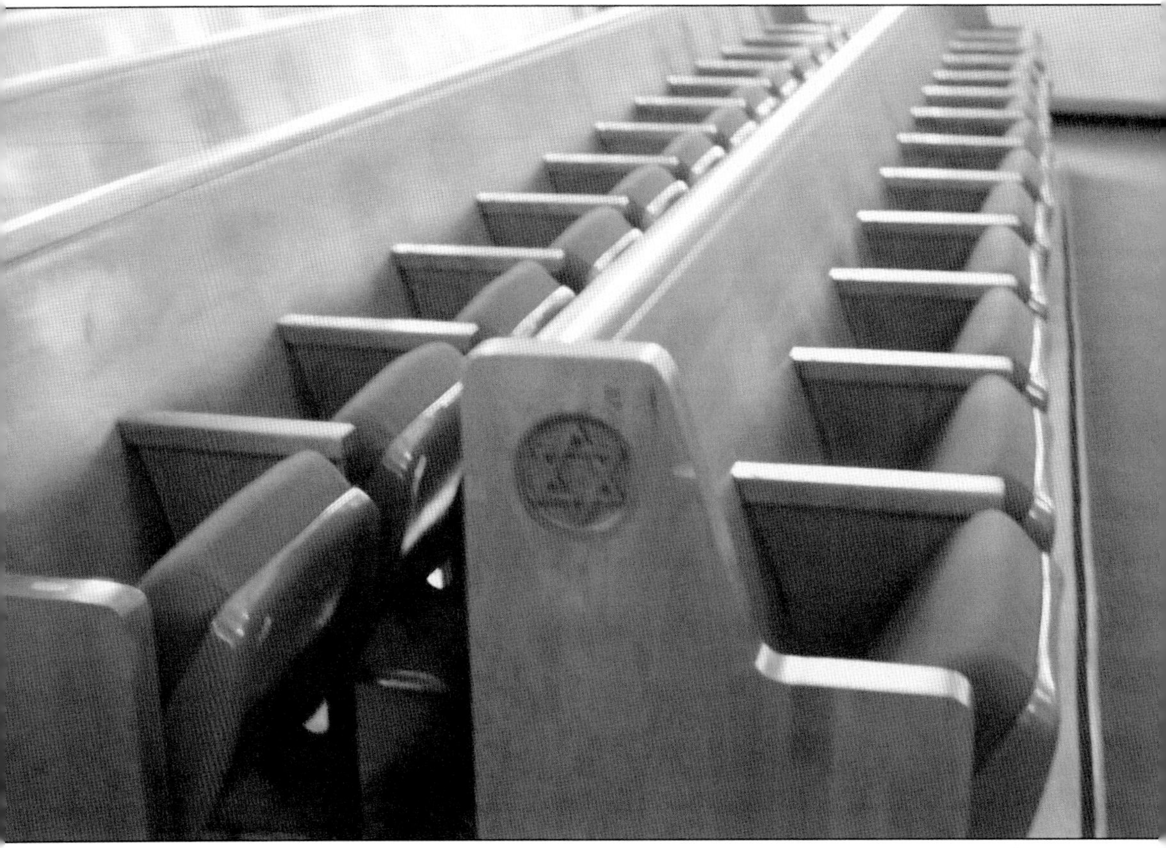

These are the pews in the main sanctuary of the Seventh-day Adventist Church. The Adventist church left many of the original details of the building as they found them, such as the Stars of David on the end pews. (Courtesy of Dasha Weinstock.)

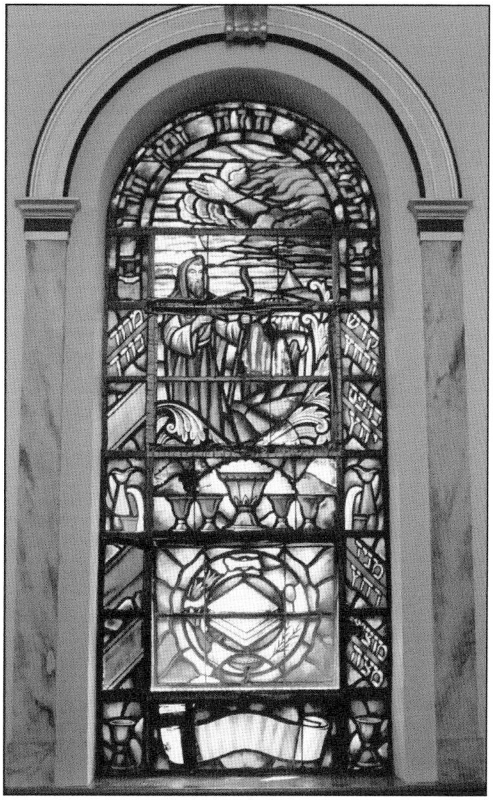

The stained glass windows in the main sanctuary, another artifact from the building's days as a synagogue, still serve the same purpose for the building's current occupants. (Courtesy of Dasha Weinstock.)

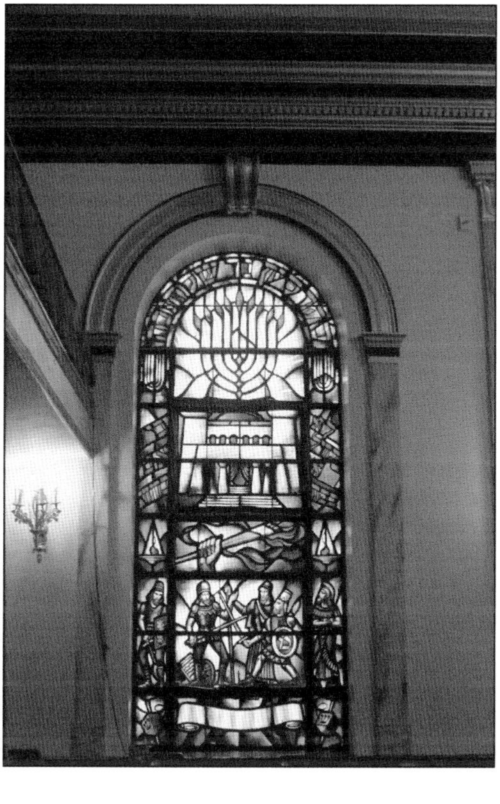

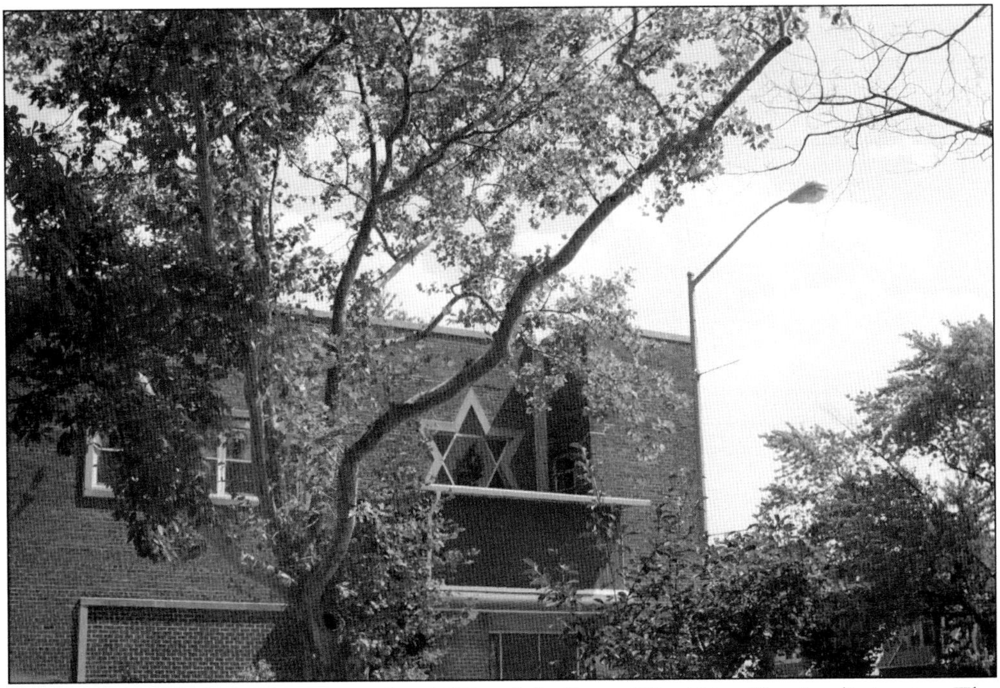

The Young Israel of Laurelton opened in 1956 and the Star of David is still quite distinctive. The Jamaica-Queens Wesleyan Church now occupies the space. (Courtesy of Dasha Weinstock.)

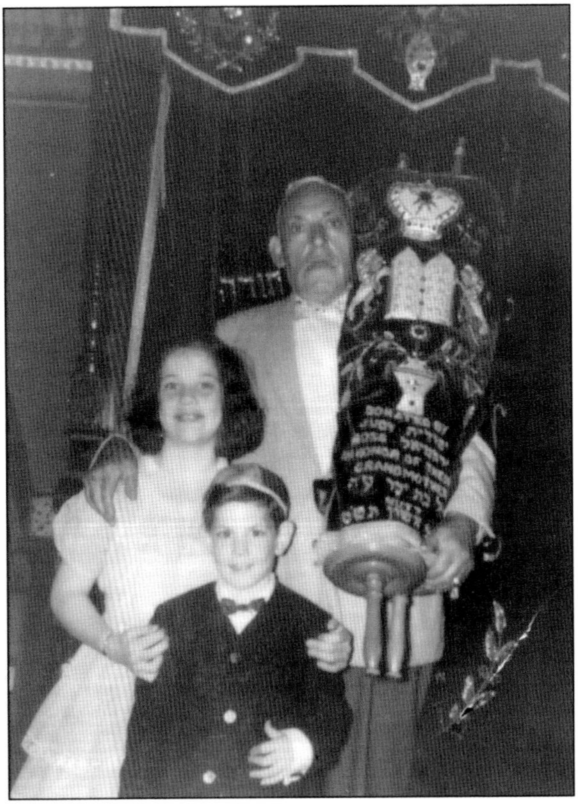

This is a photograph of Judy Rosenberg, her brother Ross, and her grandfather Max Hutt as he donates a Torah scroll to the Young Israel of Laurelton. Taken on June 9, 1955, Hutt was dedicating the scroll to his deceased wife, Rose Hutt.

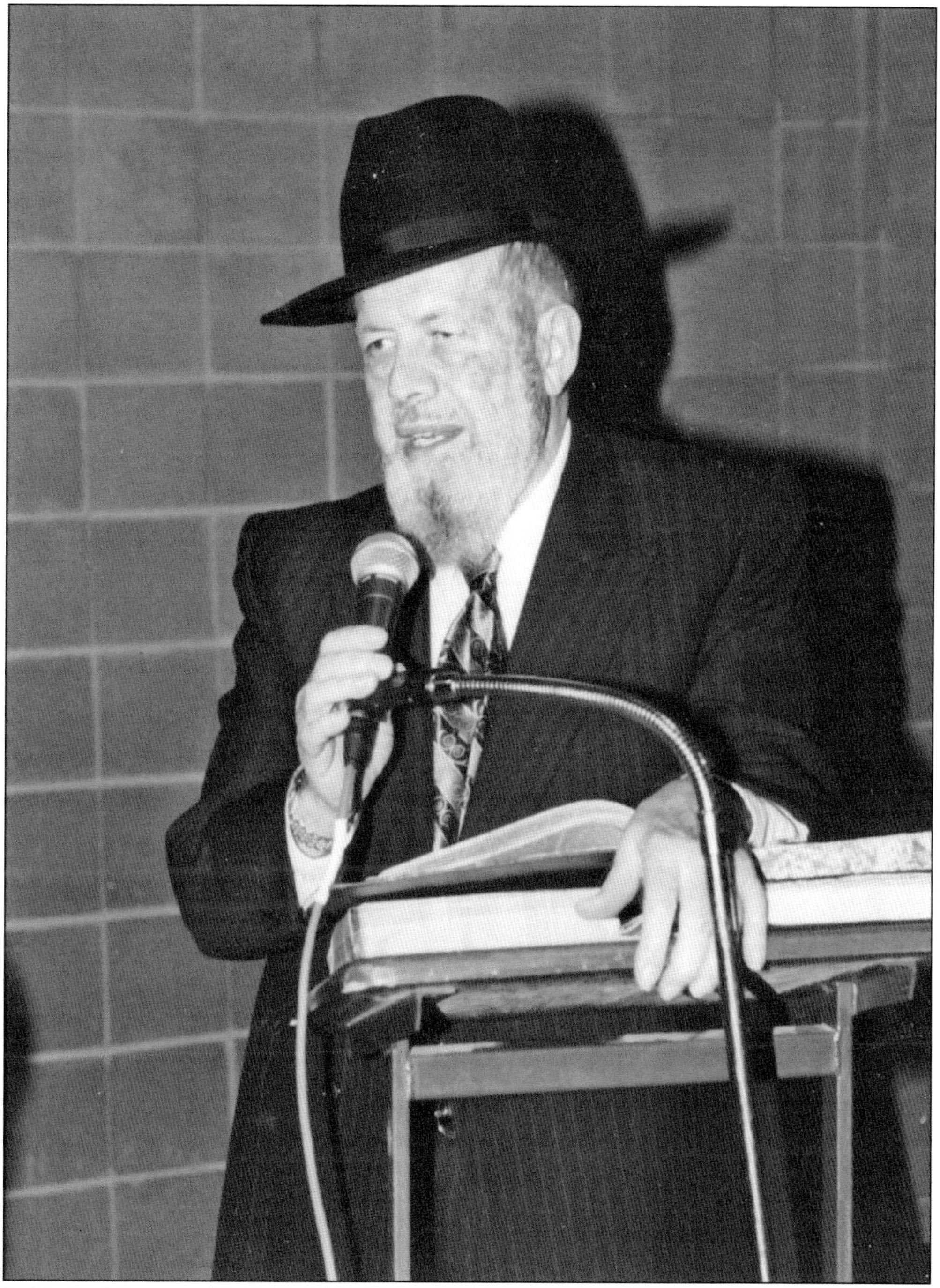
Rabbi Saul Romineck speaks a few years ago in a community synagogue. (Courtesy of Rabbi Saul Romineck.)

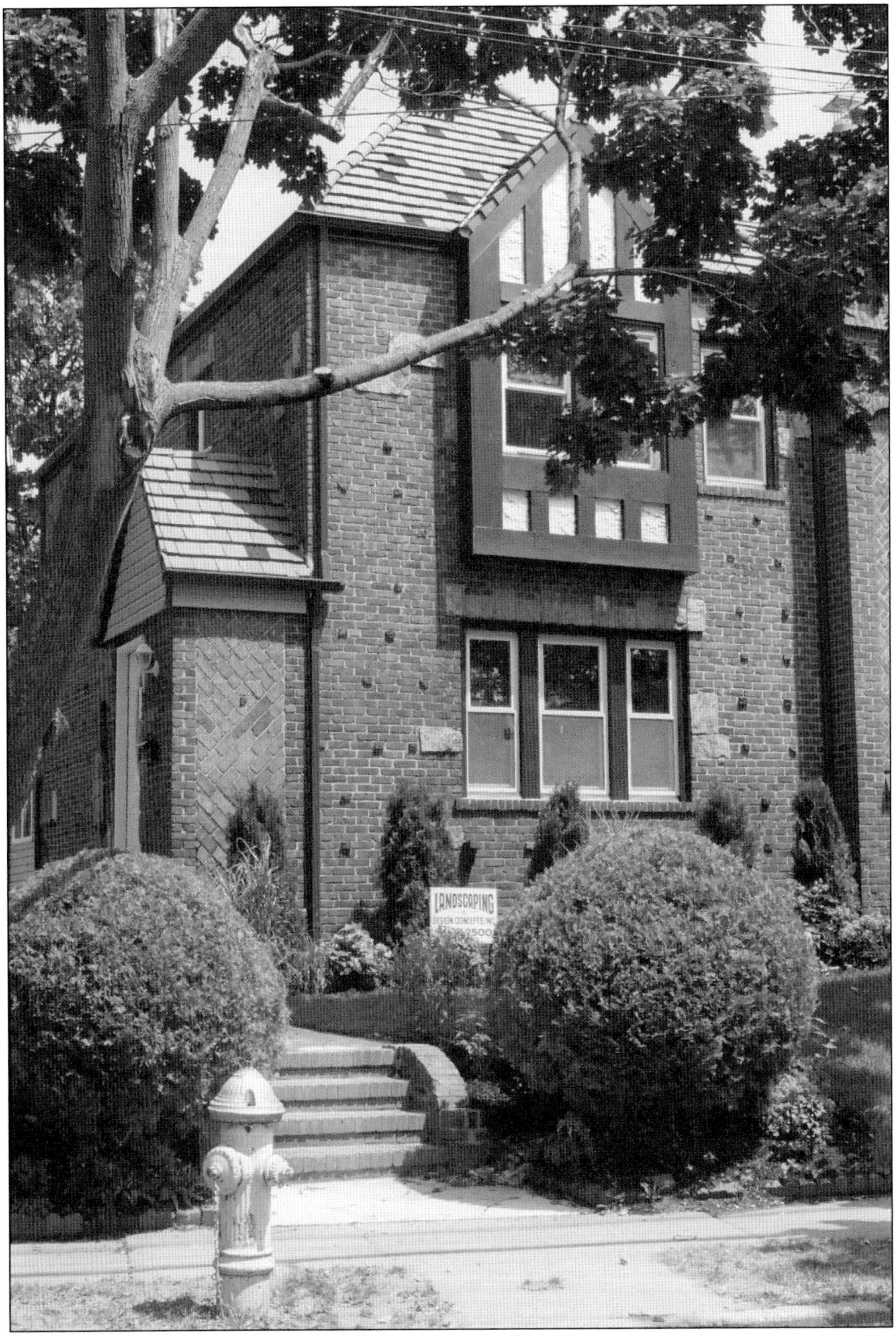

In 1931, the Henkin family purchased this home for $8,000; it is now being marketed with a purchase price of $425,000.

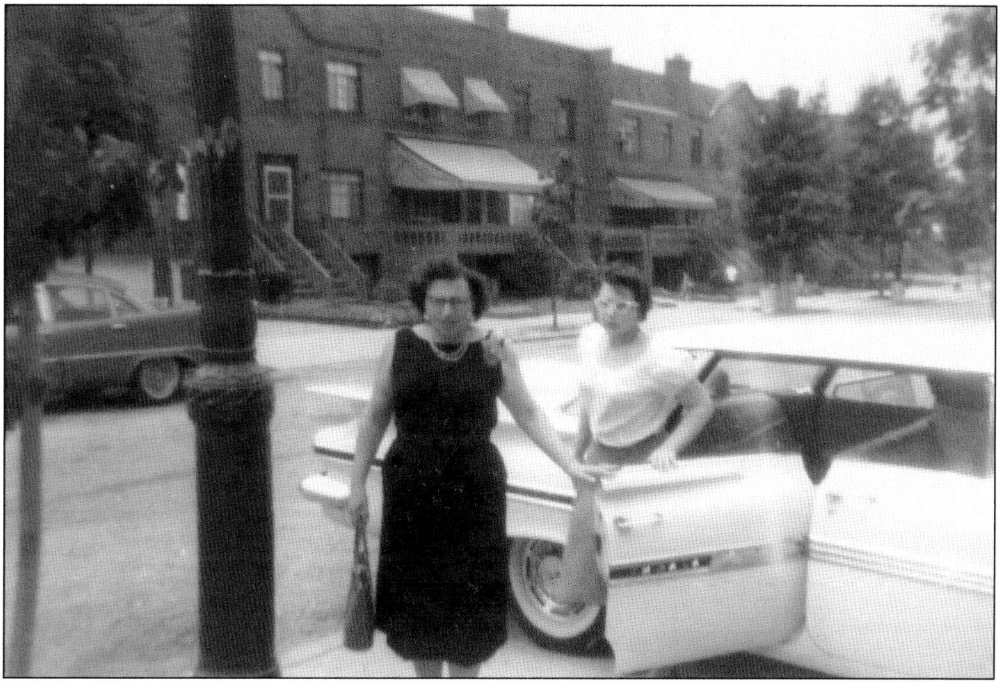

This is 225th Street looking northbound, exemplifying the uniformity of the tavern-style home, all sporting their original slate roofs. (Courtesy of Dasha Weinstock.)

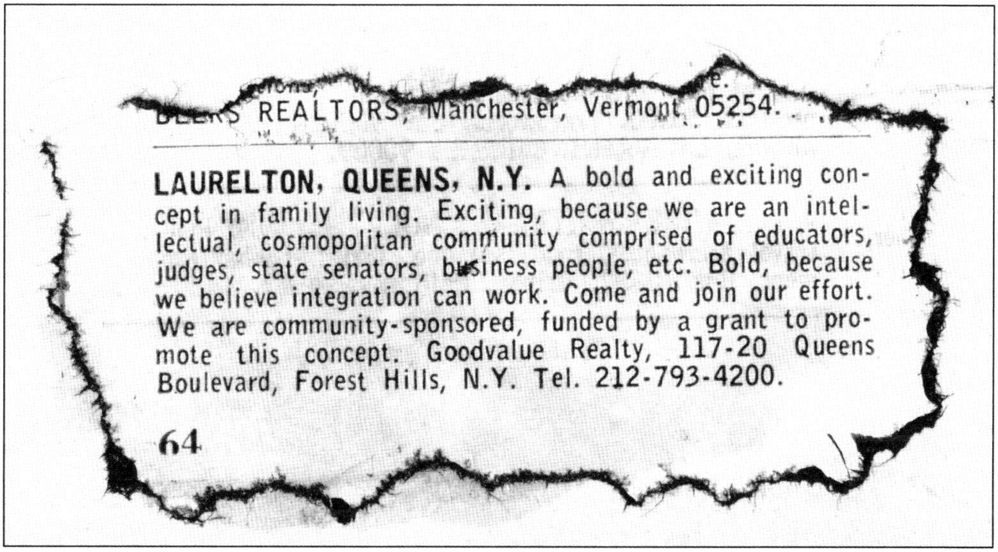

REALTORS, Manchester, Vermont 05254.

LAURELTON, QUEENS, N.Y. A bold and exciting concept in family living. Exciting, because we are an intellectual, cosmopolitan community comprised of educators, judges, state senators, business people, etc. Bold, because we believe integration can work. Come and join our effort. We are community-sponsored, funded by a grant to promote this concept. Goodvalue Realty, 117-20 Queens Boulevard, Forest Hills, N.Y. Tel. 212-793-4200.

64

This is an example of advertising to promote an integrated community. These advertisements achieved a certain amount of success but eventually failed as time took its toll on residents.

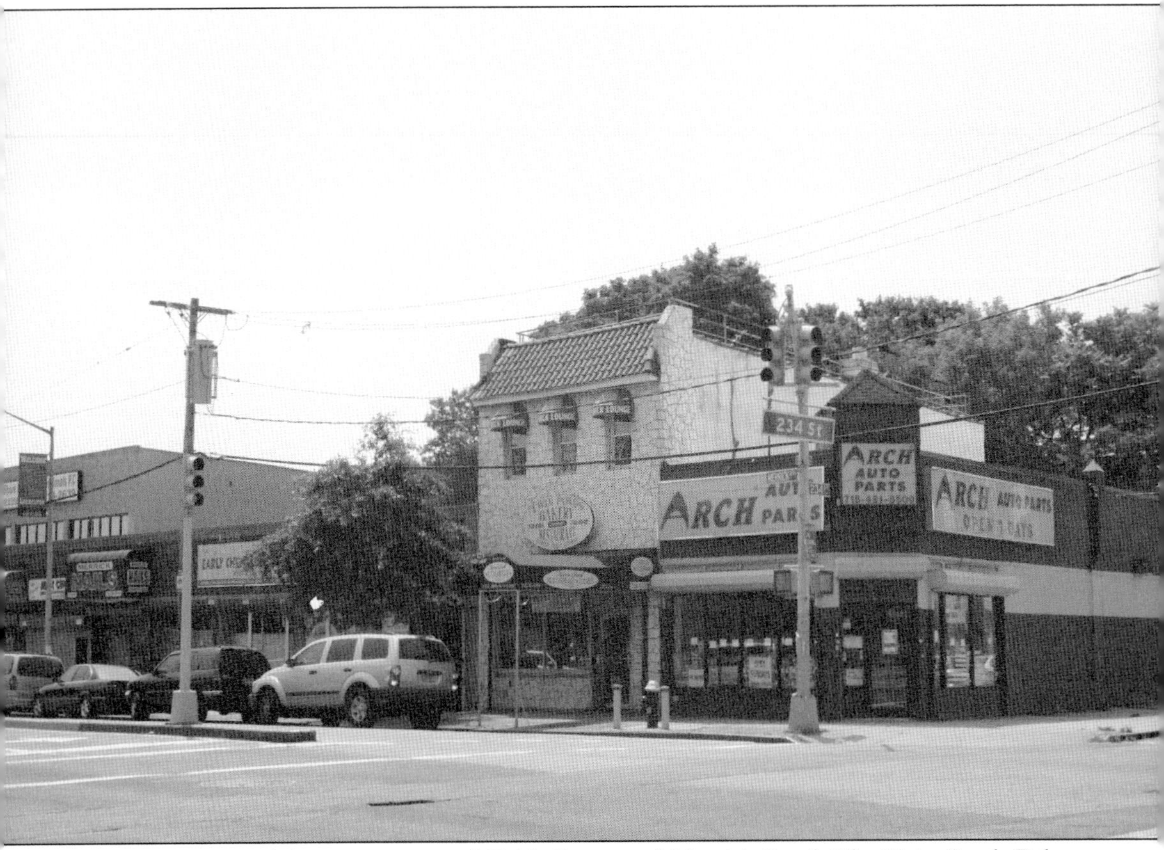

This is a view of the intersection of 234th Street and Merrick Road. The Twin Ponds Bakery still retains its pride of place, although the Schmitt farm can no longer be seen from is windows. (Courtesy of Dasha Weinstock.)

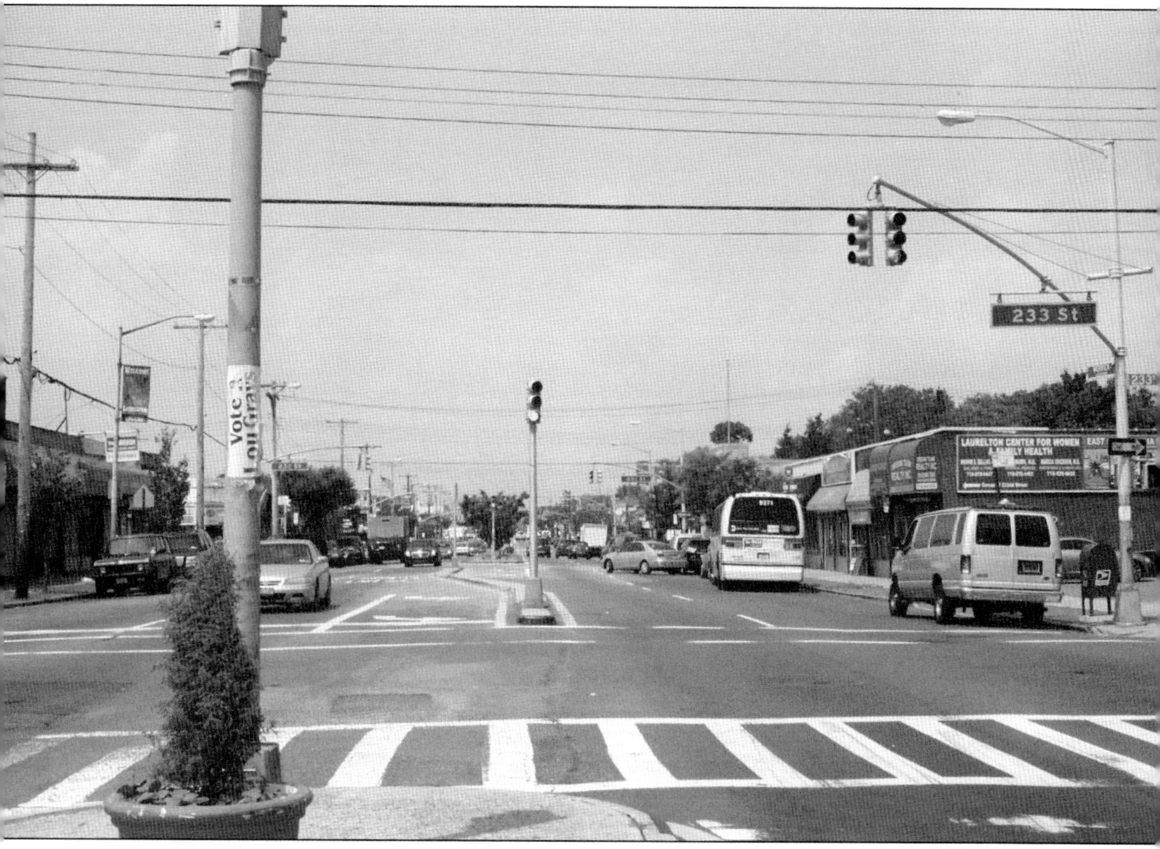

Here is another view of Merrick Road, facing eastward from 233rd Street. The constant commercial activity of Merrick Road makes an interestingly historical contrast to Albert Schmitt's description of it as "a plank one-way toll road to Jamaica." (Courtesy of Dasha Weinstock.)